PROTEST MUSIC IN FRANCE

Protest Music in France
Production, Identity and Audiences

BARBARA LEBRUN
The University of Manchester, UK

ASHGATE

Published by
Ashgate Publishing Limited
Wey Court East
Union Road
Farnham
Surrey GU9 7PT
England

Ashgate Publishing Company
Suite 420
101 Cherry Street
Burlington, VT 05401-4405
USA

www.ashgate.com

British Library Cataloguing in Publication Data
Lebrun, Barbara
    Protest music in France : production, identity and audiences. – (Ashgate popular and folk music series) 1. Protest songs – France – 20th century – History and criticism 2. Protest songs – France – 21st century – History and criticism
    I. Title
    782.4'21592'0944

Library of Congress Cataloging-in-Publication Data
Lebrun, Barbara.
    Protest music in France : production, identity and audiences / Barbara Lebrun.
       p. cm. – (Ashgate popular and folk music series)
    Includes bibliographical references and index.
    ISBN 978-0-7546-6472-7 (hardcover : alk. paper)
  1. Popular music–Political aspects–France. 2. Popular music–Social aspects–France.
3. Protest songs–France–History and criticism. I. Title.

    ML3917.F8L43 2008
    781.64'15920944–dc22

2008050805

ISBN 978 0 7546 6472 7
EISBN 978 0 7546 9464 9

Mixed Sources
Product group from well-managed forests and other controlled sources
www.fsc.org Cert no. SA-COC-1565
© 1996 Forest Stewardship Council
FSC

Printed and bound in Great Britain by
MPG Books Ltd, Bodmin, Cornwall.

Contents

List of Illustrations

General Editor's Preface

The upheaval that occurred in musicology during the last two decades of the twentieth century has created a new urgency for the study of popular music alongside the development of new critical and theoretical models. A relativistic outlook has replaced the universal perspective of modernism (the international ambitions of the 12-note style); the grand narrative of the evolution and dissolution of tonality has been challenged, and emphasis has shifted to cultural context, reception and subject position. Together, these have conspired to eat away at the status of canonical composers and categories of high and low in music. A need has arisen, also, to recognize and address the emergence of crossovers, mixed and new genres, to engage in debates concerning the vexed problem of what constitutes authenticity in music and to offer a critique of musical practice as the product of free, individual expression.

Popular musicology is now a vital and exciting area of scholarship, and the *Ashgate Popular and Folk Music Series* presents some of the best research in the field. Authors are concerned with locating musical practices, values and meanings in cultural context, and may draw upon methodologies and theories developed in cultural studies, semiotics, poststructuralism, psychology and sociology. The series focuses on popular musics of the twentieth and twenty-first centuries. It is designed to embrace the world's popular musics from Acid Jazz to Zydeco, whether high tech or low tech, commercial or non-commercial, contemporary or traditional.

Derek B. Scott
Professor of Critical Musicology
University of Leeds, UK

Acknowledgements

I would like to thank the following people for providing encouragement, useful suggestions and practical help at the various stages of this book's conception and writing: Jon Hensher, David Looseley, Bill Marshall, Lucy Mazdon, Joseph McGonagle, Richard and Ann Moncrieff, Derek Scott, Robynn Stilwell, Chris Tinker, Nuria Triana-Toribio, Darren Waldron.

Thanks are due also to the School of Modern Languages at the University of Southampton, which funded my fieldwork, and to the School of Linguistics, Languages and Cultures at the University of Manchester, which provided funding for a six-month period of research leave.

Introduction

Protest and Authenticity in Contemporary French Music Culture

In January 2008, the French conservative Head of State, Nicolas Sarkozy, married his singer-songwriter girlfriend, ex-model Carla Bruni. In the weeks following the ceremony, popular music critics in the left-wing press (*Libération*, *Télérama*, *L'Express*), wondered whether they would ever be able to listen to Bruni's music in the same way again. In *Télérama*, a journalist stated that he now found it 'very hard' to listen to her songs, even though he had enjoyed them previously, since he felt that the simple act of putting Bruni's CD into his hi-fi would amount to a declaration of support for the right-wing policies of her husband (Ferenczi, 2008).[1] In July 2008, this dilemma became more acute as Bruni released a new album, her third, and critics found themselves professionally obliged to review it. In *Télérama*, after a lengthy and circumvoluted apology, it was eventually not reviewed, but simply dismissed as 'an album of banal pop' ['un album de variété ordinaire'] (Lehoux and Cassavetti, 2008). This stood in marked contrast to the gushing reviews published in that very magazine five years earlier, when Bruni was not yet married to the President, but had just released her first album, a collection of bluesy guitar ballads accompanying her own lyrics, and been praised then as a 'pure' and 'perfect' emanation of *chanson* simplicity, in the vein of the much-revered national icon Georges Brassens (Jarno, 2003).[2] Despite the five-year gap, Bruni's 2008 album was comparable in style and content to the first one. Her music had not changed; only her personal situation.

Behind this anecdote lies a series of powerful tensions that govern the place and the values of popular music in France, and it provides a startling illustration of how the political polarization between right and left affects musical tastes, opinions and practices. It shows, firstly, how most discussions of popular music are strongly ideologically loaded in France, to the extent that the musicality of popular music is often relegated to the background when songs and artists' careers are discussed. It also indicates that 'quality' is usually perceived to be the prerogative of left-wing artists, as Bruni lost all artistic credibility when she married her right-wing husband. It is highly revealing, in this respect, that her 2008 album was dismissed

---

1   'Carla Bruni's first album, so much loved yesterday, is today difficult to put in the CD player' ['Le premier album de Carla Bruni, tant aimé hier, on a du mal, aujourd'hui, à le glisser dans la platine CD']. See also Revel, 2008.

2   On the front cover of Céline Fontana's mini-encyclopaedia of French popular music, published in 2007, Brassens' and Bruni's photographs are placed side by side.

as 'variété', a loaded and derogatory term in French which usually applies to highly mediatized, commercially successful and intellectually unchallenging songs. Regardless of her subtlety as a lyricist and skills as a singer-songwriter, Bruni's detractors considered that, since 2008, her affiliation to the political right, even by proxy, had debased her output. Their comments also imply that a powerful anti-*variété* bias exists in contemporary France which posits that high quality, prestige and 'authenticity' can only be found in consciously leftist, anti-conservative music, and in music that appears 'alternative' or non-mainstream. This book is an attempt to make sense of this paradigm, to understand its formation and resilience in France, and to question its assumptions and prejudices.

The Ordinariness of 'Protest', the Frenchness of 'Protest'

This research focus could well seem outmoded to many. In 1979, Richard Dyer had already made it clear that the anti-mainstream bias in popular music, targeting commercially successful pop music genres such as disco, was a form of terrorism on the part of left-wing intellectuals (Dyer, 1990, p. 410). Scorn for pop music was also, he argued, flawed from the start, since it was based on an unsubstantiated polarization between the 'free' or autonomous world of folk and rock (in particular), and the perverted, immoral or profit-seeking world of pop and disco (for example). The extreme rigidity of this mutually exclusive system, and its false premises, have since been revealed by various authors, including Keith Negus (1992) and David Hesmondhalgh (1999), and it is now commonly accepted that Adornian fears about mass production and mainstream music are excessive. Nonetheless, no amount of academic analysis is ever enough to change people's perceptions of the world around them, and it is a fact of life that this binary framework, however simplistic, remains highly attractive to many (perhaps because of its very simplicity). As Max Paddison (1996, p. 95) has also insisted, Theodor Adorno's criticism of consumerism and the culture industry remains relevant for those anxious about the location of quality and meaning in their musical practices, and a quest for 'authenticity' has as much topicality today as at any time in the past. The example of Carla Bruni's reception is enough to show that this quest, and its related binary discourse, still has great potency in France in the early twenty-first century.

Focusing on France from the 1980s onwards, this book looks at the constitution of a 'protest' music culture and its claims to challenge the *variété* (standardized pop) that dominates the charts and the media, and, at the same time, contest the most reactionary and socially damaging trends in current politics, such as anti-immigration policies, neo-liberalism and globalization. Squarely leftist, the participants in this 'protest' music culture equate commercially successful pop music with right-wing conservatism, and value positively the work of the artists who attempt to depart from the dominant tendency in pop music in order to question reactionary positions in contemporary French society (seemingly what Bruni failed to do by marrying a right-wing personality). The title of this book, 'Protest Music in France', should thus be understood to refer to the various ways in which chart music and political conservatism are contested in contemporary French popular music. This protest is observed through the prism of the 'alternative' rock scene of the last three decades, starting with *rock alternatif*, the post-punk French genre of the late 1980s that was defined by its production by 'independent' record labels, and continuing with *rock métis* and *chanson néo-réaliste*, two trends of the 1990s and beyond, whose artists were directly inspired by *rock alternatif* at both the stylistic and ideological levels.

Following the sociological and empirical methodology advocated by many popular music scholars, this study thus concentrates on the ideological basis and cultural constructedness of a music culture (McClary, 2000, p. 7). It considers that cultural identities, in this case the loose grouping of French artists, producers, journalists and audiences who regard 'alternative' rock music as a challenge to *variété* and reactionary politics, are the result of social, material and historical determinants (and, to a lesser extent, personal individuality). Through a series of case studies, it focuses on those instances where 'quality' and 'protest' music products do cross over to the 'mainstream', and examines the problematic, and sometimes even damaging, ways in which this shift affects the participants in this culture. More generally, this book is therefore concerned with processes of cultural validation, and the difficult juxtaposition of some people's high principles, in their quest for 'protest' and 'authenticity', with the fragile and changing context of music production, dissemination and consumption. Accordingly, attention is paid to the changes, overlaps and internal conflicts of the 'space of identity' (Morley and Robins, 1995) of France's contemporary protest music culture, locating the non-mainstream music scene of the 1980s, 1990s and early 2000s within the interplay of social, economic, political, ideological and technological factors.

French Popular Music Studies

If taking a pluridisciplinary approach is probably self-evident to most Anglo-American academics, it is still something of a novelty in the field of French (and francophone) popular music studies. There has not only been a tendency to ignore the academic study of popular music in France until recently (Teillet, 2003, p. 173), but the prevalence of a literary tradition, privileging the poetic analysis of song lyrics, has long restricted the domain. The publications of Joël July's *Esthétique de la chanson française* [Aesthetics of French *Chanson*] (2007) and Isabelle Marc Martínez's *Esthétique et poétique des textes* [Aesthetics and Poetics of [Rap] Texts] (2008), are revealing titles in this respect. This said, a number of French sociologists have started to focus on popular music from a combined perspective, privileging for instance cultural policy, the practices of musicians, or those of audiences (see Le Guern, 2003 for a brief survey). In the English language, moreover, a Cultural Studies-based approach to French popular music has grown steadily since the turn of the twenty-first century, with the publications of Peter Hawkins (2000), David Looseley (2003) and Hugh Dauncey and Steve Cannon (2003) paving the way for an assessment of the social and ideological meanings of popular music in contemporary France. In addition, the growth in the study of new music genres is particularly rich, with many titles being dedicated to the vitality of the French rap and techno scenes (Boucher, 1998; Birgy, 2001; Durand, 2002; Béthune, 2003; Huq, 2006).

While it is true that France is currently a large producer and consumer of rap music, the large output in French rap studies may have given a distorted vision, especially from abroad, of the actual patterns of production and consumption of music in the country. As we shall see, the French are also heavy consumers of other music genres, including *variété* (the best-selling category), and the more 'serious' genres of *chanson* and rock music. The recent prominence of rap studies also implies, quite erroneously, that rap is the main vehicle for an expression of 'protest' in contemporary France, with simple equations often being drawn between the music of artists from disenfranchised areas of society and the notion of 'rebellion'. This book, in part, attempts to redress this imbalance by looking at the genre of contemporary 'alternative' rock. In so doing, it asserts that forms of cultural protest can be located, clearly if paradoxically, in music genres associated with affluent, educated and intellectual artists and audiences.

The choice to focus on *rock alternatif* and its offshoots is also justified by the enormous symbolic impact of the French rock music scene generally on value judgements about popular music in France (Teillet, 2003, p. 182), and by the surprisingly sparse state of research in this area. One brief article by the late American scholar André J. M. Prévos (1991) had the merit of highlighting the emergence of alternative rock in France, although it concentrated largely on song lyrics. More recently, Cécile Péchu (2006) devoted a chapter to *rock alternatif*, but this took for granted, rather than questioned, the notion of 'resistance' in this area of music culture.[3] The aim here, then, is to explain the formation of a so-called alternative, anti-mainstream and 'protest' music culture in contemporary France, taking seriously the quest for 'authenticity' of its actors (producers, artists, audiences, critics), but also deconstructing this notion by examining the material and ideological structures that shape it, including the music industry, cultural policy, republican ideology, and social and peer pressure. Of relevance to those with an interest in French popular culture, and in popular music more broadly, this discussion of the cultural meanings attached to anti-conservative protest in contemporary French popular music combines an appraisal of the music industry with an analysis of audience practices and discourses.

---

3   Alexandre Meunier has made his unpublished BA thesis, on *rock alternatif* (1998), available online. It focuses on the relationships between key 'alternative' French artists and 'independent' record producers in the period 1983–1997.

'Protest' and 'Authenticity' in Post-war France: *Chanson*

Before charting the outline of the present research, it is worth recalling that, before the 1980s and *rock alternatif*, a discourse of 'protest' against reactionary positions and commercialization already existed in French popular music, and most evidently within the genre of *chanson* (also known as *chanson à textes*). The term 'chanson' has several meanings in French, the first one referring to any kind of popular music, including the vernacular forms of popular music developed in France since the thirteenth century.[4] A second, much more recent meaning, is that developed in the 1950s as a short-hand for *chanson à textes* (text-based *chanson*), and which has virtually supplanted the first, as most music professionals and commentators in France today, when employing the term 'chanson', have in mind the stylistic characteristics and implied connotations of this more recent usage.

The term *chanson à textes* derives from the preponderance of the lyrics, and the attention paid to careful diction for the transmission of sophisticated poetry in this genre. Often playing with different registers, *chanson* lyrics typically mix introspection with bawdiness, sentimentality with humour, and emotional fragility with intellectual literary references. Sung over a simple, acoustic melody, sometimes involving just one instrument, these lyrics can easily be heard. *Chanson* lyrics also convey a clear 'protest' message, which may not be (and indeed rarely is) party political, yet whose ideological affiliation to anti-conservatism is often explicit. Georges Brassens (1921–1981), who is unquestionably heralded in France as 'the greatest genius of French *chanson*' (Dicale, 2006, p. 165),[5] but remains a virtual unknown outside France, has epitomized this balance. His songs could be, by turns, anti-clerical, anti-militarist, anti-bourgeois and anti-nationalist, as well as subtle and moving poems (Tinker, 2005). Brassens' lyrics were considered as independent poetry from an early stage, and appeared in the prestigious 'Poets of Today' ['Poètes d'Aujourd'hui'] collection published by Seghers in the early 1960s (Looseley, 2003, p. 38). His symbolic importance as a literary and national figure is quite evident today in the many streets, public institutions and state schools named after him. Brassens has become a 'historical monument' (Calvet, quoted in Dalbavie, 2003, p. 146), and comparing Carla Bruni's first album to his work was no small praise – even if Bruni eventually gained a different form of national and symbolic prestige by marrying the President.

As well as featuring refined and politically conscious lyrics, *chanson* is also defined by its production by the lone, individual singer-songwriter, known in French as *auteur-compositeur-interprète*, henceforth ACI. Brassens embodied this all-in-one mastery, as did many of his contemporaries such as Jacques Brel, Barbara and Serge Gainsbourg. Since the 1970s and the appearance of 'new French *chanson*' ['nouvelle chanson française'], many more artists have similarly forged

---

4 Howard Mayer Brown et al., 'Chanson', *Oxford Music Online*, www. oxfordmusiconline.com, last accessed 17 March 2009.

5 '... le plus grand génie de la chanson française'.

careers as *chanson* ACIs, including Maxime Le Forestier, Renaud and Jacques Higelin, as have the more recent exponents of the sometimes awkwardly named 'new new French chanson' of the 1990s and 2000s, including Thomas Fersen, Vincent Delerm, Bénabar and Jeanne Cherhal (see Perrin, 2005; Dicale, 2006, pp. 411–16). Of course, there had been some ACI precursors before the 1950s, including the famous Charles Trenet, but combining the previously separate professional roles of lyricist, composer, singer and musician was new to post-war France, and contingent on the growth of mass entertainment in the years following the Liberation.

Indeed, text-based *chanson* only emerged in post-war France when, after years of privation and curfews during the Occupation, the eating, drinking and singing establishments of Paris gradually re-opened. The trend, already established before the war, which opposed the larger, wealthier music halls, with a seating capacity in the hundreds, to the smaller, often pokey and run-down cabarets, which could only sit a few dozen people, increased. After the war, while some savvy entrepreneurs set out to improve the lighting, sound and décor of their music halls (most famously perhaps, Bobino and L'Olympia), equally enterprising bar-tenders, working on a much smaller scale, opened the main rooms, backrooms and cellars of their cafés to music performers, in order to attract a slightly different clientele, often (but not necessarily) less wealthy patrons, finishing their night out with a casual form of entertainment. These new cafés were the reincarnation of the late nineteenth- and early twentieth-century cabarets, which had in the past been mainly situated in Montmartre and on the periphery of Paris, but started opening in the city centre for the first time after the war (Calvet, 1981, p. 71).

The new-look cabarets were often very small, with a confined stage space and poor acoustics that only allowed one artist to play at a time. As a result, singers had to accompany themselves, typically on the guitar, which they could bring along, and sometimes on the piano if the cabaret owner had one. The spatial and material constraints of cabarets thus determined the development of *chanson à textes* as a solo art form (Calvet, 1981, p. 72). The very high popular demand for this form of cheap entertainment also meant that, after the war, many artists tried their luck in such places, and many lyricists would learn a few basic guitar chords to provide a background for their songs on stage. Among the most successful cabarets of that period (1947 to the late 1950s) were L'Ecole Buissonière, L'Ecluse and Les Trois Baudets (Dicale, 2006, pp. 145–9).

The confined stage space, by necessity, imposed great economy on musical orchestration. As a result, artists compensated for the lack of instruments by a richness of words (Calvet, 1981, p. 72). Moreover, the high demand for new songs (also spurred by the growth in radio broadcasting – see below) forced many artists to add already existing poems, famous or lesser-known, to their repertoire: text-based *chanson* was born (Dicale, 2006, p. 150). Finally, most of these cabarets were situated on the left bank of Paris, in the now-famous areas of the Quartier Latin and Saint-Germain-des-Prés, where rental space was cheaper than on the right bank. There, many vanguard artists, left-wing sympathizers and high-profile intellectuals, including the philosopher Jean-Paul Sartre, also congregated. In these conditions, the genre of *chanson à textes*, born in left-bank cabarets, became associated with intellectual and poetic sensibility (in the lyrics), artistic autonomy (the ACI, the stage), and leftism (anti-conservative 'protest'). From then on, the phrases *chanson rive gauche* (left-bank song), *chanson de qualité* (quality song) and *chanson à textes* (text-based song) all became essentially synonymous, and 'chanson' came to be used as a shorthand for all of these. Material conditions, then, established the background for a series of assumptions to flourish, most powerfully the idea that only *chanson*, as a lyrics-oriented solo genre, could represent 'quality', and that only *chanson* had the ability to challenge dominant discourse. In other words, only *chanson* was 'authentic'.

Anti-*Variété* Prejudice, *Yéyé* and Mediatization

These assumptions are evident in the *chanson* rhetoric that David Looseley (2003, pp. 65–84) has already scrutinized. Looseley quotes many French music professionals, artists and critics who esteem *chanson* as a 'morally superior' art form. Among them, one could cite Fred Hidalgo, the editor of *Chorus*, the first French monthly dedicated to *chanson*, considered by the profession as the magazine of reference in this domain (Dicale, 2006, p. 465). For Hidalgo, the genre of *chanson* is epitomized by Brassens, summarized by its 'proud, nonconformist, rebellious, free' character (Hidalgo, 1991, p. 110),[6] and constitutes an emanation of the French national character. Furthermore, for Marc Robine, the author of an anthology of French popular music, *chanson* is 'the culture of the poor and their natural expression' (Robine, 1994, p. 9).[7] Although Robine's book focuses on the earlier period, from the Middle Ages to the late nineteenth century, his introduction charts contemporary developments and clearly uses the term 'chanson' with implied post-war, 'authentic' connotations. Indeed, Robine argues that technological developments such as 'the radio, the television, the walkman have silenced the people [of France]',[8] and his simplistic polarization between *chanson* on the one hand, as the supposed emanation of a sense of national bonding, and 'modernity' on the other, as a destructive force killing this solidarity, is typical of the *chanson* rhetoric that developed in the late 1950s and early 1960s.

Robine's anthology was published in 1994, and one might think that, by the mid-1990s, French music critics would have been able to reach beyond this simplistic prejudice against 'modernity'. Nonetheless, behind the bold claim that *chanson* has never been, and should not now be, contaminated by technology, lies the assumption, still extremely powerful, that the popular music dominant in contemporary France is unnatural, artificial and inauthentic. Implied in Robine's

---

6   '… l'essence même de celle-ci [la chanson], fière, anticonformiste, révoltée, libre'.
7   'La chanson était la culture du pauvre et son expression naturelle'.
8   'La radio, la télévision, le walkman ont rendu le peuple muet'.

statement is the lowly status of *variété*, the term now favoured by the French to refer to any heavily mediatized and/or intellectually unchallenging popular music which is, by virtue of being heavily mediatized, often highly successful. The term *variété(s)*, whether written in the singular or plural form, was initially descriptive in French, and referred to the variety of acts showcased on the music hall stage of the late nineteenth century onwards – the English language has retained this usage when talking of 'variety acts'. From the 1950s onwards, however, the term began to take on pejorative undertones by contrast to the elaboration of *chanson* as a supposedly 'purer', more personal and more complete song form, disseminated outside the music hall network and, presumably, outside the process of mediatization (Calvet, 1981, p. 70). This is the binary that Robine hints at when he opposes *chanson* to radio and television, following the widespread assumption that *chanson* is the natural expression of a poet, and the 'authentic' reflection of a French popular art form, while *variété*, by contrast, is its debased, unsophisticated, newer and mediatized avatar. 'Variety song' ['la chanson de variété'], 'les variétés' or 'la variété', are terms that today apply to various music genres, from the *yéyé* of the 1960s, the disco of the 1970s, to the made-for-TV pop music of the 2000s, but what all these genres have in common is the large amount of airtime they receive on radio and television, the 'starification' of their performers in a combination of new media, and their usually subsequent, but by no means always guaranteed, high sales.

It is thus important to stress that the discourse of 'authenticity' surrounding French *chanson* is historically grounded in the late 1950s and early 1960s, when cabarets not only gave birth to *chanson à textes* in stylistic terms, but new technology (including the portable radio, the turntable, the television, the youth and music press) also created a favourable terrain for the mass-mediatization of all music genres, and, consequently, for the elaboration of a defensive discourse against this mass-mediatization. Indeed, just as rock music was making its first appearance in France in the late 1950s, radio station promoters, record producers, music hall owners, television programmers, and journalists both of the generalist and burgeoning specialist music press, all started to work in partnership with a view to increasing the mediatization of popular music artists, and the sales of their respective businesses. The phenomenon of mass-mediatization was particularly evident in the promotion of *yéyé* music, the French response to rock music that intentionally copied US and UK rock hits, with French lyrics ('yeah, yeah!', hence the genre's name) sung by French artists.

Johnny Hallyday, the first and most successful *yéyé* star, has, more than Brassens, achieved a modicum of recognition abroad, if only as the butt of sniggering comments (Looseley, 2005). His success in France, however, and that of other such artists, was due to the role of French record producers who bought the copyright to American songs, and hired teams of translators to create French versions. From 1960 onwards, year of the first recording contract for Hallyday, the turntable and the portable radio were also selling strongly, so that a variety of professionals, working in and around the music industry (record producers, radio managers, television directors, press editors, music-playing equipment sellers) had clear pathways for the dissemination of a new 'youth' culture, mediatized in multiple and intensive ways (Dicale, 2006, p. 203). *Yéyé* stars were also, typically, younger and more physically active performers than had previously been the case in French popular music, using their whole body in ways that contrasted particularly sharply with the often staid (yet subtle) performances of *chanson* artists, including Edith Piaf and Brassens.[9] What the example of *yéyé* music reveals, then, is that by the time rock music arrived in France, and by the time French professionals cottoned on to the fact that it was there to stay, the reinforcement of a sense of 'authenticity' in the cabaret-born, lyrically subtle *chanson* (a few years older than *yéyé*), and of a sense of artificiality in the imitative, non-author based and ever-present *yéyé*, was inevitable. By contrast to *chanson*, *yéyé* was derided in the 'serious' music press as 'vacuous and embarrassingly inauthentic, a colonised music that eternally misses the point' (Looseley, 2003, p. 30).

Nonetheless, the dialectical system opposing *chanson* to mainstream pop music (*yéyé* in particular, *variété* in general) constitutes a generalising, simplistic proposition. It is easy to criticize it by recalling that, in the early 1950s, the careers of *chanson* artists were already inseparable from the music industry. For instance, in 1952, Brassens was introduced to Jacques Canetti, who simultaneously launched him on the stage of his cabaret Les Trois Baudets, and gave him a recording contract with Polydor, the branch of the multinational company Philips for which he worked as creative director. By 1954, Brassens had contracts to perform at the upmarket music halls of L'Olympia, and later Bobino, and would never return to the small-scale cabarets of his beginnings (Dicale, 2006, pp. 168–9 and p. 182). In the early 1960s, Philips also signed Hallyday, and these two artists, Brassens the national *chanson* icon, and Hallyday the quintessential *yéyé* fraudster, were both produced by the same multinational conglomerate throughout the 1960s and 1970s.

This simple fact is enough to show that the 'authenticity' of *chanson*, partly derived from its supposed absence of interaction with the commercial side of the music profession, is questionable. It also illustrates perfectly the point that the *chanson* rhetoric, structured around a basic binary, is often factually incorrect, a simplified version of complex events, or a 'national myth' as Looseley (2003, p. 63) puts it. Nonetheless, like all myths, this idea is also highly attractive, powerful and significant to many people, and was given gravitas in the early 1960s by the highly visible promotion of *yéyé* music on various fronts by some commercial producers. The rhetoric of *chanson* authenticity is thus occasionally grounded in reality, and is a defensive notion invented in the late 1950s and early 1960s in reaction to *yéyé*'s supposed lack of literariness and wit, absence of ACI skill, and its insertion within an efficient network of commercialization. The construction of this 'artificial' pole allows *chanson* to shine through as 'authentic' in contrast,

---

9 The role of the mind/body polarization in this rhetoric would deserve its own book-length study, and can only be hinted at in the following pages.

and to be construed as a tool of 'protest' against the artificiality of the *variété* pop. In the early 1980s, the emergence of *rock alternatif* would give a new lease of life to this discourse of authenticity.

Chapter Outline

With this background in mind, the present study charts the resilience of the myth of 'authenticity' in contemporary French popular music, paying attention to its factual inaccuracies, its contradictions and paradoxes, as well as its material resilience, and ideological and symbolic impact. This short historical presentation has also highlighted that France is an ideal national context in which to observe the play of tensions between popular music and social protest, augmenting existing Anglo-American-centred research in this area (see Peddie, 2006).

Chapter 1 maps out the private and public determinants that have contributed to the production of French rock music from 1981 onwards, and examines their relation to the wider 'mainstreamization' of popular music in France. Exploring the intricacies of the music industry in contemporary France, it focuses on the close yet conflictual relationships between foreign-owned major companies and local independent labels, arguing that so-called 'alternative' rock music, in France in the 1980s and 1990s, covered various conflicting zones of interests. This chapter also interrogates the influence of the French state in propagating a sense of anti-mainstream 'resistance', in particular through the measures of decentralization and the 'liberalization' of the airwaves. While the presence of this state sponsor calls into question French rock's autonomy, a series of case studies on the production of French rock acts (Bérurier Noir, Mano Negra, Têtes Raides, Louise Attaque) highlight the fact that the notions of anti-commercialism and 'authenticity' are at once a specificity of the 'independent' music sector, and part of the larger endeavour of the global music industry to maintain its diversity.

The following three chapters all focus on questions of national identity, showing that, after *rock alternatif*, different protest music genres found new ways of expressing the notions of 'protest' and 'authenticity', thereby challenging as much as reproducing the supposedly 'national' character of French *chanson*. Concentrating on *chanson néo-réaliste*, a genre characterized by its intentional references to the realist song of the inter-war period, Chapter 2 examines the ways in which the notion of nostalgia was, in the 1990s and beyond, used by artists, producers and critics to construct a sense of 'resistance' against mainstream pop music, 'modernity' and consumerism. Dwelling on a series of old-fashioned stereotypes, this genre is, however, problematic in its depiction of contemporary reality, and the chapter underlines the uneasy relationship of *chanson néo-réaliste* artists to France's post-colonial identity.

The place of post-colonial minorities and the representation of multi-ethnicity in contemporary French 'protest' music are developed in Chapter 3, with reference to the genre of *rock métis*. Squarely leftist in its combination of anti-commercial ideals with an anti-racist agenda, *rock métis* is a music genre mixing rock and *chanson* with the musical instruments, genres and languages of previously colonial locations. This compositional hybridity, or *métissage* as the French call it, challenges official republican doctrine by calling into question the supposed neutrality of French identity. Nonetheless, with specific reference to the group Zebda, composed of French-Algerian artists, Chapter 3 also argues that the exploration of ethnic difference, and in particular of 'Arabness', remains controversial in contemporary French culture, as *beur* artists find it impossible to gain both commercial success and critical acclaim while retaining a sense of 'difference'.

The problematic relations between fame and critical recognition form the heart of Chapter 4, in which the Franco-Spanish artist Manu Chao provides a paradigmatic example of the contradictory position of 'resistance' in French music culture and in the wider global music industry. Playing in the *rock métis* style, Chao has achieved a relatively large degree of commercial success in France and abroad, indicating that *métissage*, despite being an intentionally contestatory mode of expression, can appeal to large sections of the public. His success, however, was not simply due to the 'authentic' sound of his music or the sincerity of his pro-migration arguments, but also to his inscription into the wider protest movement of anti-globalization, whose well-off, educated and left-wing participants constitute a highly receptive audience for the idea of *métissage* and for the ill-defined genre of 'world music'.

The last two chapters develop the place of the audience in the formation of a widespread taste for French 'protest' music in France. Chapter 5 presents innovative fieldwork in French music studies by providing transcriptions of interviews, the qualitative analysis of which reveals the importance of cultural antecedence, peer-pressure and prestige in shaping 'alternative' or 'anti-mainstream' music tastes. Building upon existing studies of music audiences, but emphasizing the national specificities of respondents, this chapter stresses the fluidity of 'alternative' music identities as audiences react to the growing success of some 'protest' artists and re-position themselves. Examining the choice of media outlets that audiences also claim as representative of anti-mainstream music tastes, outlets which are in many cases state-sponsored, Chapter 5 also echoes Chapter 1 in its demonstration of the links between France's official and elite culture, and the notions of anti-commercial 'resistance' and anti-mainstream criticism.

Finally, Chapter 6 focuses on French popular music festivals as sites where the notion of anti-mainstream 'authenticity' and leftist ideology converge particularly intensely, and interviews with festival participants are quoted as evidence of this connection. While audiences declare their pleasure in taking part in an experience of 'destabilization' of dominant norms, the structural, political and commercial reality of festivals reveals that they constitute, in particular in France where the state is an important financial partner, regulated and fashionable events. Examining the tensions between the imagined roles of marginality and solidarity adopted by festival-goers, and the reality of marketing forces and social exclusion, this chapter problematizes the part played by festivals in France's protest music culture. In explaining why the ideas of resistance, destabilization, protest and authenticity appeal to French artists, producers, critics and audiences, while examining the contradictions hidden behind these notions, all six chapters emphasize the ambivalent, complex and subtle formation of 'alternative' music identities in contemporary France.

PART I
Serious Business.
The Production of Protest in the French Music Industry

Chapter 1
Independent Labels, Music Policy and
Rock Alternatif

In the early 1980s in France, a shift became perceptible in the discourse of artists, producers and journalists alike regarding exactly what constituted 'authenticity' in French popular music. From the 1950s up until the late 1970s, there was a wide consensus that musical 'authenticity' was the preserve of *chanson*, and that it manifested itself in the artist's poetic sensibility, hard graft and multi-tasking skills as composer, author and interpreter (Looseley, 2003, pp. 66–9). The conditions of production of *chanson*, in small or larger companies, did not come into the equation. Yet, like other popular music genres, *chanson* was a commercial artefact, produced by profit-driven record labels. Georges Brassens, Barbara and Jacques Brel were all signed to subsidiaries of the large international conglomerate Philips, while the self-proclaimed anarchist singer and poet Léo Ferré was produced by Barclay, the largest post-war French record company.[1] Philips also produced the *yéyé* star Johnny Hallyday, and the similar conditions of production for both *chanson* and *yéyé* music never prevented the former from reaching the status of a national signifier of artistic quality. Up until the late 1970s, then, the inevitable subordination of *chanson* artists to market forces did not affect their creative output and their reception as models of 'authenticity' (Yonnet, 1985, p. 193).

In the 1980s, however, due to a convergence of structural, political and ideological factors, the perceived authenticity of certain French artists was increasingly perceived as being dependent on the autonomy of their production, and since all the large multinational music companies were, by this time, foreign, the local 'independent' French record labels, whose number also increased in this period, came to be seen as the bulwarks of a French way of supporting music and doing business. While artists working with large, foreign 'major' companies were stripped of their cultural and national prestige by this anti-commercial bias, one music genre in particular, *rock alternatif*, crystallized the emerging notion of 'resistance' to the global industry. As a post-punk genre, *rock alternatif* developed an exclusive relationship with local independent labels, and accumulated a series of 'authentic' values based on its combination of the virtues of *chanson* (the foregrounding of poetic and political lyrics), of rock (energy, anger), and of a renewed sense of ethics in its challenging of international economic pressures. Taking into consideration the changes that affected the French music industry in

---

1   In his trademark irony, Ferré composed a song about the profit-driven ambitions of Barclay's producer, Eddie Barclay, which itself became a hit ('Monsieur Barclay', 1965).

the second half of the twentieth century, and the cultural policies relating to popular music since 1981, this chapter explains how *rock alternatif* became a catalyst for this renewal of a French 'protest' discourse, with case-studies of independent rock labels of the 1980s and 1990s providing concrete evidence of this shift.

Major Production Labels and French Popular Music

Since its very inception at the end of the nineteenth century, when the licence to produce Edison sound recording machines was sold to American, German, British, Dutch and French companies, the music industry has been an international affair. France was a major player from the start, with competitive music companies, a vibrant national music scene and a large audience ready to buy new products. As early as 1896, the French company Pathé had bought British-made gramophones, obtained the rights from the US company Columbia to promote American artists in France, and begun manufacturing its own cylinders and recording home artists. By 1910, Pathé was exporting these to Italy and Russia (Lefeuvre, 1998, pp. 8–15).[2] At the same time, foreign companies such as Columbia (US) and His Master's Voice (UK) were opening branches in France and recording, producing and selling French artists to the French public. Throughout the twentieth century, the music recorded, sold and listened to in France was the product of foreign-owned companies, as well as of French companies with local and/or international interests. In terms of record production, therefore, there never was a purely 'national' music market, in which local artists would only be released through local companies.[3]

Nonetheless, the twentieth century did witness a gradual decline in the national music market share controlled by French production labels. In the late 1930s, Pathé was the main French film and music production company, but it was forbidden by the state from holding a monopoly over both cinema production and music recording (Farchy, 1999, p. 55). Pathé chose to concentrate on film, dismantling its music branches and selling them off to its richest, foreign competitors. No French company was subsequently strong enough to buy back the majority of the market share in French music, and there has been no French brand able to compete on a global scale ever since. After the Second World War, the large European and North American music companies started to merge with one another in order to access new markets, vying for the control of international music sales

---

2   Howard Rye, 'Pathé', *The New Grove Dictionary of Jazz* (2nd edn), reproduced in Oxford Music Online, www.oxfordmusiconline.com, last accessed 20 March 2009.

3   A problem arises in translating the French term *producteur*, which does not cover the same reality as 'producer'. In an independent French production label, the manager or *producteur* may combine the Anglo-American skills of financial producer, A&R manager and sound technician. For a clearer distinction, see Hennion (1990 [1983]), note 1, p. 206. To simplify here, we use the English 'producer'.

as popular music consumption increased. The most powerful of these companies became known as the 'majors'. The majors are international conglomerates which achieve a synergy through their control of all the stages of music development. They own pressing plants, recording equipment and studios, produce software and hardware (vinyl, cassettes, CDs, MP3s, hi-fi equipment), and control advertising and distribution via contracted media and retailers (TV, radio, the press, music shops, e-commerce). Over the period of our study (1981–2008), the number of majors went down from six to four. These were Polygram/Philips (Netherlands), EMI (GB), BMG (Germany), Universal (USA), Warner (USA) and Sony (Japan) (Lefeuvre, 1998, p. 71). In 1998, Universal acquired Polygram, becoming in effect the world leader in music sales. In 2004, BMG merged with Sony, and EMI and Warner have subsequently been discussing a possible merger (Hopkins, 2004; Byrne, 2007, p. 9).

It was in the late 1970s and during the 1980s that the last large French record companies were bought out by the majors. In 1978, the main French post-war record producer, Barclay (founded in 1948), was bought by Polygram. In the mid-1980s, Trema, an important producer of French *variétés*, sold some of its shares to Sony and EMI. In 1992, the French label Vogue, created in the 1950s and initially specializing in jazz, filed for bankruptcy and sold its shares to BMG. As a result of these and other buyouts, the music produced and sold in France came to be predominantly controlled by the majors, who would, by 1996, account for up to 99 per cent of music in the French charts, and control about 95 per cent of the national market share in music sales generally (Lefeuvre, 1998, p. 72). This rampant presence in France can be explained by a historical lack of protectionism, in contrast to the state's earlier regulation of the film industry. However, it is also due to the combined role of the majors as record producers and distributors. Music distribution includes the negotiation of access to publicity networks and the supply of recorded music to retailers. In France, this chain is virtually monopolized by the majors, and even the music produced by independent producers gets distributed by majors, with some rare exceptions. Paradoxically, then, even if French consumers choose to purchase French over non-French music, their money still goes overwhelmingly to foreign-owned majors and, likewise, many of the French artists selling records on the national territory also contribute to these companies' financial success (Lefeuvre, 1998, p. 111). This dominance has had several consequences for the national music landscape. One has been the vitality of the French music scene in general, which majors see as being in their interest to boost. Another is the resilience and high symbolic value of national independence in music production, as 'independent' labels now provide one of the very few spaces for doing business autonomously (or appearing to do so at any rate). As will be seen, a fierce sentiment of self-righteous 'resistance' to the power of the majors established itself in France from the 1980s onwards.

The presence of the majors in France, as part of the general phenomenon of globalization, has not actually led to the sidelining or disappearance of French popular music. *Au contraire*. Because the French are rather heavy music consumers, with France rating fifth in terms of units sold in the world (Lefeuvre, 1998, p. 22), and because they also tend to favour home-grown artists and songs with French lyrics, the majors, despite being foreign-owned, protect and encourage the consumption of French music in order to enhance their profits. In the mid-1980s, 45 per cent of all record sales in France were by French artists, while only 20 per cent were by Anglo-American artists (the rest being made up of classical, jazz, humour and other repertories not classified as 'popular music') (Mermet, 1985, p. 372). The so-called 'Loi Toubon' of 1994, which stipulated that a minimum of 40 per cent of the music broadcast on French radio must be of French origin, only increased this trend (Looseley, 2003, pp. 153–4). By 1998, the proportion of French and francophone albums sold in France had reached 54 per cent, with the 10 best-selling French albums of that year all being produced and/or distributed by majors (*L'Année du disque 1999*, p. 134). By 2005, 61.4 per cent of music units sold in France were by national artists (Dicale, 2006, p. 411). It is in this dual context of the hold of the majors in France, and of the success of French music on the national territory, that the production of the most popular French artists of the 1980s and 1990s must be seen. During the 1980s and 1990s, three of the best-selling French artists were Michel Sardou, Jean-Jacques Goldman and Mylène Farmer, and all were produced by majors (subsidiaries of Sony for the first two, Polydor/Universal for the latter). In 1998, Céline Dion was nominated as the nation's favourite female artist, and she, too, was produced by the major Columbia/Sony.[4]

None of these artists corresponds, however, to the 'quality' models of the *chanson* canon, for different reasons. Although he is a singer-songwriter, Sardou has been affiliated to mainstream music through the innumerable chart successes he has achieved since the 1960s, and to reactionary ideology through his right-wing declarations in favour of the death penalty and against feminism (Calvet and Klein, 1978). Despite being associated with left-wing movements, Goldman is, for his part, generally derided by the music press for composing 'conventional', bland pop ballads (Saka and Plougastel, 1999, p. 257). Farmer and Dion are, moreover, 'mere' interpreters, whose fame has relied on erotic provocation (Farmer) and vocal prowess and showmanship (Dion), rather than personal creativity or lyrical subtlety. Since the output of these artists, the most commercially successful music in France, is produced and distributed by the majors, its exposure on prime-time TV shows, commercial radios and the like is guaranteed, thus increasing its chances of further success.

One could argue, too, that this music is also representative of a dominant ideology, with the style and content of the songs often repeating prevailing gender codes (the erotically charged lyrics and videos of Mylène Farmer reinforce a certain objectification of women), and does not obviously question the neo-liberal status quo. There is, then, such a thing as the dominance of mainstream pop, or *variété*,

---

4   *Les goûts musicaux des français*, Sofrès survey for SACEM, SACEM publication, January 1999.

in France, even though the artists producing it may be left-wing (as in the case of Goldman), singer-songwriters (as in the case of Goldman and Sardou), 'skilled' (as in the case of Dion), and its music and lyrics may include a degree of provocation and controversy (as in the case of Farmer). What really matters is that this type of popular music is featured on mainstream prime-time media, is highly successful, and its artists do not engage in open criticism of their modes of production. As we shall see, many counter-examples also exist, to show that it is possible to combine fame and 'protest' in contemporary France, yet the resulting balancing act also proves highly problematic for those artists whose central ambition in composing music is to mark their difference from mainstream pop.

From the 1980s onwards, then, the majors unarguably disseminated a form of conservative pop through the mainstream media, and a 'resistance' discourse started to take shape which targeted *variété*, taking issue with its supposed lack of artistic sophistication, its production by the majors, and the right-wing ideology visibly embedded in it (economic liberalism, social and cultural convention). This discourse of contestation is loosely left-wing, anti-capitalist in orientation, and rooted in an Adornian mistrust of the mass media. While such a discourse has been central to the elaboration of rock music culture in the USA and the UK (Negus, 1992, p. 16; Shuker, 1998, p. 21), its impact and significance in France was arguably greater, from the 1980s onwards, due to a series of nationally specific cultural and political factors. These included the launch of the French charts in the mid-1980s, which rendered the success of the majors all the more transparent, the inclusion of rock music within the prestigious official realm of public spending from 1981 onwards, and, paradoxically given the growing power of *variété*, the vitality of the French music scene in general, whose relative economic good health provided a space for the formulation and solidification of this 'protest' identity. These factors all converged to reinforce the legitimacy of any challenge to the power of the majors.

'Resistance' in the French Music Industry

The year 1984 saw the launch of the Top 50, the first national music chart, the results of which were compiled without consulting independent record producers and retailers (Lacoeuilhe, 1987). Through its retransmission on prime-time television (Canal +), commercial radio (Europe 1) and the national press (the highly popular TV guide *Télé 7 Jours*), the Top 50 effectively provided publicity for the already best-selling music products of the major labels, encouraging their further consumption. The chart also threw into sharp relief the fact that the French were buying 'mainstream' artists en masse, privileging the music produced by the majors (Dicale, 2006, p. 341). A number of critics saw in this the shocking sign of the encroachment of these foreign companies on French territory. For Brigitte Kernel (1987, p. 9), a presenter on the national radio station France Inter, the Top 50 represented a purely artificial way of gauging success, a sign of the tragically changed times in which the intrinsic value of a song and its 'author' no longer mattered.[5] For Fred Hidalgo (1991, pp. 93–4), the birth of the charts in France 'marked the beginning of the end for all those authentic artists for whom *chanson*-making is first and foremost a pressing urge to express themselves'.[6] Kernel and Hidalgo both pitted, in a defensive manner, the supposed 'authenticity' of French popular music, its originality and integrity, against the majors' apparently unique focus on short-term profits. Both took for granted the existence of an 'essence' of French song-making, suggesting that commercial considerations had never before come into the equation, and that a truly French approach to music respected the intellectual preoccupations and emotional impulses of artists. They opposed human creativity to the mechanization of profitability, and a French national sensibility to foreign (Anglo-American) business requirements. Since the charts were compiled with the exclusive support of the majors, the independent sector gained, by implication, 'authentic' credibility. As we shall see, such opinions have become extremely widespread (also Lledo, 1991, p. 123; Klein, 1995, p. 64).

In 1985, a survey of patterns of music consumption and 'lifestyles' in France similarly suggested that the charts were for conservative listeners and were about 'pure' entertainment rather than reflection, conferring by contrast the positive values of 'adventure' and 'rigour' upon rock music (Mermet, 1985, p. 366). Drawn up in a supposedly impartial way, this survey nonetheless took for granted many parameters, including the idea that hedonism and seriousness could never go together, and that rock music never featured in the charts, which it in fact did. While it is true that this survey also pointed to broad tendencies in the organization of music tastes in France, which the present study confirms to an extent, this kind of polarization is also overly simplistic and does not take into account its own binary limitations. What these examples reveal, then, is that the hold of the majors over France, and the establishment of the charts system in the 1980s, forged a relatively new cultural split with key commentators such as Kernel and Hidalgo, and the sociologist Mermet, taking anxious and unproblematic positions against the presence of new production and media systems. In these conditions, the independent production labels that started to emerge at that time, mainly producing a French version of punk called *rock alternatif*, became the repositories of a romanticized, supposedly natural, 'French' way of making and promoting 'authentic' popular music (Lefeuvre, 1998, p. 112). *Rock alternatif* broadly encapsulated the twin 'authentic' discourses of *chanson* and rock, with its attention to sophisticated and politically charged lyrics, and its energy and criticism of dominant society.

---

5 'The Top 50 and other such fake signs of success are deceptive. The "made to measure" [songs] of today only erode the core value of a song, an author.' ['Les Top 50 et autres ersatz de réussite faussent les jugements. Le "cousu sur mesure" de l'époque ne fait plus qu'éroder la valeur intrinsèque d'une chanson, d'un auteur.'].

6 '… le début d'une longue traversée du désert pour l'ensemble des artistes authentiques, pour qui la chanson est d'abord la forme aboutie d'une incontournable urgence d'exprimer'.

As this book reveals, it had a tremendous impact upon, and lent resilience to, a particularly French 'protest' discourse throughout the 1990s and beyond.[7]

Before looking at this discourse in its specific context of 'independent' production, it needs to be pointed out that the setting-up of independent labels in France in the 1980s was assisted by the general good health of the music industry. Prior to that period, there had been independent producers (and to a lesser extent, distributors), whose companies functioned without being controlled by larger conglomerates. The 1980s, however, after the slump following the oil crisis of 1973–4, was generally a prosperous time for the music industry. In France alone, music-listening was the leisure activity that increased the most between the 1970s and the 1990s (Mermet, 1998, p. 379), with sales of music units in France growing from 100 million in 1981 to 150 million in 1997 (D'Angelo, 1997, p. 178).[8] Moreover, and despite the independents' relegation to second place in terms of economic impact, being a small music producer in the 1980s was a potentially profitable operation. Without ever entering the charts, the third album of the *rock alternatif* act Bérurier Noir, produced by the French independent label Bondage, sold over 200,000 copies overall (Verlant, 2000, p. 127). Likewise, in the UK in the 1980s, the independent rock label Rough Trade also met its sales targets easily (Reynolds, 2005, p. 107). In addition to this, the majors were becoming aware of the shortcomings of their overgrown organizations, and entered a period of 'flexibilization' by splitting up into a multitude of small sub-labels, some of which were able to pass for independents although they were technically 'integrated' (Negus, 1992, p. 14). Finally, the groundwork covered by the independents, whose managers and talent spotters do actually listen to demo tapes and tour the music festivals, is also acknowledged by the majors, who regularly work in partnership with indie labels and step in once new or outlandish artists have obtained a degree of success (Laing, 1986, p. 335; Frith, 1992, p. 65; Lefeuvre, 1998, p. 155). These structural inter-dependencies mean that major and independent companies are not in direct confrontation with each other, and that, in a highly competitive business where the success of a given act is often quite unpredictable, there have been plenty of opportunities for new, small-scale producers to try their luck.

It is also important not to regard the independent music sector as homogeneous, since among the 1,000 or so independent labels active in France during the 1980s and 1990s, vast structural disparities existed (Lefeuvre, 1998, p. 114). On the one hand, the general tendency for independent record companies was to make do with low staff numbers (often fewer than 50), focus on a musical niche, and have yearly turnovers which rarely exceeded 45 million francs

---

7   Other music genres were affected by this 'protest' discourse, including *chanson minimaliste* (Reins, 2003; Barbot, 2003; Lehoux, 2004) and some sections of rap and electro (Jouvenet, 2006).

8   The growth of free music download from the Internet gradually changed this situation, but the present study really focuses on the 1990s, when the Internet had not yet had a clear impact on the music industry.

(Lefeuvre, 1998, p. 71).[9] Boucherie Production, one of the most famous French *indés* of the 1980s and 1990s, was in this sense typical. Structured around 6 employees, it mainly produced rock and *chanson* (as opposed to 'pop') and declared a turnover of 9.5 million Francs in 1998. This stands in sharp contrast to the majors' control of the recording technology and international distribution networks, their production of artists from all musical styles, and their turnovers expressed in billions of Francs. On the other hand, some independents occasionally reproduced the structural features of the majors, including the French independent label Musisoft which was set up in 1998 by the ex-general manager of Sony France, was not dedicated to any music genre in particular, employed 110 staff and had a turnover similar to that of a major, reaching 200 million francs in 1999 (Jammet, 1999, p. 33). Given their control of the distribution networks, the majors have also often contributed to the success of 'independent' acts produced on small labels, as was the case in 1998 with the post-*rock alternatif* band Louise Attaque, produced by the label Atmosphériques and distributed by Sony (see below). Thus, there is no simple definition of economic independence in popular music, and the relationships between majors and independents are far more intricate than might at first seem.

This said, however, the independent sector is often treated as a coherent whole, mostly because its rock music labels have been guided, for the most part, by an ideal of structural autonomy, and have refused to be linked to the production system of the majors (Lefeuvre, 1998, pp. 110–12). For the music journalist Christian Eudeline (in Verlant, 2000, p. 127), these labels unquestionably constituted a form of resistance because of their focus on 'autonomy and craftsmanship' ['autonomie et artisanat']. Philippe Teillet, the analyst of cultural policy in French popular music, agreed that the 'resistance' discourse, prevalent among French music professionals, took a fiercer turn during the 1980s and gradually achieved a 'considerable impact symbolically' by the end of the century (Teillet, 2003, p. 182). Because this discourse appropriates the notion of 'authenticity' already at the heart of *chanson*, it is no surprise that it would become more defensive at the turn of the 1980s, as the two 'greats' of French *chanson*, Jacques Brel and Georges Brassens, died around this time (in 1978 and 1981 respectively). To sum up, then, while a 'rock prejudice' exists elsewhere in the West, which rejects the majors *en bloc* (Negus, 1992, p. 61), it crystallized in France in the French independent labels of the 1980s because of a number of factors. The 1980s witnessed the buying-out of the last important French record companies by the majors, the growth of the Top 50 and the passing of national *chanson* icons, all of which triggered protectionist fears in some quarters. At the same time, however, it was due to the relatively healthy state of the industry that a space developed for the expression of resistance in small labels, where left-field music professionals could

---

9   Because this study concentrates on the 1990s in France, before the country changed its currency to the euro in 2000, we refer throughout to French francs, unless otherwise specified. During the period, the value of 10 francs approached that of £1.

find structural and ideological refuge. This was also helped very concretely by the French state. Indeed, rock music and its ideology of 'resistance' became, from 1981 onwards, the recipient of the largesse of the Ministry of Culture, arguably 'the most powerful agency of legitimation' in France (Looseley, 2003, p. 204), and this aspect of national specificity requires further investigation.

Cultural Policy and French Rock Music

In the early 1980s, the French state started to consider popular music as a legitimate area for public spending. This allowed the left-wing preoccupations of 'independent' (or independent-minded) music professionals to merge with the somewhat protectionist measures implemented by the government, influenced perceptions of rock music as a prestigious and 'serious' music genre, and conferred a degree of moral superiority upon the discourse of 'resistance' against mainstream pop. To explain this evolution, its apparent contradictions and its impact on the French music landscape, it is necessary to briefly retrace the evolution of these national music policies. Philippe Teillet (2003) and David Looseley (1995 and 2003) have examined the cultural policy of this period in great detail, and this section owes much to their research. Nonetheless, the emphasis here is placed on those measures that contributed, intentionally or otherwise, to legitimizing a 'protest' culture in the music sector, providing official and culturally dominant avenues for its expression.

The growing globalization of consumer society has long been a *bête noire* of the French state, due to the republican fear that mass consumption would atomize the nation's (supposedly) unified socio-economic community (Kelly, 2001, p. 120). The French state is renowned for its controlling attitude towards the arts, which may be seen to date back as far as the sixteenth century (Looseley, 1995, p. 11), but this became more formalized with the protectionist measures put in place in the 1940s around the national film industry. Despite being based on a simplistic antagonism towards US cultural imperialism (Mazdon, 2000, p. 9), these measures were exacerbated after 1981 when the Parti Socialiste (PS) won the presidency with a neo-Marxist agenda (at least initially), and its Ministry of Culture started to take an active interest in popular music. Before 1981, popular music and the music industry had not really featured on the agenda of the Ministry of Culture/Cultural Affairs. The state's general argument was that popular forms of entertainment, such as music, could sustain themselves economically without public protection. During the 1960s, for the most part, only classical and 'proper' music concerts (those where the audience remained seated), were encouraged via small subsidies, and up until 1981, government involvement in popular music remained confined to the spheres of taxation (box-office entries) and occasional censorship (Looseley, 2003, p. 119).

During the 1970s, however, a shift had started to occur within what was then known as the Ministry of Cultural Affairs, as advisors, influenced by the anti-conservatism of May 1968 and led by the influential sociologist Michel de Certeau, argued against the policy of democratization (one culture for all), and for the recognition of cultural pluralism (all cultures are valid). This new programme sought to encourage youth culture and amateur practices, and also to include popular music within the realm of public spending (Looseley, 1995, p. 113). In 1981, with the election of the PS, the newly renamed Ministry of Culture embarked upon an enthusiastic overhaul of previous cultural policies, driven by the idea of pluralism, under the colourful leadership of the new Minister of Culture, Jack Lang. With a bigger budget, reaching almost 1 per cent of national spending, the Ministry developed an active policy of support for popular music which boosted France's national music output over the following two decades (Looseley, 2003, pp. 152–3). However, because the decision to support popular music had arrived so late, when the majors were already more or less in control of the national music industry, pure protectionism, as had been the case with cinema before, was out of the question. Furthermore, since the music industry was in full bloom, the Ministry realised that its policy for popular music would have to generate 'some form of palpable return' (Looseley, 2003, p. 168).

From 1981 onwards, then, the Ministry proposed to subsidize all forms of music, classical and popular, 'mainstream' and 'quality', so as to increase national levels of music practice and consumption across all tastes, ages and classes. French popular music was addressed under the general heading of 'jazz, chanson et variétés', without discriminating between genres. The policy for performing arts ['spectacle vivant'] applied to all arts performed live on stage, including pop concerts, opera and dance. With regards to the music industry itself, the state developed a 'mixed economy' approach, favouring partnerships with the majors as well as giving funds for the promotion of new talents and the support of small (independent) labels. In doing so, it followed free-market logic even as it sought to 'correct [its] worst effects' (Teillet, 2003, p. 184). Some conservative commentators regarded this new approach as a dangerous erosion of hierarchies and a general dumbing-down of national quality (Finkielkraut, 1987; Fumaroli, 1992). What is clear, however, is that independent record producers, while not being the unique beneficiaries of the Ministry's policy, received some direct subsidies, encouragement and, above all, symbolic support. In addition, the Ministry set out to reconcile the market value of music with the safeguarding of a sense of prestige and 'difference' in the production of French cultural goods (Looseley, 2003, pp. 134–5). It did this by funding its 'rock policy' considerably less generously than other 'high' forms of music, notably opera.[10] This very discrepancy ensured that rock purists never saw the involvement of the state as compromising their declared autonomy (Teillet, 2003, p. 182). As a result, those music producers claiming to offer 'resistance' benefited from this policy, yet could declare that their hostile attitude to the Establishment and economic liberalism was left more or less intact. Two measures

---

10   For the period concerned, the state funds for 'popular music' averaged at only 2 per cent of those for opera (Looseley, 2003, p. 160).

in particular, decentralization and the 'liberalization' of radio, helped them develop alternative networks of promotion that made French 'indie' music stand out as a bastion of structural and ideological authenticity, while stabilizing it economically as a viable alternative to the major companies and the mainstream media.

Decentralization and the 'Liberalization' of Radio

Decentralization was one of the chief innovations of the PS, involving a general reorganization of public funds and decision-making from the Parisian centre to the regional and municipal peripheries (Cole, 1998, p. 119). This measure mostly affected urban planning and industrial development, but also had an impact on culture, as local government became responsible for devising policies and allocating funds within its sphere of influence. Without necessarily seeing their role as being that of challengers of globalization, regional and municipal authorities started spending money on the development of local infrastructure such as concert halls and rehearsal studios, giving subsidies to small production companies and independent radio shows, and generally encouraging the practice and consumption of music by the local population. Competition for tourist revenue also played a part, and Chapter 6 explores the role of decentralization in boosting the creation of music festivals in this period.

In the context of these initiatives, it is certainly the case that many new acts emerged in the provinces in the 1980s, such as Carte de Séjour in Lyons, Zebda in Toulouse and Noir Désir in Bordeaux, all of which were able to develop a following and attract interest outside the charts, at least initially, and without relying exclusively on mainstream producers and media. The French record label Bondage, one of the first and fiercest anti-capitalist producers of the 1980s, had its head offices just outside Paris, but its managers stressed that 'ever since the "alternative" scene [of the 1980s], there's been loads of stuff happening in the regions. Bondage at least managed to challenge the hegemony of Paris' (Tellier, 1999, p. 36).[11] The 'alternative' scene referred to here was synchronous with, and sustained by, the measures of decentralization. Similarly, the members of the 'alternative' rock band Têtes Raides, who started touring in the 1980s, claimed that they owed their success to 'people in the regions' ['les gens dans les régions'],[12] suggesting that the explosion of 'protest' rock music was made possible at this time, due to the increased musical activity and concert-going practices of the public in the provinces.

A second important change implemented by the PS concerned radio broadcasting. Before 1981, radio broadcasting in France was the monopoly of

---

11   'Depuis la scène alternative il se passe des tas de choses dans les régions. Bondage a au moins servi à contester l'hégémonie de Paris.'

12   Interviewed by Albert Algoud, 'La partie continue', *France Inter*, 20 March 2001.

one state-owned company, Télédiffusion de France (TDF). TDF forbade all other stations from broadcasting, with the exception of some 'peripheral' stations situated outside the frontiers, in Luxembourg and Monte Carlo for instance. This meant that pirate radio stations flourished, especially in the 1970s, influenced by British models such as Radio Caroline and often set up in support of regional separatist groups or workers' rights, in the wake of May 1968 and its challenging of official media (Collin, 1982, p. 22). French pirate stations were the forerunners of the *radios libres* of the early 1980s, ex-pirate stations that became legalized after 1981 when, despite some hesitation from the newly elected PS government, the radio wavelengths were 'liberated'. The *radios libres* were typically small-scale stations that combined an interest in anti-establishment politics with a taste for rock music (Collin, 1982, p. 33), and small record producers were now free to give exposure to their sometimes controversial artists, ensuring a degree of mediatization for them. *Rock alternatif*, along with other genres, benefited from this measure, and the producers of Bondage recalled that broadcasting their bands on *radios libres* helped to promote them (Tellier, 1999, p. 34). Meanwhile, the binary discourse opposing 'quality' to 'commercial' music grafted itself onto this new system, with national and peripheral stations representing 'a uniform culture aimed at undifferentiated masses', and *radios libres* standing out as exponents of originality and specialism (Mermet, 1985, p. 363).

The 'authenticity' of the *radios libres*, however, was short-lived. In 1984, the PS authorised commercial advertising on local and private stations, which led to a remapping of this dialectical approach to music broadcasting. Most *radios libres* managers opted to work with sponsors, and competition for audiences led to a 'mainstreaming' of music programmes, with new stations such as NRJ playing 'hit music only' (in English in the original), by artists described as 'big names' ['valeurs sûres'] that were expected to attract vast audiences (Bouton, 1999, p. 64; Arteta, 2003, p. 18). NRJ quickly became France's largest radio station, attracting 14 per cent of all radio listeners, with a potential 120 million listeners across Europe by 2003 due to its merger with various foreign stations (Arteta, 2003, p. 18). However, NRJ is presented by critics as the absolute model of mediocrity due to its refusal to broadcast original, 'true' artists, such as the post-*rock alternatif* band Têtes Raides (Lehoux, 2008a). Conversely, since 1984, only those radio stations that remained fully or partly publicly funded, including the regional outposts of Radio France (the new incarnation of TDF), could broadcast music without needing to chase profits. As a result, unlike the earlier scenario, state-funded stations became, from the mid-1980s onwards, the guardians of original, adventurous and 'quality' music programming, and the representatives of a broadcast alternative to mainstream pop music.[13] In particular, the general-interest branch of Radio France, the station France Inter, regularly emphasizes its 'eclectic' playlist and its opposition to

---

13   A similar trajectory occurred in the UK, albeit 15 years earlier, when the dismantling of Radio Caroline led to the creation, in 1967, of the new, 'cool' station, Radio 1, an outpost of the publicly funded BBC. Radio 1 recruited the DJs who previously broadcasted rock

the commercial stations. The producer of the independent label Boucherie has recognized this station's specificity: 'apart from France Inter, Boucherie's artists were never played on the big [commercial] radios'.[14] In May 2000, when the FIP stations, local outposts of Radio France, fell victim to closures, many French rock bands played in support of the staff on strike, and the 'alternative' bands Zebda and Louise Attaque stressed the usefulness and validity of 'the French public service and its cultural exceptionalism'.[15] These examples show that, even as the Ministry devised policies that encouraged the commercialization and mainstreaming of popular music in some media, public stations now found themselves in the position of being standard-bearers of 'quality', places of refuge for a defensive discourse against the power of money. In France therefore, at least in recent years, the state has helped consolidate a 'resistance' discourse opposing rock and *chanson* to 'mainstream' pop, in quite simple but, for this reason perhaps, durable terms. Four case studies of French independent producers of rock music will now assess the significance, efficacy and resilience of this 'protest' position.

Bondage Records and Bérurier Noir

The association Rock Radical Records, which later became known as Bondage, was set up in 1982 as a non-profit-making music organization. It was founded by Jean-Yves Prieur, a musician playing punk music with friends under the name Les Brigades, whose group had gathered enough money to record and produce their first single. Thanks to other friends, who were DJs on *radios libres*, the group achieved reasonable sales, and the money was re-injected into the production of new groups. In 1984, with the addition of two new members, Marsu and Philippe Baia, the association turned semi-professional, changing its name to Bondage to evoke punk's SM aesthetic and its challenging of the 'chains' of consumerism. For Marsu, Bondage's ambition was to 'let the groups exist autonomously, in an uncompromising system that would be strong enough to avoid the mainstream network [of distribution and mediatization]' (in Tellier, 1999, p. 34).[16] This profession of faith was not innovative *per se*, as it paralleled the arguments central to the rock subculture of the late 1970s on the other side of the Channel and the Atlantic (Negus, 1992, p. 16). Nevertheless, the repercussions of punk culture in

---

music from the offshore pirate station, the latter 'going legit' under the auspices of the state-funded broadcasting house (Garfield, 2007, p. 20).

14   '... à part sur France-Inter, Boucherie n'a jamais eu droit à l'accueil des grosses radios du circuit', *L'Echo des Côtelettes*, 12, Autumn 1998, p. 14.

15   *Libération*, 25 May 2000, p. 31.

16   '... notre envie était de faire exister les groupes de manière autonome, de proposer un système sans concession suffisamment solide et efficace pour éviter le circuit normalisé'.

France, lagging a few years behind Britain and the US, contributed to the birth and dissemination of an 'alternative' ethos in the 1980s (Looseley, 2003, p. 47).

Indeed, the managers of Bondage quoted the UK and US independent labels Rough Trade and Alternative Tentacles as direct sources of influence (Tellier, 1999, p. 34). Alternative Tentacles, label of the US punk band Dead Kennedys, mixed left-wing anti-Establishment sentiment with the pursuit of economic independence (Benetollo, 1999, pp. 114–15). Rough Trade, an independent label founded in London in 1976, created a distribution network outside the hold of the majors, and a 'democratic' form of management by sharing profits equally between artists and producers (Reynolds, 2005, p. 104; Hesmondhalgh, 1997, p. 260). Marsu saw these two companies as prime examples of 'political rigour' and 'musical seriousness', which have managed to challenge the status quo of the dominant music industry by holding irreproachable moral principles. Bondage thus modelled itself on Rough Trade, devising unwritten contracts between producers and artists, insisting on the 'collegiality' of the venture, celebrating the fact that 'we were all great friends' ['on était tous vraiment potes'] (Baia in Tellier, 1999, p. 34). Ludwig Von 88, one of the bands produced by Bondage, qualified the relationships with the producers as 'direct', praising the presence of 'a manager, not a boss', and the absence of 'marketing imperatives or deadlines' (in H.M., 1992c, p. 55). In effect, Bondage bypassed the mainstream broadcast system by developing stage concerts rather than TV or commercial radio play, and sold records to the public directly afterwards, via mail order or through independent distributors and small record retailers such as New Rose in Paris.

This strategy paid off, especially for the band Bérurier Noir, whose punk sound, anti-fascist declarations and somewhat violent theatrical style also played a part in their self-promotion (Prévos, 1991; Marcil, 1997). Such was the band's success that in 1986 Bondage changed their status to that of a profit-making company. In 1987, Bérurier Noir's third album *Abracadaboum* sold 60,000 copies, allegedly in a few hours and without any mainstream promotion (Prieur in Tellier, 1999, p. 36), and went on to sell 200,000 copies in total (Verlant, 2000, p. 127). The same year, Bérurier Noir played live at the high-profile Printemps de Bourges music festival, with a line-up of other *rock alternatif* bands, helping to bring this music and its left-wing identity a degree of national recognition. In February 1989, Bondage secured the Zénith concert hall in Paris (around 6,000 seats back then) for Bérurier Noir, and the band's continuing rise not only signalled to sceptics that a 'non-mainstream' music network did exist, but also that independent production structures could be effective.

Nonetheless, with success came problems. Independent producers are frequently overwhelmed by the growing success of their artists (Lefeuvre, 1998, p. 117). In material as much as in 'human' terms, success is often accompanied by a change of expectations from managers and artists, and it is at such times that small structures are confronted with their own limits. In 1987, the members of Bérurier Noir went on strike, asking for a rise in their wages. This early confrontation marked the beginning of the end for Bondage, as the producers argued about which course to take. On the one hand, Prieur thought that signing a distribution deal with a major would help to bring the band to a wider audience, guarantee greater profits and allow a wage increase. This was a strong possibility since the major Sony, upon realising the growth of Bérurier Noir, had contacted Bondage in the hope to sign the group (Tellier, 1999, p. 36). However, Baia and Marsu rejected this idea, which they saw as a compromise and a form of 'selling out'. In 1989, after two years of internal conflict, Bérurier Noir split up, Prieur left Bondage, and the other producers carried on, though with lower and less reliable profits. Bondage continued to exist for a few years under Marsu's management, and was still referred to in 1992 as 'the symbol of the French alternative scene' (H.M., 1992c, p. 53). Nonetheless, its shares were gradually sold to other companies during the 1990s, including the major Warner.

The episode of Bondage's short-lived autonomy reveals, rather touchingly, how artists' and producers' dreams of commercial autonomy were tested by the commercial success of the 'resistance' they championed. It was because their methods had initially allowed Bérurier Noir to develop a wide following that a major took an interest, and conflicts arose. This also shows that the ideal of resistance, invoking a chivalric vocabulary of integrity and heroism, produced some results, but not unproblematically. The years of conflict over the possible involvement of the majors were messy – Marsu compared this period to the rivalry of a 'Sicilian village', while Prieur regretted the intractable positions of his colleagues (in Tellier, 1999, p. 36). This also demonstrates that 'independence' itself was (and still is) a fluid notion, as Prieur and Marsu held two differing interpretations of the term, yet also managed to work alongside one another for some time. An examination of the functioning of Boucherie Production, a company closer to Prieur's position in their readiness to negotiate with the 'enemy', will allow us to pursue the analysis of the ambivalences present within France's 'protest' rock music culture further.

Boucherie Production and Mano Negra

From the outset, many parallels existed between Boucherie Production and Bondage. Like Bondage, Boucherie Production was set up as a label to promote French punk music. The singer-songwriter François Hadji-Lazaro, who fronted the comic punk band Les Garçons Bouchers, had been unsuccessful in finding a record deal for his band and, after several refusals, decided to create his own production company in 1986, the same year that Bondage turned fully professional. Boucherie's ambition, taking a similar line of argument to Bondage's producers, was to hold 'the means to function [economically] without being a slave to the system of the money society'.[17] Openly voicing his left-wing sympathies, Hadji-Lazaro was introduced in *L'Humanité*, the Parti Communiste's newspaper, as

---

17   '… les moyens de fonctionner sans être esclave du système imposé par la société de l'argent', *L'Echo des Côtelettes*, 12, Autumn 1998, p. 14.

'not the kind of guy who composes commercial ditties; protest songs are what he's about' (Chérel, 1992).[18] Such statements, and many others to the same effect, established the existence of an anti-major 'protest' discourse, firmly anchored on the left, and set up a clear distinction between commercially successful music on the one hand, and more difficult, meaningful or contestatory genres on the other. In 1988, Boucherie produced the first album of the *rock alternatif* band Mano Negra, *Patchanka*. The brainchild of the Franco-Spanish artist Manu Chao (see Chapter 4), Mano Negra had been playing the bar circuit, mainly in Paris and its suburbs, under different names since the early 1980s. The group performed fast rock music with politically charged lyrics, with a Latin horn section and mixture of French, English and Spanish lending it a distinctive 'exotic' flavour. In 1988, Boucherie was invited to present its artists, including Mano Negra, at the state-sponsored Printemps de Bourges festival, and this series of concerts, taking place only one year after Bérurier Noir's performance there, sealed the coherence of France's alternative rock culture as rebellious, creative and 'authentic' (Davet and Tenaille, 1996, pp. 48–51).

However, divergences also existed between the two production companies, and they were often seen as rivals within the 'independent' music scene. Firstly, Boucherie was set up from the start as a registered company (*société civile*), allowing it to take profits. This gave the label 'the means to fight in show-business, which must be fought with its own weapons'.[19] For Hadji-Lazaro, the commercial side of his project was self-evident, and he understood that his company would still be a platform for the development of newcomers. His intention was to discover and produce unusual artists, hoping that they would eventually reach beyond the 'alternative' milieu, and leave him for a wider audience.[20] Consequently, Boucherie welcomed a series of partnerships with the majors for the distribution of its artists, including Polygram and BMG. In the 1990s, it released the first album by Paris Combo, which went on to gain a high degree of international success as a result of its distribution via Universal (see Seery, 2007). In addition, since it was in the hands of a single manager, Boucherie did not suffer from internal conflict, and appeared more professional than Bondage to its business partners. In 1989, it was identified by the Ministry of Culture as an efficient company meriting financial encouragement, under the *Plan Label* policy (Roussel, 1995, 50). In 1990, Boucherie also received subsidies from the newly created export bureau, the French Music Office, to organize tours for its artists in Quebec and New York (Micaeli, 1990). As a result, it became a higher-profile indie label than Bondage, just as the latter was crumbling under the weight of its ideological divisions.

---

18   'Le leader de Pigalle n'est pas du genre à écrire des ritournelles commerciales; son truc, c'est plutôt la chanson … engagée, au bon sens du terme'.

19   '… les moyens de battre le système show-biznessien qu'il faut affronter sur son propre terrain', *L'Echo des Côtelettes*, 12, Autumn 1998, 12.

20   'Boucherie veut développer des musiques difficiles à diffuser, sans restriction de style et en tentant d'atteindre toutes les oreilles'. *L'Echo des Côtelettes* 12, 1998, p. 12.

Boucherie's fame was also boosted by its association with the group Mano Negra. In 1988, the track 'Mala Vida' from *Patchanka* was released as a single, and Boucherie budgeted both for the production of a music video, and a long French tour for the band. The song consequently benefited from airplay on some national radio stations and TV channels. Arriving on the post-punk scene just as Bérurier Noir were facing difficulties, Mano Negra's success was certainly due to the music's originality and to Chao's highly energetic performance style. It was also, undoubtedly, helped by Boucherie's clear marketing strategies. Soon, the British label Virgin (which was bought by EMI in 1992) approached Boucherie, and Hadji-Lazaro, in agreement with Mano Negra, sold the band's production contract. The money from Virgin was re-injected into the production of new 'challenging' acts, and enabled Boucherie to perform well for a few more years. It also allowed Mano Negra to benefit from better recording conditions and wider promotion for their subsequent albums. Indeed, as Manu Chao has often stressed since, working with Virgin always gave him total freedom in artistic creation (Belhaddad, 2003, p. 42; Manche, 2004, p. 54).

Comparing Mano Negra and Bérurier Noir's trajectories, Prieur from Bondage recognised the benefits of this strategy, regretting Bérurier Noir's refusal to sign with a major and the consequent lack of critical or commercial acclaim for a band which he considered at least as interesting as Mano Negra (in Tellier, 1999, p. 37). Indeed, as a result of this deal with Virgin, Mano Negra's second album, *Puta's Fever* (1989), sold around 350,000 copies (Rigoulet, 1998, p. 32). It has been regularly re-issued since, and the website of Fnac, France's main record retailer, advertised it in 2007 as 'a classic', the most ground-breaking French rock album of all time, due to its innovative inclusion of Hispanic influences.[21] Mano Negra became one of the best-selling groups of the early 1990s, and still managed to sell 100,000 copies of their 'best of' album in 1998, four years after they had split up (*L'Année du disque 1999*, p. 134).

During the 1990s, Boucherie remained a relatively viable outsider in the French music industry, facing regular financial difficulties yet managing to stay afloat due to the marked originality of its image, and the strong personality of Hadji-Lazaro, who also obtained critical acclaim as an artist in his own right with his other band Pigalle, a *néo-réaliste* group (see Chapter 2), and various solo projects. Nonetheless, as the state had authorized the broadcasting of record advertising on television in 1989, the 1990s were also a period of increased competition for record producers. After the departure of Mano Negra, Boucherie was unable to afford TV exposure, and went into gradual decline. In a 1998 edition of *L'Echo des Côtelettes*, Boucherie's quarterly newsletter, the anonymous editor (possibly Hadji-Lazaro) bitterly regretted not having been able to promote the label's artists on the 'popular' medium of TV more often.[22] In 2001, the label filed for bankruptcy,

---

21   See www.fnac.com, key in 'Puta's fever' under the rubric 'Disques'.

22   'Télé: combat éternel à Boucherie pour pénétrer cet écran populaire. A part quelques clips et apparitions dans quelques émissions, dur combat', *L'Echo des Côtelettes*, 12, Autumn 1998, 14.

announcing that the pressures from distributors and record retailers had become too difficult to handle.

Compared to Bondage, Boucherie's longer lifespan, as well as its ultimate failure, demonstrates some further points about the meaning and efficacy of 'resistance' in the (French) music industry. First, it once again underlines the fact that there is such a thing as the global domination of the music industry by major companies and mainstream media, and that within the independent sector, there are individuals, producers and artists, who play a critical, political role in attempting to challenge that power. It also shows that 'resistance' can take several forms, from the economic naivety of Bondage to Boucherie's greater flexibility, although it cannot function in absolute terms, at least not in the long run. Innovative artists are still produced by independents and released all the time, but their longevity is dependent on the majors taking an interest in, and a financial risk on, their broader market appeal. Thirdly, the occasional access of non-mainstream acts to wider fame, usually through the selective marketing strategies of their independent producers, means that opposition to the majors sometimes becomes highly visible, frequently enough to seem 'real' for audiences and to signify the apparent power of this 'alternative' identity.

In this sense, the year 1989, which some commentators have seen as a 'turning point' for protest rock music in France (Belhaddad, 2003, p. 45; Péchu, 2006, p. 613), marked both the consecration of *rock alternatif* and its demise. On the one hand, the growing sales of Bérurier Noir and the national success of Mano Negra sparked off a tremendous amount of enthusiasm for an 'alternative' rock culture, and a new confidence in the future of 'quality' (read 'protest') music in France. On the other hand, the split of Bérurier Noir, Bondage's gradual acquisition by majors and Mano Negra's 'selling out' to Virgin, signalled the end of the initially autonomous conditions of production of these artists.[23] Good sales, fame and recognition are thus at once the signs of the existence of 'protest', but also of its imminent negation. The 1990s exemplified this paradox to a far greater extent. The brief commercial success of *rock alternatif* groups led the majors to capitalize on a 'non-mainstream' rock identity, and while the Ministry of Culture followed its policy of support for both independent and major companies, rock and *variété*, the 'alternative' culture of French rock music gained further cultural legitimacy just as it became even more entwined within the web of the majors. The inherent paradox of this governmentally and commercially sanctioned 'subversion' is clearly visible in the careers of Têtes Raides and Louise Attaque.

---

23   The label of 'rock alternatif' only applies to those groups working with independent record labels in the mid- to late 1980s, and the French groups of the 1990s looking up to this earlier trend evolved into different music genres, among which *chanson néo-réaliste* and *rock métis* chiefly stood.

Tôt ou Tard and Têtes Raides

Têtes Raides are a French rock band that reached fame in the mid-1990s, and that have been described by some as the standard-bearers of the 'alternative' spirit of France's counter-culture (Saka and Plougastel, 1999, p. 411). Alongside Pigalle and Négresses Vertes, they revived the use of the accordion and adopted the nostalgic imagery of the 'realist' French song of the 1930s, as Chapter 2 describes in more detail. Like most bands emerging in the *rock alternatif* scene, Têtes Raides toured the bar circuit for several years, self-producing their first album with a small budget, before being given a distribution deal by an independent label, Just'In, in 1989. Their first two albums, *Not dead but bien raides* (1989) and *Mange tes morts* (1990), were only marginally successful, but the group's heavy touring schedule, which included such major dates as the Printemps de Bourges festival in 1989, meant that they started to attract a respectable following. In 1991, the group's efforts received dual recognition in that they were selected by the FAIR (Fonds d'Aide et d'Initiative pour le Rock [Rock Music Initiative Fund]), the Ministry of Culture's 'unequivocal' programme of direct financial aid to creation in rock music (Looseley, 2003, p. 143), and also spotted by Vincent Frèrebeau, the artistic director of the French branch of the major Warner. Not only did the FAIR selection boost Têtes Raides' profile, but Frèrebeau offered them a contract for two more albums, giving them access to the logistics available to a major and helping the band reach a greater degree of national fame.

Frèrebeau certainly foresaw the profits to be made in producing kindred spirits to the already successful Négresses Vertes, yet he also stressed his pleasure and bewilderment at seeing them perform live for the first time: 'I saw them, I liked them, but I didn't understand a thing. I signed them without realising the importance they would have in my life' (in Paquotte, 2001, p. 58).[24] In 1996, without splitting from Warner, Frèrebeau set up and headed an 'integrated label' within the major, called Tôt ou Tard. Tôt ou Tard took on the appearance of an 'independent' company, focusing on the development of author-based French music and trading on the success of Têtes Raides and other 'serious' rock and *chanson* artists, including the veteran Jacques Higelin and the newcomer Thomas Fersen, both being singer-songwriters. The label was introduced as an 'adult' niche, based on its interest in the poetic and political maturity of its artists (Lefeuvre, 1998, p. 87). Frèrebeau insisted that Tôt ou Tard was a 'quality' company, exhibiting the same 'immediacy, craftsmanship and perfectionism' that these artists put into their creative work (in Paquotte, 2001, p. 59).[25] In parallel, he upheld the reputation of Têtes Raides as a 'real' band, whose prestige was derived from the artists' hard work (they were 'grafters' ['des bosseurs']), their avoidance of the mainstream media, and their 'sincerity' (in Gonot, 2004, p. 111). These terms stressed the

---

24   '... je les ai vus ..., j'ai aimé, mais je n'ai pas compris. Je les ai signés sans mesurer l'importance qu'ils auraient dans ma vie'.

25   '... le travail du label est calqué sur le leur: contact direct, artisanat, opiniâtreté'.

relevance of the discourse of 'authenticity' for music producers, as Frèrebeau's 'organic' approach to production paralleled the discourse of many independent rock producers (Negus, 1992, pp. 54–5), but also attempted to show the human face of his label.

The decision to dedicate a new label to 'alternative' or 'serious' French music also reflected the saleability of this protest identity, which was carefully engineered in the case of Têtes Raides, and sustained economically with the support of Warner. For instance, in the late 1990s, the tour managers were able to fix a maximum price of 130 francs per concert ticket, in agreement with the artists, who accepted individual fees of less than 1,200 francs per concert (Paquotte, 2001, p. 59). This confirmed Têtes Raides as an approachable band, refusing to increase their fees despite their increasing success. Another marketing decision was to re-issue all the band's previous albums in brown paper and cardboard packaging, bringing a degree of 'naturalness' to the group's image by contrast to the usual plastic cases of CDs. This, twinned with the band's striking visual presentation through the use of sepia colours and child-like collages (see Chapter 2), had a noticeable impact on the public. One of my interviewees, a fan of Têtes Raides, explained that he enjoyed the 'rough' feel of the cardboard packaging, and associated 'alternative' music styles with this presentational device. This carefully constructed 'authentic' identity paid off, and Têtes Raides' sales gradually increased. The album *Gratte poil*, released in 2000, sold 90,000 copies in less than four months, and in 2001, it sold another 100,000 units, and so did the band's previous album of 1998, *Chamboultou* (Perrin, 2001a). Also in 2001, Têtes Raides were granted a long, eulogizing article in France's leading cultural weekly *Télérama*, were selected by the Ministry of Culture to head the bill of the Fête de la Musique festivities in Paris, and nominated for the televised *Victoires de la Musique* Awards, which enhanced their success even further.

The example of Tôt ou Tard reveals that there is, under the aegis of the majors, room for the long-term support of a supposedly non-mainstream group. Têtes Raides' success did not happen overnight, and the label was cautious in its management of their mediatization, targeting an 'alternative' audience with appropriate visually based strategies (such as packaging), as well as privileging touring over mainstream broadcast for instance. This also corresponded to the desire of the artists, for whom musicianship is 'a form of danger, challenging the danger of routine', including the routine of mass media exposure (in Paquotte, 2001, p. 59).[26] In Autumn 2001, Tôt ou Tard celebrated its fifth anniversary by fixing specially low prices on its CDs for a few weeks (59 francs in Fnac shops), and giving away a compilation of their house artists for free with each album bought. Such a public-friendly measure was only possible with the support of a major, and contrasts unfavourably with Boucherie's decision to raise the retail

26   'On est tous dans cet état d'esprit, cette mise en danger qui rompt avec le danger de la routine'.

price of its CDs to 110 francs in the late 1990s, simply to get by.[27] The group Louise Attaque, who have occasionally shared the bill with Têtes Raides, is another (and our final) example of the marketability of protest rock music in France.

Atmosphériques and Louise Attaque

Atmosphériques is a production company set up by Marc Thonon in 1996, which employed eight staff in 1999 and falls under the category of an independent label. It works, however, in close partnership with Trema, a large French producer of *variété*, 15 per cent of whose shares belong to Sony.[28] Consequently, Atmosphériques benefits from distribution by Sony, who shares the label's turnover with Trema. For two years, Atmosphériques did poorly, but in 1998, the band Louise Attaque, whom they had signed the year before, started selling extremely well and eventually became the second best-selling French album of that year, selling nearly three million copies of their first, eponymous album (Verlant, 2000, p. 154).

According to Prieur, the ex-manager of Bondage, the success of Louise Attaque was due to the initiative of Bondage and Bérurier Noir, who opened up an 'alternative' space for the dissemination of unusual music acts, essentially through live performance and word of mouth (in Tellier, 1999, p. 37). This has been a commonly held view about Louise Attaque's rise to fame. A journalist for *Libération* remarked in 1998 that the band were never heard on mainstream radio, never seen on television, owing their fame and credibility to the stage circuit and to an 'old-fashioned' conception of the music profession (Rigoulet, 1998, p. 32).[29] Elsewhere, the band has been introduced as 'real', owing to their avoidance of commercial mediatization (Saka and Plougastel, 1999, p. 310). These statements, like others highlighted above, contrast today's mass-mediatization, perceived as artificial, with a supposedly promotion-free, pre-modern age, the latter standing out as more 'authentic' than the former. Such views are erroneously nostalgic, since it was the technological and social developments of the industrial era which brought about the conditions for the elaboration and reception of live performance as more desirable, even more 'resistant', than its mediatized equivalent (Auslander, 1999, p. 11 and p. 70). Nonetheless, such declarations confer an aura of authenticity upon the band in question.

In fact, Louise Attaque's success in 1998 was not as unexpected or detached from commercial imperatives as it might seem. Set up in 1994 in Paris, this four-man band played an acoustic rock style which followed a trend already set by earlier *rock alternatif* bands, including Négresses Vertes and Têtes Raides. The lyrics, casting the singer as an anxious, depressive male, were sung with a trembling

---

27   *L'Echo des Côtelettes*, 12, Autumn 1998, 14.
28   Personal communication with Marc Thonon, email, 12 January 2000.
29   '… un concept du métier à l'ancienne'.

voice recalling Jacques Brel's whine. This asserted the group's preoccupation with 'quality' *chanson* and their marginal status vis-à-vis the mainstream pop milieu. Similarly, the band's trademark violin, played very fast and often taking the place of the lead guitar, forged a connection with 'authentic' folk music traditions, including Irish country song and 'Gypsy' tunes, which had been enjoying a revival since the 1980s (see Chapter 6). The group also claimed the US 1980s folk-rock band Violent Femmes as their main influence, an underground trio with a cult following who played acoustic music and presented themselves, not entirely seriously, as 'the sonic personification of anxiety'.[30] All of these aspects reinforced the 'protest' credibility of Louise Attaque, and ensured their success among the 'alternative' rock crowd.

The label Atmosphériques, also, followed a well-thought-out strategy. Its marketing director, Laurent Macherey, explained how Louise Attaque's success was the culmination of a year and a half of relentless promotion on the stage circuit, which entailed securing venues and contracts with touring managers. Among other concerts, Louise Attaque performed in August 1997 at the elitist festival La Route du Rock, a concert that was broadcast live on the national radio station France Inter, and heavily marketed in the music weekly *Les Inrockuptibles* (see Chapter 5 on the popularity and consumption of these media). The producers also targeted key newspapers and magazines for reviews, consciously avoiding, although they could afford it, advertising on TV because it 'did not correspond' to the group's image and their likely fans (Macherey, quoted in Lefeuvre, 1999, p. 45).[31] Similarly, they refused to release a single until later on in 1998, in order to avoid broadcast on commercial radios and a 'mainstreaming' of the band's image. By the end of the summer 1997, the sales of Louise Attaque's first album had reached 200,000 (Verlant, 2000, p. 154), and the distribution via Sony allowed the label to provide the retailers with CDs efficiently, avoiding the kind of panic that Bondage was thrown into when its sales of Bérurier Noir started to increase.

Other touches signalled the producers' great care in marketing this 'alternative' product. Louise Attaque's first album, although packaged in a standard plastic CD case, featured an insert printed on rough brown paper, reminiscent of the cardboard packaging of Têtes Raides, and fitting into an already existing trend for 'natural-looking' CDs. The seemingly hand-written name of the band, in thick white, irregular letters, gave a child-like, innocent feel to the product. In addition, the absence of any photograph of the artists, or any recognizable album title, as well as the mysterious, apparently female name of the band, confused rather than comforted the audience (Rigoulet, 1998, p. 32). Atmosphériques was also able to fix the album's price at 99 francs for a while, a clever and symbolic marketing coup which ensured wide sales, but was only possible with the major's support.

---

30   www.vfemmes.com, under 'band info', last accessed 18 March 2009.

31   '… une promotion et un marketing ciblé, des opérations commerciales discrètes …. Nous ne sommes pas tombés dans le travers de la pub TV. Artistiquement, cela ne correspondait pas!'

After 1998, two singles were released and commercial radios started to broadcast Louise Attaque, increasing their success even more and moving the band into the mainstream. Many of their initial followers rejected this mediatization, distinguishing themselves from the 'masses' who discovered the band not in rock festivals, but through prime-time TV and radio exposure (see Chapter 5).

Nonetheless, Atmosphériques reaped the benefits of its discreet marketing strategies which, despite remaining invisible to the general buying public, sprung from their careful consideration of the commercial impact and cultural meanings of 'protest' music and an 'alternative' music culture. In a personal communication, the label's boss Thonon explained that he signed new acts 'for the love of music and according to their economic potential', interestingly combining the 'organic' approach of authenticity with commercial considerations.[32] His statement had the merit of honesty, and illuminated the harsh reality of the music industry, where passion alone cannot sustain success, and financial investment alone cannot guarantee longevity. This also reinforces the point that independent producers can work with majors without this necessarily being an aesthetic compromise (Hesmondhalgh, 1999). Indeed, in this case, Thonon's pragmatic approach, combined with the structural means to pursue it through an 'independent' subsidiary label, produced one of France's best-selling and most original acts of the 1990s, without any undue idealism or illusions about the purity of 'national' or independent music.

This chapter has shown that the material conditions for the emergence and relative success of an 'alternative' music scene in France in the 1980s and beyond were to a large extent determined by the hold of the major companies over national music production, and the widespread success of *variété*. Opposing the power of the majors only made sense in the context of increasing mass-mediatization, and this 'resistance' could only be sustained economically because music production was a relatively profitable business. It was also demonstrated that the definition of 'independence' at the production level varies for different professionals, from a purist interpretation which considers any interaction with major companies to be a form of immoral compromise (Bondage), to a more flexible understanding that accepts the necessity of selective partnerships with conglomerates (Boucherie, and the subsequent 'integrated' labels of the 1990s). Despite this structural difference, both models have allowed for the occasional success of their artistically original and politically engaged artists. When success and/or national recognition are achieved, however, as they were throughout the 1980s and 1990s for the various groups examined, the central contradiction of the notion of 'resistance' becomes apparent, for as the saleability of these groups' music comes to the fore, their core value of anti-commercialism is compromised.

If, according to purists, the genre of *rock alternatif* reached its zenith in 1989, just as it self-destructed, two music genres in particular have continued to forge

32   '... au coup de cœur et selon la validité économique', personal communication with Marc Thonon, email 12 January 2000.

a 'protest' identity since. These are *chanson néo-réaliste*, based on a nostalgic representation of the working classes and a supposedly lost era of solidarity, and *rock métis*, which considers multi-ethnicity as a tool of protest against republicanism. Both followed the ideological precepts of *rock alternatif* in claiming to be anti-mainstream and anti-conservative, even if their involvement with production labels grew increasingly confused. Focusing on these trends, the next three chapters pursue the analysis of the internal ambivalence of 'protest' music by looking at the notion of national identity in greater depth, stressing in particular the vulnerability of 'protest' or 'alternative' music cultures which is at once upheld as an essential feature of their authenticity, in contrast to the apparent power of *variété*, and lamented, because of the way it relegates 'authentic' popular music to a secondary role in terms of commercial and popular impact.

PART II
Protest Identities.
Nostalgia, Multiculturalism and
Success Abroad

Chapter 2
Authenticity and Nostalgia in
Chanson Néo-réaliste

Chanson néo-réaliste, one of the two genres (the other being *rock métis*) that branched out of *rock alternatif* in the 1990s, is characterized by a system of references to the inter-war genre of *chanson réaliste*.[1] In the 1930s, *chanson réaliste* evoked the Parisian underclass of the nineteenth century, dwelling in particular on its 'suffering and rebellion' (Conway, 2004, p. 42). This strategy had evident melodramatic qualities, but also provided a commentary on the evolution of urbanization and its detrimental effects on the social fabric. When, in the 1990s, *chanson néo-réaliste* artists started copying many lyrical and musical elements of this earlier genre, they too composed songs focusing on hardship and a sense of lost conviviality, often to the tune of a waltzing accordion. By consciously reviving a musical genre from the past, along with its accompanying instruments, they sought to show that similar social tensions were shaping contemporary society. They asserted these ideological concerns through a form of 'protest' song, in keeping with their roots in the left-wing fringes of the French 'alternative' rock scene of the late 1980s.

Given its musical idiosyncrasies and its ideological earnestness, it is perhaps surprising that *chanson néo-réaliste* has encountered a large degree of success, spearheaded by bands such as Pigalle, Négresses Vertes and Têtes Raides. In 2001, two albums by Têtes Raides turned 'Gold' as they passed the 100,000 mark for the number of copies sold (according to the French classification system).[2] At the turn of the twenty-first century, many journalists began to remark upon the growing slew of *néo-réaliste* groups, arguing that the genre was suffering from 'traffic congestion' and 'obesity' because of its swollen ranks, with many new groups emerging in the mid- to late 1990s including La Tordue, Casse-Pipe, Paris Combo, Ogres de Barback, Padam and many more (Perrin, 2001a; Lehoux, 2008b). Writing in 2002, one critic warned that while the *néo-réaliste* style had once been

---

1   A French-language version of this chapter is forthcoming, entitled 'René, Ginette, Louise et les autres. Nostalgie et contestation dans la chanson néo-réaliste', *French Politics, Culture and Society* (Lebrun, forthcoming 2009). The genre is referred to as 'chanson' in France, mostly because of its frequently acoustic sound, but belongs to the larger category of 'rock' given its roots in *rock alternatif* and its insistence on oppositional meanings (against *variété*, against conservatism).

2   Certified 'Gold' albums in France (2001): www.disqueenfrance.com (select 'classifications', then '2001' then 'album or'), last accessed 24 March 2009.

'fine cuisine', it had become, apart from some notable exceptions, a fast-food recipe (Paquotte, 2002). These derogatory comparisons (junk food, obesity) signalled the critics' fears that in achieving a high degree of success, the style was losing its earlier, 'authentic' credentials. What critics might have underlined, too, was that *chanson néo-réaliste*, because of its stylistic choices, also appeared intentionally nostalgic, and for this reason potentially regressive.

It is surely something of a curiosity, then, that at the turn of the twenty-first century, playing the accordion would not only appeal to a relatively large audience, but also signify social and political rebellion, and that a genre whose main *raison d'être* appeared to be its 'pastness' would constitute a significant 'protest' subculture in France. Nonetheless, the key to understanding the growth of *chanson néo-réaliste* lies in its ability to connect overtly nostalgic elements with a contemporary discourse of resistance. Like all forms of art, including nostalgic forms of expression, the genre articulates 'meaning, purpose, and value' in the present (Lowenthal, 1985, p. 41). This chapter examines the resonance of *chanson néo-réaliste* in present-day France, its discourse and figures of contestation, while paying attention to its sometimes reactionary aspects, as the genre tends to engage rather selectively with chosen elements of the national past.

Chanson Réaliste, Nostalgia and Authenticity in the Inter-War Period

The notion of nostalgia is traditionally defined as the consciousness of a malaise in the present, and as the selective and imaginary mental reconstruction of the past in order to alleviate this unease (Lowenthal, 1985, p. xix and p. 13). According to this definition, a nostalgic work of art is one which sentimentalizes the past, opting to represent it with fondness and melancholy. In the late nineteenth and early twentieth century, the genre of *chanson réaliste* certainly was nostalgic, lamenting as it did the development of industrialization, and harking back to a time when the city, Paris, was supposedly a convivial village. Realist songs depicted life trajectories ruined by rural exodus, individualism, poverty and doomed love. The origins of this genre lay in 1880s Paris and the development of *cabarets artistiques* as places of amusement for a socially mixed audience (Hawkins, 2000, p. 72). Aristide Bruant (1851–1925), one of the owners of such a cabaret, Le Mirliton, became famous for the aggressive delivery of his own compositions, a mix of bawdy and comic as well as melodramatic songs. The latter repertoire was adopted by a few female singers at the very end of the nineteenth century, including Eugénie Buffet (1866–1934) and Yvette Guilbert (1867–1944), who paved the way for the creation of a distinct, female-only 'realist' style. The songs they picked, written by Bruant and other composers, would typically describe life on the margins, poor social conditions, and offer a gallery of outcast types including pimps and prostitutes, sailors, working-class girls and alcoholics of both sexes. After the First World War, the genre became codified and interpreted by specialized female singers, the *chanteuses réalistes*, who self-consciously played with 'the codes of realism and melodrama already circulating in literature, film and the music hall' (Conway, 2004, p. 95). These singers included Damia (1889–1978), Fréhel (1891–1951) and of course, although some time later, Edith Piaf (1915–1963), and clear material conditions explain the establishment of *chanson réaliste* as a genre in its own right in the inter-war period.

Firstly, a clearer distinction emerged in the 1920s between cabarets (and *café-concerts*) and music halls, two types of venue that had, roughly up until the First World War, welcomed live performances by realist singers. With the development of electricity and of more sophisticated machinery, the already wealthier music halls emphasized the visual spectacle of their music shows, leading to the creation of the *revue* and the 'starification' of visual performers such as Mistinguett and Josephine Baker. Cast in the role of the poor relation by these developments, mainly because they were initially eating and drinking places that did not charge an entrance fee, cabarets declined. Those that survived deployed two, apparently contradictory, strategies: emulating the music hall extravaganzas, or appealing to the public's sense of nostalgia by staging 'realist' performances (Conway, 2004, p. 131). It is in the context of the latter that Damia, Fréhel, and then Piaf, started to perform. Meanwhile, the 1920s and especially the 1930s saw the development of music recording, thanks to the electric phonograph, and the growing popularity of cinema and the 'talkies', whose projection of *chansons filmées* gave singers an opportunity to reach a wider audience. Damia and Fréhel boosted their careers by appearing in many films, often in the 'true-to-life' roles of *chanteuses réalistes*, and the success of the realist genre in the inter-war period was, somewhat paradoxically, dependent on the culture industry and the progression of consumerism and technology. Furthermore, personal trajectories are important in explaining the enduring success of *chanson réaliste* in French popular culture, as these female singers all suffered, in varying degrees, from poverty, solitude and alcoholism, like the characters of their songs. Their often poor childhoods and difficult private lives were reported in the burgeoning sensationalist press, and their deliberate choice to interpret songs that narrated similar life stories to their own solidified the audience's impression that they were witnessing a seamless transition between life and stage. *Chanson réaliste* therefore became the accepted, albeit mythic, performance of 'authenticity' (Vincendeau, 1987, p. 114).

This said, the genre had been contradictory from the start, staging 'authenticity' in the most self-conscious, artificial way, as might be expected of an artistic performance. Bruant invented sordid stories to thrill his mostly bourgeois audience (Hawkins, 2000, p. 72), while Buffet and Guilbert followed prostitutes at night in order to copy their demeanour and costume (Conway, 2004, p. 47 and p. 50). In the 1920s, *chanson réaliste* became successful and recognizable as a distinct style just as it was turning into a parody of itself. As early as 1920, the song 'Mon homme', interpreted by Mistinguett and telling the story of a down-on-her-luck prostitute, was intended as a realist pastiche. Moreover, singers were not detached from the lucrative possibilities of *la vie d'artiste*, Fréhel for instance being renowned for her 'keen sense of marketing' (Conway, 2004, p. 95).

Despite these evident contradictions and the somewhat formulaic nature of realist songs, critics and audiences enjoyed the genre's depiction of drama and misery, and seemed to encounter 'a genuine experience and emotion' (Conway, 2004, p. 50) in its presence.

Chanson Néo-Réaliste and Nostalgia in 1990s France

It is the nature of this emotion that is interesting, for its resurgence in the 1990s under the guise of *chanson néo-réaliste* reveals an ongoing interest in the evocation of hackneyed clichés (the whore with a heart, conviviality among the destitute, the destructiveness of modernity) and in the staging of 'authenticity'. Before examining the forms that this renewed interest in 'realism' takes, and the reasons for it, it is worth noting that, more generally, nostalgic cultural forms have been hugely popular in France from the 1980s onwards, especially in the audio-visual domain. In 2001, *Amélie* (directed by Jean-Pierre Jeunet) was the most successful French film of the year, with box-office sales of over 8.5 million nationwide.[3] Depicting the tribulations of a generous young woman in the working-class *quartier* of Montmartre, the film was set in 1997 while its photography, décor and costumes recalled the inter-war period. Its success, critics have argued, relied on conveying the expression of conviviality through retro imagery, which comforted contemporary feelings of destabilization by invoking a better, sweeter past (Vincendeau, 2001; Austin, 2003). Indeed, French cinema of the late twentieth century has in general been characterized by its emphasis on 'heritage', its frequent adaptation of works from the literary canon and its representation of past historical events (Powrie, 1999).

French popular music, for its part, has perhaps been even more nostalgic in this period. Compilations of hits of the earlier period fill the shelves of record shops, and anthologies of 'la chanson française' are regularly released. In 2002, the most successful French album of the year was *Entre-Deux*, a compilation of cover-versions by Patrick Bruel of 1930s numbers, initially performed by the likes of Maurice Chevalier and Edith Piaf. With 'swing' acoustic guitars and waltzing accordions, its orchestration closely followed the original versions and this unabashed homage to the popular music of the inter-war period sold 1 million copies in the first few months of its release (Lebrun, 2009).[4] More generally, though, the most obvious sign of musical nostalgia in contemporary France has been the growing success of *chanson néo-réaliste*, and its explicit reprisal of key lyrical, musical and performance elements of the earlier realist genre.

Like many *néo-réaliste* bands and artists, Pigalle, Têtes Raides, La Tordue and others come from the left-wing, anti-capitalist background of *rock alternatif*

3   www.allocine.fr/film/fichefilm_gen_cfilm=27063.html.
4   Classification of album sales (2002), www.ifop.com/europe/sondages/DISCANNU/albums02.stm.

(see Chapter 1). With its fascination with poverty, fragility and 'authenticity', the realist song provides a perfect parallel to their own preoccupation with anti-consumerism, independence and solidarity. By modelling themselves on realist singers, the *néo-réaliste* artists have developed an explicitly nostalgic identity which gives them the opportunity to counter, at least symbolically, the development of mainstream pop music in France, whose obsession with novelty, success, youth and good looks supposedly typifies the evils of modernity. On the outset, it is thus important to stress that it was through the prism of punk music and the contestatory values attached to independent production that their appropriation of the realist genre took place, for, in keeping with their leftist ideals of social solidarity and anti-capitalist protest, they were drawn to the realist song because of its emphasis on fragility (the destitute characters) and destabilization and threat (life on the margins). The group Têtes Raides, for instance, started by playing punk-rock music while being produced by an independent label (see Chapter 1), before developing a more acoustic and consciously nostalgic style over the 1990s.

One of the most surprising aspects of *chanson néo-réaliste* is that, while its performers are almost all male, they refer to the realist song whose interpreters were almost exclusively female. This discrepancy has been examined, albeit briefly, elsewhere (Lebrun, 2005b, p. 216; Seery, 2007, p. 161; Cecchetto, 2007, p. 8). While they certainly acknowledge their predecessors' gender, these male singers tend to idealize the personal lives and performance styles of dead female artists, drawing sometimes far-fetched connections between the realist genre and their own, present, 'alternative' aspirations. In 1992, the independent label Boucherie released a compilation of cover versions of songs by Piaf and Fréhel, entitled *Ma grand'mère est une rockeuse* ('My granny is a rocker'). The album featured several *rock alternatif* bands, and the orchestration of the covers updated the original versions by including electric guitars, drums and bass, and by speeding up the tempo. Behind the humour lay a conscious strategy of establishing a direct affiliation with these dead artists, and to define the realist genre as a relevant model for contemporary protest, full of vitality, anger and rebellion. This re-evaluation of *chanteuses réalistes* as modern and credible 'protest' models has in fact become a commonly held perception in certain quarters of French music culture, with artists like Rachid Taha claiming that 'Piaf was rock' (in Pascaud, 2007), and critics insisting that Fréhel's life of debauchery made her 'a sort of punk' (Dicale, 2006, p. 91), while Piaf's drug addiction and self-destructive lifestyle lay down the premises for the subsequent rock culture (Fontana, 2007, p. 36). As well as keeping *chanteuses réalistes* very much 'alive' in contemporary French culture (the highly successful 2007 biopic on Piaf, *La vie en rose*, is the latest demonstration of this phenomenon), these comments legitimize the systematic engagement of today's artists with the past. At the same time, the past in which *néo-réaliste* artists are interested is not perceived as being more carefree or less problematic than the present. It is, on the contrary, picked up today for its (imagined) confrontational and non-conventional qualities. The nostalgia of *néo-réaliste* artists for the realist genre is thus, as the following sections will emphasize, an affirmation of the antecedence of 'protest' and 'authentic' principles in French music history, and forms part of their attempts to legitimize their own current 'authenticity'.

Another aspect of the *néo-réaliste* artists' 'nostalgic' approach is their concentration on the notions of social and physical marginality, including old age, deformity and their focus on characters from the underclass. Like the realist songs of the inter-war period, these contemporary songs are peopled with sailors, pimps and prostitutes ('Gino' by Têtes Raides; 'Stilitano' by Casse-Pipe; 'Régina' by Jack O'Lanternes), homeless people and tramps, such as 'Roger Cageot' (Mano Negra) and 'Evariste le Charlot' (Jack O'Lanternes), and drunks of both sexes, including 'Ginette' (Têtes Raides), 'Louise' (Hurlements d'Léo) and 'René Bouteille' (La Tordue). These drop-outs and petty criminals create continuity with the realist genre, but more importantly perhaps, become abstract notions, symbols of poverty, injustice and isolation, whose accumulation serves the contemporary artists' commitment to leftist causes and social justice (Lebrun, 2005a). At the level of onomastics, many *néo-réaliste* bands' names also evoke a working-class, even low-life, context. The name of the band Les Escrocs means 'the crooks', while Garage Rigaud conjures up image of a mechanic's workshop. Many *néo-réaliste* names also evoke physical deformity. The name of the band Têtes Raides (literally 'the stiff heads') suggests a state of drunkenness or being stoned, as well as moral intransigence, a punk-inspired idea that was confirmed by the jokey *franglais* title of their first album, *Not Dead but Bien Raides* ('bien raides' translating as 'well stoned', 'well dead' or 'well stubborn').

Two other bands' names, Les Hurleurs ('the screamers') and Hurlements d'Léo ('Léo's screams') hint at anger and despair. The name of the band Ogres de Barback is a pun on the musical instrument known in French as an 'orgue de Barbarie' (the barrel organ), with connotations of street performance and fairground amusement. This name also evokes cannibal ogres (orgue/ogre), since 'barback' sounds like 'barbaque', a slang word for raw meat, bringing to mind images of gory children's tales along with the notion of pastness closely associated with macabre references. The name of the band La Tordue is equally multi-layered. It literally means 'twisted' or 'sprained', in keeping with the evocation of the bizarre, but also sounds like the name of the 1880s music hall star and cancan dancer La Goulue ('big mouth'), who was renowned for her heavy drinking and immortalized in Toulouse-Lautrec's posters. The name of the band Casse-Pipe, our final example, refers to death through the slang expression of 'casser sa pipe' ('kicking the bucket'), while also invoking the novel of the same name by Louis-Ferdinand Céline, published in 1952, which describes in harrowing detail the author's army training in 1912. The evident literariness of some of these names not only signals the high-brow milieu of *chanson néo-réaliste* (more of this later), but also the artists' clear preference for sombre elements. Their nostalgia is thus not one of comfort and facility, but is rather expressed in the 'anti-escapist' mode (Lowenthal, 1985, p. 62), refusing to refer to the past simply for its pastness, but selecting and valuing only those past features that can connote social and physical fragility, potential conflict and destabilization.

Têtes Raides: Destabilization through Performance

The trope of destabilization features prominently in the musical composition and stage performance of many *néo-réaliste* songs, and is epitomized by the style of Têtes Raides. One song by Têtes Raides, 'Ginette', clearly illustrates the punk-infused style of *chanson néo-réaliste*, and its 'non-escapist' approach to nostalgia. 'Ginette' was initially released on Têtes Raides's first album *Not Dead but Bien Raides* (1989), and is a rock-waltz hybrid that has, over the years, acquired iconic status (Seery, 2007, p. 143). The group's ten-year compilation released in 2000 was named after this song, and it is invariably asked for as an encore by audiences. Without providing a full musicological analysis of this piece, it is possible to identify briefly some of the features that contribute to the intentional creation of a nostalgia of destabilization, rather than a nostalgia of comfort.

The music of 'Ginette' starts slowly, a melancholy waltz on the accordion and cello. The choice of the accordion is obviously a nod to realist song, and other retro elements are conveyed through a direct reference to Charles Baudelaire's poem 'L'Albatros' (1859),[5] with a dark, melancholy storyline, and the introduction of a stereotypical character, Ginette. Through somewhat obscure lyrics, using approximate syntax and a slurring delivery, Ginette is conjured up as a drunk woman, stumbling like an albatross on the ground, dancing in a cabaret where musicians play their sad tune for her. In this song, Têtes Raides are staging themselves as 'real-life' musicians playing for Ginette, and the audience is invited to listen to the band's 'tune of scrap iron and broken glass' ['cet air de ferraille et de verre cassé'] as if they themselves were Ginette. The singer and composer Christian Olivier stutters in order to render the drunkenness of Ginette, and mimics, in live performances, the unstable gait of a drunk.[6] This song within a song thus attempts to give a mirror image of the human condition, as poets, characters, as well as 'real' singers, musicians and the audience, walk the line between comfort and despair, serenity and chaos. Musically, the song is a single long waltz that slows down and accelerates, with a swelling effect provided by the gradual addition of instruments, including the drums, an acoustic guitar, the cello, the trombone and a saxophone played with a distorted effect. After about four minutes, the band suddenly falls silent, before the whole effect starts all over again, the singer this time stepping away from the microphone and shouting the name 'Ginette' from a distance. Finally, after some even faster accordion swirls, the music stops abruptly, and the singer concludes with a deadpan 'and that's it' ['et c'est tout']. Perhaps signalling Ginette's eventual fall to the ground, during

---

5   The final line of Baudelaire's poem is the most representative of the depiction of the powerlessness of man/the Poet: 'His giant wings prevent him from flying' ['Ses ailes de géant l'empêchent de voler'].

6   Seery (2007) has noted the role of the hurricane lamp on stage, which swings above the heads of the musicians and is another accessory of destabilization.

live performance this highly frustrating finish always prompts the audience into cheering and clapping.

Like other songs by Têtes Raides, and as has become common in the *néo-réaliste* genre since, 'Ginette' is a polished, highly controlled music performance which excitingly juxtaposes teasing with dissatisfaction, enthusiasm (especially through the swelling effect of the waltz), and despair (in the lyrics and sonic confusion). This style is not straightforwardly nostalgic in the common acceptation of providing comfort, and the self-conscious irony underlying it is rather typical of the post-punk era. For critics, Têtes Raides create, primarily, a 'topsy-turvy' world (Seery, 2007, p. 136). They are a 'dis-concerting' group displaying a 'taste for risk-taking' (Pantchenko, 2004, p. 96), who force upon their listeners a durable impression of 'nausea', of life-like flirting with disquiet and a looming death (Gonot, 2005, pp. 84–5).[7] These features of destabilization consecrate Têtes Raides as a serious group, whose engagement with retro and stereotypical elements (the waltz, the accordion, a drunk) does not culminate in a sentimentalizing nostalgia, but rather in a complex understanding of life, where past and present both appear problematic. Têtes Raides are perceived as being 'radical' and 'uncompromising' (Paquotte, 2001, p. 59), 'true' (Gonot, 2005, p. 111), 'authentic' (Perrin, 2001a).

There is insufficient space here to conduct an exhaustive analysis of all the performance choices of the band, and of *néo-réaliste* groups more generally, but generally speaking all reinforce this specific, uncomfortable engagement with nostalgia. When playing 'Ginette' live, for instance, Têtes Raides's light technician, aptly nicknamed Fantôme, produces a 'slow-mo' effect, alternating zones of light and shade, recalling the expressionist style of silent movies. This brings the band's style closer to theatre performance than rock music concerts (Hazera, 1999), and clarifies their goal of fitting into the tradition of the cabaret, when songs were staged as pared-down 'mini-dramas' (Hawkins, 2000, p. 79).[8] This technique also characterizes the group's ambition to decompartmentalize genre conventions, to 'seek danger' and to break away from 'the danger of routine' (in Paquotte, 2001, p. 59). We shall see in Chapter 5 that this discourse is characteristic of the artistic vanguard, and that it in fact constructs its own routine, its own set of conventions, by being quite widespread among a clearly defined socio-cultural group. This does not, however, invalidate the group's originality, nor does it prevent us from accepting the 'alternative' characteristics of *chanson néo-réaliste*, especially by contrast to more mediatized, commercially successful pop.

---

7   'Têtes Raides dé-concerte', their 'indéfectible goût du risque'; 'une encre nausée', 'la mort … comme une entité avec laquelle on doit vivre', 'étrange impression … de subites inquiétudes'.

8   The UK group Tiger Lillies and the Russo-German combo ErsatzMusika, also influenced by the theatricality of the cabaret, would provide an interesting comparison with Têtes Raides.

Popular Authenticity

The 'non-escapist' nostalgia of *chanson néo-réaliste* co-exists, nevertheless, with a more sentimental vision of the past. In their declarations, many *néo-réaliste* artists present the inter-war period as a time of intense social relationships, of solidarity among the classes, in contrast with the contemporary period when consumerism and individualism have allegedly broken the social fabric. This basic and squarely leftist analysis of society conveys an idealized 'popular' authenticity, which is another feature of the complex nostalgic identity of the genre. For instance, the *néo-réaliste* and fellow-traveller François Hadji-Lazaro, founder of Boucherie Production and singer/composer for Pigalle, argued that capitalism has brought social division. To challenge and provide a respite from this, his intention with the band Pigalle was to forge a 'popular rock' ['un rock populaire'], a music genre able to unite a wide cross-section of society, and modelled precisely on the 'old realist songs' (in Chérel, 1992).[9] His interpretation of the ability of realist songs to significantly unite social classes, however, was rather questionable. Already in the 1840s, at the height of the Parisian craze for *guinguettes* (outdoor drinking and dancing venues that are another topos of *chanson néo-réaliste*), different venues catered for different audiences, which were distinct in terms of professional and regional backgrounds. In most cases, people would congregate to dance with an already-gathered group of friends and relatives (Gasnault, 1986, pp. 40–41). In the late nineteenth and early twentieth century, at least as much social separation as apparent 'bonding' existed during a realist cabaret performance (Scott, 2008). This has not changed much today: as Chapter 6 demonstrates, there is a major discrepancy between the (relative) social fragmentation of contemporary festival audiences, and the (imagined) conviviality they nonetheless represent.

In any case, Hadji-Lazaro's idealization of the inter-war period was typical of the discourse surrounding *chanson néo-réaliste*, and more generally of the 'alternative', 'anti-mainstream' music culture of late twentieth-century France. Seery (2007, p. 121) has demonstrated the vagueness of the inter-war anchorage of the group Paris Combo, whose first album was released by Hadji-Lazaro's

---

9   It is worth quoting Hadji-Lazaro (in Chérel, 1992) at length on this point: 'We were the first, with the singer from Négresses Vertes, to sing old realist songs. We claim to follow a popular rock; not just for an elite, the microcosm of Parisian trendies, or snobbish specialists… That's why we perform at the Fête de l'Huma [the Parti Communiste's own music festival]. … We live in a world where people's only ideals seem to be Coca-Cola and individual success, surrounded by triumphant capitalism. We're heading towards a generation of disillusioned individualists' ['Nous avions été les premiers, avec le chanteur des Négresses Vertes, à chanter de vieilles chansons réalistes. Nous nous réclamons d'un rock populaire; pas réservé à une élite, au microcosme des branchés parisiens, ni à des spécialistes snobinards... C'est pour ça que nous allons jouer à la Fête de l'Huma. … On est dans un univers où il semble n'y avoir plus comme idéal que Coca-Cola et la réussite individuelle dans le capitalisme triomphant. On va vers une génération individualiste et désabusée'].

label Boucherie. For Têtes Raides, whose twin musical influences are punk (The Clash) and the realist song (in particular, Marianne Oswald, Damia, Fréhel), the 1930s in France gave rise to 'a truly popular song' ['une vraie chanson populaire'] (Hache, 2006).[10] More specifically, in 2006, Têtes Raides organized, in conjunction with the annual Communist-sponsored Fête de l'Huma, the celebration of 1936, the year when the Front Populaire, a left-wing coalition, was first elected in France. Grégoire Simon, the saxophonist of the group, declared that that year was 'sharply resonant today' ['cruellement d'actualité'] (Hache, 2006). For the younger band Ogres de Barback, their self-proclaimed 'punk spirit' and 'truly alternative' identity equally have their origins in the realist genre, which was 'popular in the noble sense of the term'.[11] Here too, the inter-war period, the realist song and the idea of working-class fraternity are fused together with idealism, so as to achieve antecedence and, by extension, cultural legitimacy, for present-day leftism. The Ogres de Barback insist on their contemporary political commitment by stressing for instance that their songs 'bear the mark of the citizen-centred preoccupations of responsible and committed people'.[12] Clearly, then, the inter-war nostalgia of *chanson néo-réaliste* is not formulated in a vacuum, but is, rather, characteristic of post-1981 French politics, when the Socialists in power asserted their own credibility by situating themselves in continuity with the Front Populaire. For Cornick (1998, p. 301), a sentiment of 'nostalgia for the great days of the 1936 Popular Front' is characteristic of left-wing intellectuals in 1980s and 1990s France, and *chanson néo-réaliste* largely echoes this trend.

The reappraisal of the adjective 'popular' (*populaire*) in many groups' declarations effectively sidelines the difficult polysemy of the term in French, so as to retain only its 'authentic' and 'honest' connotations, its echoes of a fraternal and victimized working class. This use of the adjective, with connotations of a working-class pastness, is particularly interesting, as it contrasts with the more widespread and often pejorative use of the same term in contemporary speech, among the same socio-cultural group, to refer to the apparently dominant population ('the masses') that listens to the popular music played on commercial media (see Chapter 5). This second and more widespread meaning of the adjective 'popular' evokes the 'mainstreamization' of cultural tastes in France, and is fiercely rejected by self-defined alternative locutors. Thus, when Hadji-Lazaro and the members of Têtes Raides and Ogres de Barback praise the notion of a 'popular' culture, as above, they idealize a time when, presumably, mass-mediatization was not yet an

---

10   Interview of the singer Christian Olivier and the musicians Grégoire and Iso for *Le Hall de la Chanson* (11 February 2004), audible online on www.lehall.com (select '20 ans de chansons actuelles', then 'Têtes Raides', then 'L'interview'), Questions 4, 6 and 7, last accessed 24 March 2009.

11   '... la chronique réaliste, populaire au sens noble du terme', www.lesogres.com, select 'Bio'.

12   '... la marque des préoccupations citoyennes des gens impliqués et responsables', www.lesogres.com, 'Bio'.

issue, and when music identities were not divided by their loyalty to 'authentic' and 'resistant' music on the one hand, and their opposition to a homogenized mass-culture notions on the other. Given their contribution to the edification and perpetuation of this cultural split in France today, it is perhaps ironic that they seem to regret the passing of this supposed monoculture.

Finally, the evocation of collective solidarity and communal participation in *chanson néo-réaliste* is also bound up with references to alcohol consumption, as heavy drinking can imply, at once, individual depravity and solitude, social gathering and conviviality. The name of the band Blankass, for instance, is an approximate phonetic transcription of the abbreviation of 'blanc-cassis', a white wine and blackcurrant liqueur *apéritif*, while that of another band, Debout sur le Zinc ('Dancing on the counter') associates the festive practice of dancing with the setting of a bar (the 'zinc' counter is a synecdoche for the bar itself and more generally any drinking place). This key word is also present in the name of two compilations featuring *néo-réaliste* artists, *Chansons du Bord de Zinc*, volumes 1 and 2 (1999 and 2001), and *Zic de Zinc*, volumes 1 and 2 (2006 and 2007). Both titles refer to 'songs from the bar counter', and hammer home the idea that social bonding happens through music-playing and drinking in public places. Many *néo-réaliste* album covers depict café scenes, with a bistro table, a wine glass, dominos or a smiling crowd surrounding bar musicians, illustrating the pleasure of togetherness in contrast to the presumed individualism of domestic life and contemporary consumerism.

Instruments, Simplicity and Mobility

In the 1930s, the 'city idyll' already mixed Parisian urban décors with elements of the countryside, so as to juxtapose feelings of conviviality with a critique of urbanization, and to represent the working class as somehow 'innocent', suffering from, rather than being complicit in, the process of industrialization (Rifkin, 1991, p. 206). In the 1990s and 2000s, the portrayal of working-class life as 'authentic' and linked to a disappearing countryside is repeated in the *néo-réaliste* artists' passion for outdoor music festivals, and in their enthusiasm for transient lifestyles and travelling communities (see Chapter 6). Meanwhile, the instruments played in *chanson néo-réaliste* are selected for their capacity to foster a supposedly direct relationship with the audience, through an idealization of collective music-playing in an outdoor setting. Rather than using heavy, fixed instruments such as the cello and the piano, which are traditionally associated with the domestic space of bourgeois sociability,[13] *néo-réaliste* artists privilege the use of small, light, portable instruments, which are also rarely heard in mainstream pop. These include the accordion, the barrel organ, the xylophone, the helicon, the banjo,

---

13   See Scott (2001, pp. 50–51) for parallels with the bourgeois use of the piano in mid-nineteenth century England.

the jew's harp, the musical saw, the harmonica and the *contrebassine*, a home-made double bass whose sound box is an upturned plastic bucket. The *contrebassine* (a play-on-word on the French for double-bass, *contrebasse*, and the word for washing-up bowl, *bassine*) was popularized in France by the *rock alternatif* bands Les VRP and Nonnes Troppo in the 1980s. It is the latest incarnation of the early twentieth-century washtub-bass of blues, and of the 1950s tea-chest bass of skiffle music in the UK, two genres which are often lauded for their 'authentic' and DIY connotations. Portable instruments obviously allow for mobility, and the accumulation of such small, usually cheap instruments signals, in contemporary France, the craving of 'non-mainstream' artists and audiences for the disappearing outdoor practices of street singing, Gypsy music, brass bands, fairgrounds, the circus and *bals musettes*.[14] These instruments also allow the artists, through their portability and capacity to be played outside, to make a statement against the implicitly poorer experience of 'modern', domestic and individualized music consumption.

Even in the 1920s, though, outdoor music-playing had already become something of a rarity, and street singing, which was never a particularly popular or lucrative profession, had been superseded by the phonograph. Piaf abandoned street singing as soon as she could get a contract for an indoor venue, and in their memoirs, Eugénie Buffet and Fréhel both recount the precariousness of such an existence (Conway, 2004, p. 50 and p. 93). Between 1900 and 1930, when phonographs were not yet affordable for many private individuals, café owners would buy these 'modern' machines and play music with loudspeakers in order to attract their clientele. The realist singer Fréhel recounts that the street music of her childhood was, already, that of the phonographs played in bistros (in Conway, 2004, p. 104). Moreover, the domestic activity of record-listening contributed to forging strong and arguably 'authentic' feelings of intimacy between the audience and the piece of recorded music, as was the case for many French jazz lovers in the 1930s (Tournès, 2005, p. 145). These points demonstrate that outdoor music-listening has long been inseparable from recorded music, and that indoor, domestic music practices can also generate collective bonding and feelings of 'authenticity'.

Regardless of the actual situation in the inter-war years, the image that contemporary *néo-réaliste* artists convey of this period, of the realist song and of street singing and outdoor music-playing more generally, is one of authenticity and desirable freedom. In 1997, the singer and lyricist of Paris Combo, Belle du Berry, underlined that her inspiration was situated in the 1930s because she was attracted to the 'free-spirited' quality of the era.[15] Bypassing the fact that the period had seen an increase in unemployment, anti-Semitism and the continuation of the colonial

---

14   The revival of circus attractions (*le nouveau cirque*) and street theatre in contemporary France is a clear indication of this general trend (see Chapter 6; also Seery 2007, p. 139 and Cecchetto, 2007, fn. 53).

15   'Notre esprit était très proche de celui des années 1930. On aimait cette idée de la vie libre', the singer Belle du Berry, interviewed for the festival Printemps de Bourges (1997), www.reseau-printemps.com/rpb/cyber/home_1997.html.

empire, she characterized the period through a single, simple and rather erroneous notion of liberty. In a 1992 interview, Hadji-Lazaro proudly pointed out that one of his artists, the lead singer of 10 Petits Indiens, had been a street singer before joining his label.[16] Many album sleeves pursue this theme visually through the juxtaposition of conviviality with outdoor settings. Street scenes, Gypsy caravans and street accordionists illustrate the albums of Têtes Raides (1998), Jack O'Lanternes (1998) and Ogres de Barback (1997 and 2001). Refusing to a certain extent to engage with the latest technology, such as the electronic samples dominant in rap music of the 1990s, these artists also usually prefer to play acoustic gigs. As an exercise in such 'pastness', Têtes Raides toured in 1999 with an entirely unplugged show, 'Non!', without any amps or microphones, in an attempt to re-create the 'unmediated' feel of cabaret performance. The nostalgia of *néo-réaliste* artists for certain instruments is also most obvious in their frequent playing of the accordion, an instrument singled out for its emblematic old-fashionedness and 'popular' appeal.

The Accordion: Ultimate 'Authentic' Frenchness?

Developed in Austria in 1829, the accordion was popularized in France thanks to a Parisian patent to reproduce it as early as 1830, but documentary evidence of the instrument's penetration of popular music culture is scarce. The polka dance craze of the 1840s and 1950s did not seem to be performed on the accordion, but rather on the violin and drums (Gasnault, 1986, p. 184). The instrument is also notably absent from illustrations of collective music scenes in the second half of the nineteenth century, and how the fast waltz of *la java* came to be performed on this instrument has yet to be precisely ascertained. Nonetheless, the portability of the accordion suggests that it would have been perfect for the outdoor performances of *guinguettes*, and it would seem that, by 1900, it had become systematically associated with the working classes and street music, and commonly accepted as a metaphor for a 'popular' identity.[17] By the beginning of the twentieth century, it had certainly become part of the orchestration of some realist songs, including the most heavily nostalgic recordings of Fréhel and Piaf that evoked the waltzes of yore ('Dans un bouge du vieux port', 1937; 'L'accordéoniste', 1942). In the post-war period and up until the 1980s, the female accordionist Yvette Horner continued to popularize this instrument in France, while giving it a series of right-wing connotations because of her support for the conservative president Giscard d'Estaing, and her participation, the instrument slung across her chest, at various

---

16   Chérel (1992).

17   Helmi Strahl Harrington, 'Accordion', Grove Music Online, available through www.oxfordmusiconline.com, last accessed 24 March 2009; Rifkin (1991). In Marcel Aymé's novel *La rue sans nom* (1930), Italian immigrants live in a sordid Paris street and play the accordion all day. In the eponymous film adaptation (dir. Pierre Chenal, 1934), the realist singer Fréhel plays the wife of the central character.

Tours de France. In the 1950 and 1960s, with the advent of rock music and electric guitars, the accordion gradually fell out of fashion and was only occasionally used in French popular music, Jacques Brel's 'Amsterdam' (1964) being one notable exception.

It is customary, in nostalgic cultural forms, to appropriate 'past' elements once a certain temporal distance has been covered, and once these elements have in effect become *passé* (Lowenthal, 1985, p. 51). This was certainly the case with the accordion by the late 1980s, when *rock alternatif* and *chanson néo-réaliste* artists decided to (re)appropriate it. By then, the instrument had seemingly lost any credibility or relevance to youth culture.[18] In 1982, the French singer-songwriter Gérard Blanchard had a hit with 'Rock Amadour', a fast rock-steady song whose melody was followed up on the accordion, which he played himself. By all accounts, this was a comic 'novelty' song, but Blanchard was retrospectively credited as the 'father' of *rock alternatif* and *chanson néo-réaliste* for his unheard-of juxtaposition of this instrument with punk rock.[19] Now, many *rock alternatif* groups were not without a sense of humour, especially Bérurier Noir, Garçons Bouchers and Les VRP, but the evolution of the 'alternative' creed into a more systematic opposition to modernity through the development of a nostalgic 'protest' was meant, above all, to be a serious proposition. Generally speaking, then, in *chanson néo-réaliste* the accordion constitutes a flagrant anti-mainstream and anti-consensus statement. For Hadji-Lazaro, his intention in picking up the accordion was to react against the sectarianism of music categories, including those employed by punk music lovers, and to prove that various instruments and styles, old and new, could mix well together (in Chérel, 1992). For Têtes Raides, the accordion was also a means to challenge the rock music crowd and their preconceptions (Paquotte, 2001, p. 57), while at the same time establishing a connection with the high status of *chanson* by hiring, from 1995 onwards, the accordionist Jean Corti who had accompanied Jacques Brel on stage in the 1960s (Pantchenko, 2004, p. 105).

As Pigalle, Négresses Vertes, Têtes Raides, La Tordue, Ogres de Barback and other bands adopted the accordion within an alternative culture and protest discourse, so the instrument became the sign of a new Frenchness, one positively associated with leftism, intellectual critique, radicalism and *métissage*. We discuss

---

18   The major exception to this is the singer-songwriter Renaud who, in the mid-1970s, voluntarily revived the stereotype of the Parisian street urchin and played on the accordion a series of provocative songs (Harrison, 2003, p. 71). Renaud is sometimes quoted as a source of influence for *néo-réaliste* artists.

19   The music journalist Hélène Hazera presenting Blanchard for her 'Chanson Boum!' programme on the radio channel France Culture (19 November 2006), text reproduced online at: www.radiofrance.fr/chaines/france-culture2/emissions/chansons/fiche.php?diffusion_id=45869&pg=avenir. For other, non-French juxtapositions of rock music with the accordion, see the Cajun bands of the US, and the Irish band The Pogues, to whom Négresses Vertes and Têtes Raides are often compared for their similar 'raw energy' alongside a folk, nostalgic identity.

the implications of this new self-proclaimed multicultural 'authenticity' in the next chapter, but it is telling that, in 1987, the accordionist Yvette Horner agreed to play with the Maghrebi-French rock-rap band Kous Kous Klan, in a fusion that would have been unimaginable, let alone 'alternative', a few years earlier (Moreira, 1987, p. 21). For these artists, then, playing the accordion was not only an aspect of their musical sensibility, but also of the intellectual project of disrupting prejudices, including those of the 'indie' crowd, and more generally of challenging present-day certainties. Playing the accordion in the 1990s was, of course, a nostalgic gesture, based on the flawed assumption that the accordion was central to the realist song, but it also fitted well into a more generally left-wing agenda, critical of dominant 'mainstream' popular music, consumerism and modernity at large, since the instrument could evoke working-class solidarity.

The first album by Ogres de Barback, *Rue du Temps* (1997), typifies this cultural ensemble. The record sleeve shows a circus tent, a prostitute in front of an hotel and an accordionist on the pavement, while one song is entitled 'Rue de Panam'.

Illustration 2.1   Ogres de Barback. Front cover of album *Rue du Temps* (1997). Reproduced by kind permission of Yannick Legrain, on behalf of the production company Irfan.

These signifiers build up an archetypal *néo-réaliste* identity. The key word 'rue' (street) is repeated twice and sets out the importance of urban life, and obviously of Paris, since 'Panam(e)' is slang for the capital. Social marginality and poverty are also present through the references to busking and prostitution, while nomadism is evoked by the circus (and looking for a pick-up is also an ambulatory practice). Finally, the word 'temps' (the time that passes) wraps up these elements in a nostalgic feel, which the hand-drawn, sepia-coloured iconography of the record sleeve also stresses. On their website (for even 'nostalgic' artists must keep up with technology), the band specify that 'Rue de Panam' has become their most iconic song, consistently demanded as an encore by audiences (also Cecchetto, 2007, p. 8). It is a waltz on the accordion whose lyrics are narrated by a Parisian pimp, wary of the city's modernization. It concludes with a hymn to 'joy and anarchy'. This song is, basically, a *néo-réaliste* cliché, yet the band take pride in considering it the most representative title of their contemporary and 'radical' identity. The highly positive reception among a dedicated crowd of 'alternative' music-lovers suggests that the song's obvious pastness, and more generally the evident nostalgia of the *néo-réaliste* genre, works as something other than an old-fashioned stereotype.[20] For their fans, Ogres de Barback and other *néo-réaliste* groups convey a potent protest message through the subtle dissemination of key markers. A hand-drawn picture on a cardboard album sleeve, the sound of a waltz, the story of a homeless drunk, a call for anarchy, are all vague references that manage, in their cumulative effect, to conjure up notions of dissatisfaction with modernity, and to suggest that marginality and collectivity are topical anwers to consensus and individualism. In this, *chanson néo-réaliste* is very much a contemporary 'protest' music genre.

Nostalgia, Ethnicity and *Métissage*

Nostalgia and *métissage* (multiculturalism/hybridity) are arguably the two most obvious tendencies in the evolution of French popular music in the 1990s (Bonnieux, Cordereix and Giuliani, 2004, p. 101; also Looseley, 2003, pp. 37–62). *Chanson néo-réaliste* is, as we have seen, turned towards the French, even Parisian, past of the 1920s and 1930s (nostalgia), but it is also peppered with non-traditionally French sounds and historical references (*métissage*). These features are perhaps present in most artistic representations of any given period, as the tendency to mix classical trends with new and foreign influences has existed in the past, but this tendency achieved a new poignancy in late twentieth-century France when ethnic minorities from a colonial background reached adulthood, and when left-wing artists and intellectuals had to situate themselves in debates regarding the place of multiculturalism in French society.

---

20   See for example the highly enthusiastic messages posted by young fans on http://musique.ados.fr/Les-Ogres-de-Barback/commentaires-1253.html, last accessed 21 March 2009.

In the inter-war period, the realist song was already 'hybrid' to an extent. If the confined nature of cabaret venues initially limited the genre musically (Calvet, 1981, p. 72), with typical instruments including the piano, the violin and the accordion,[21] after the First World War the development of recording techniques, boosted by the electrification of the phonograph in the late 1920s, meant that realist orchestration gradually became fuller and more diverse. The waltz and the faster lilt of the java continued to dominate, but the use of woodwind, violins and other string instruments also became very common. In the 1920s, the Argentine tango and Afro-American blues started to arrive in France, and a few composers included these sounds in their realist creations, alongside the touches of orientalism already present (Terrasse, 1995). Indeed, the realist genre included some 'oriental' songs, even if these went along with the dominant colonialist views of the time, representing the indigenous population through the twin registers of comedy and the exotic (Liauzu and Liauzu, 2002, p. 85). In many ways, the 1930s signalled the decline of colonialist mentalities, and some songs, such as 'Mon légionnaire', 'Mon amant de la coloniale' or 'Le grand voyage du pauvre nègre' (all penned by Raymond Asso and performed by Marie Dubas and Piaf in 1935–7), started to depict the colonies as places of melancholy and uncertainty, and the oriental 'other' as a complex and suffering individual (Liauzu and Liauzu, 2002, p. 138). Nonetheless, the relative musical hybridity of the realist genre served to hide an overall orientalist ideology, as befits a genre shaped during the colonial period, and the exclusively white singers of the realist genre never hinted, for instance, at the possibility of inter-racial equality or love. In the 1990s, the appropriation by leftist bands of this cultural past, with its underlying rearguard discourse vis-à-vis ethnic difference, is highly problematic.

On the one hand, most *néo-réaliste* artists do not confine themselves to a nostalgic evocation of the inter-war period, but explore, at least musically, the genres of non-French cultures. The band Hurlements d'Léo uses a brass section that bridges the gap between military march bands, Gypsy music and British-Jamaican ska. Many other groups, such as Nonnes Troppo, Les Pires and Ogres de Barback, incorporate yiddish and kletzmer music. Reggae music is also widely present (La Tordue, Têtes Raides), as is flamenco ('Manuela', Têtes Raides, 1996) and Middle-Eastern percussions, as in 'Istanbul' by Paris Combo (1997) and 'Leïla' (1999) by Négresses Vertes. The artists also translate and cover foreign songs, such as La Tordue's 'Grand Père' (2000), the original version of which was composed by the Spanish singer-songwriter Paco Ibañez. These borrowings and musical crossovers demonstrate that, despite its nostalgic elements, *chanson néo-réaliste* does not map out a narrow Frenchness.[22] Furthermore, many bands appear influenced by North African music, and interested in related issues of

---

21   Bruant hired a brass-band during his recordings of the 1900s.

22   Ross (2007) makes a similar point when he underlines the centrality of the Portuguese grand-mother character in *Belleville Rendez-Vous* (dir. Sylvain Chomet, 2003), an animation film nostalgic about inter-war France.

post-colonial migration. The groups Mano Negra and Négresses Vertes were among the first artists in France, in the late 1980s, to borrow the derbouki percussions and oud guitar of the Maghreb, to sing in Arabic, and to give an oriental layer to their music alongside their re-evaluation of the realist heritage. In 1998, Têtes Raides composed music for the poem 'Dans la gueule du loup', written by the Algerian Kateb Yacine, and repeatedly explored the limitations of a strict understanding of republicanism in France, with special reference to the situation of Maghrebi minorities ('L'Iditenté', 2001, 'Des accords', 2004). Many bands have also actively campaigned against racism and for the right to stay of illegal immigrants (Lebrun, 2005a and 2006a).

Like the left-wing intellectualism identified earlier, this tendency fits into a broad cultural response to the rise of the Front National in France since the 1980s, and a general reflection about France's self-discovery as a multicultural country since decolonization. Incorporating musical influences drawn from North Africa and further afield, *néo-réaliste* artists produce a musical and ideological *métissage* that is both a reflection of the period, and controversial in its attempted challenge of dominant positions, whether traditional republicanism or the most exclusionary tendencies of society exemplified by the far right. More than the *chanteuses réalistes* of the 1930s, therefore, the *néo-réaliste* groups of today engage with the diasporic formation of the French nation, often in an open-minded and critical fashion, furthering their credentials as 'alternative' and 'radical' artists.

On the other hand, the place of post-colonial ethnicity in the *néo-réaliste* genre is very much wrapped up in an overall 'realist', passeist package, and despite the points made above, the vast majority of the cultural references in these songs come from the historically and ethnically circumscribed context of France between the two world wars. On the whole, *chanson néo-réaliste* only engages with ethnic diversity in specific and isolated efforts, which are often somewhat obscure in their formulation and secondary to the artists' interests, and it does not really convey a multicultural image of contemporary France – explaining, perhaps, its lack of success abroad.[23] Most song characters, for instance, bear names that are 'typically' French, such as René, Ginette, Louise, Evariste, Jeannette and Oscar, and these bind the present-day songs into an unquestionably white genealogy. As a result, a debate exists among journalists and academics about the possible incapacity of the genre to provide a properly 'radical' identity in the contemporary period, and a degree of unease is evident in their discussions surrounding the 'retro' and 'nostalgic' labels attributed to the genre.

---

23   In 2002, the US label Luaka Bop released *Cuisine Non-Stop*, a compilation of music from 'the French nouvelle generation', featuring Têtes Raides, Louise Attaque, La Tordue and other 1990s *chanson*-rock artists. The liner notes were provided by David Byrne, mastermind of the avant-garde rock band Talking Heads, who was quoted on the front sleeve saying that 'it's all about being alternative'. The album did not have much success, and the label closed down a few years later.

The implied whiteness and traditional 'Frenchness' of *chanson néo-réaliste* can indeed appear problematic when it apparently excludes from the 'pleasure of recognition', even only symbolically, immigrants and French nationals of post-colonial extraction (Lowenthal, 1985, p. 39; Morley and Robins, 1995, p. 41 and p. 46). For Lowenthal (1985, pp. 47–8), it is familiarity with the past that creates pleasure from its evocation in the present, and immigrants who have not shared in this past, simply because their ancestors were not in France at the time, or because that cultural heritage has not been passed down, cannot participate in a nostalgic culture on the same level as the majority population. A debate arose in France in 2001 precisely about this point, after the release of the film *Amélie*. Although it was generally very well received by critics and audiences alike, one sector of the French left-wing press took issue with its overt visual passeism. In a scathing attack led by two *Inrockuptibles* journalists, the film was dubbed a neo-colonial product and, provocatively, a piece of Front National propaganda.[24] More cautiously, a few academics agreed that the film was conservative in its refusal to engage with today's multicultural reality (Vincendeau, 2001; Austin, 2003, p. 135). Popular music journalism is less well established in France than its cinema counterpart, and *chanson néo-réaliste* has not generated the same amount of debate and degree of condemnation as *Amélie*. Nonetheless, some critics have expressed concerns about the pastness of *chanson néo-réaliste*, wondering how an evident nostalgia for pre-decolonization France could square up with the artists' leftism in the present.

In 1999, writing for the left-wing journal *Esprit*, Paul Garapon noted that the choice made by Négresses Vertes to play the accordion raised the possibility of conservatism. At the same time, he denied vehemently that the group were guilty of cultural *revivalisme* (in *franglais* in the original). Choosing to play the accordion, he argued, did not prove the band's reactionary understanding of national identity, but conjured up instead a broad cultural system based on the French working class, the Popular Front, the films of Renoir and the *bals musettes* of the Marne river banks (Garapon, 1999, p. 101). In other words, the band was 'saved' from being labelled 'reactionary' because of its nostalgia for supposedly 'popular' (as in working-class, and therefore left-wing) features. Ten years earlier, in *Actuel*, the self-appointed 'magazine of counter-culture', the critics Philippe Vandel and Paul Rambali (1988) had already introduced Négresses Vertes in the same enthusiastic yet confused way. On the one hand, they acknowledged that playing the accordion could be seen as a 'benighted Franco-centrist attitude' ['beaufitude franchouillarde']; on the other, they refuted this accusation by praising the group's ability to counter far-right ideologies: 'the true java, the popular and cheeky java,

---

24 See Bonnaud (2001) and Kaganski (2001). The fact that this anti-nostalgic criticism emerged from *Les Inrockuptibles* is significant in sociological terms, and a point to bear in mind for Chapter 5 when we discuss the impact of this magazine on French music audiences.

threatens Le Pen much more than any political discourse'.[25] More recently, yet following a similar line of argument, the *Télérama* journalist Anne-Marie Paquotte (1999) reviewed the band Paris Combo. The group openly admires the 1930s jazz guitarist Django Reinhardt, but Paquotte insisted that this attitude 'was not revivalist' (also Seery, 2007, p. 108). Similarly, when interviewed about Têtes Raides, the producer Vincent Frèrebeau rejected the use of the label *néo-réaliste* to describe the group, because it implied 'passeism and a closed nostalgia'. For him, above all, the group were in fact forward-looking and dynamic (in Gonot, 2005, p. 112). In all these cases, the critics underlined, quite rightly, that these bands were not rearguard or racist, but their dialectical arguments and heavy use of denegations also revealed their defensiveness regarding the artists' taste for the accordion, and for a markedly 'French' past. The term *revivalisme* is a pejorative anglicism in French, and all these critics sought to pre-empt the possibility of any criticism based on an analogy between supposedly stereotypical French music and the expression of far-right views. Their declarations, therefore, show that the chosen mode of representation of *chanson néo-réaliste*, nostalgia, can be problematic when coming from otherwise left-wing groups claiming fraternity and 'sharing' ['le partage'] as their central driving force (Paquotte, 2001, p. 59).

Cultural Participation and Social Exclusion

The question of potential audience exclusion can be assessed in more concrete, sociological terms with reference to the public that actually appreciates these groups' nostalgia – even if is it a nostalgia of protest. Audience reception is examined in detail in Chapter 5, yet a few starting points can be made here. In their ultimate praise of *chanson néo-réaliste*, the critics quoted above suggested, for instance, that all audiences could relate to the cultural world evoked in the *néo-réaliste* songs, and understand the 'popular' authenticity conveyed by their working-class cultural heritage (the films of Renoir, the Popular Front, the *guinguettes*, etc.). This follows the common view that 'we can be nostalgic about, or invest in, an experience that we have not actually had, or a period never personally experienced' (Drake, 2003, p. 198). In other words, even if one's own grand-parents were not dancing to the tune of the accordion in 1936, were not called Oscar and Ginette, and did not live in a popular *quartier* of Paris between the wars, one can still appreciate the full cultural and emotional depth of *chanson néo-réaliste* today.

Unfortunately, this upbeat approach to nostalgia bypasses the fact that the pleasure derived from nostalgic works of art is usually the result of a 'composite' of personal experience and of mediated knowledge (Lowenthal, 1985, p. 40).

---

25   'La vraie java, la java populo et gouailleuse menace plus Le Pen que tous les discours politiques' (Vandel and Rambali, 1988, p. 112). On the 'beauf' as absolute enemy to the 'alternative' mentality, an approach which characterizes the cultural snobbism of *Les Inrockuptibles*, see Andrews (2000, p. 243).

For this reason, not all audiences are on the same footing with regards to its evocation. Indeed, it has been clear, at least since the publication of Bourdieu's seminal work *La Distinction* in 1979, that not all consumers are equal before cultural knowledge. Bourdieu demonstrated that different socio-economic groups tended to have different cultural experiences and tastes, and that cultural capital is as unequally shared among the French population as is economic wealth. More recently, other studies have shown that, as ethnic inequalities progress along socio-economic lines, migrants and those of migrant origin, especially in the post-colonial context, often fall within the least educated sectors of French society, and are the most likely to be unemployed and excluded from the cultural capital of the elite (Hargreaves, 2007).[26] Thus, not all audiences are equal in terms of the cultural knowledge required to decode the mediated and composite nature of nostalgia in general, and of *chanson néo-réaliste* in particular. To hope that the question of exclusion can be sidestepped by emphasizing the universal nature of this nostalgic recollection is, in sociological terms, wishful thinking. Indeed, and rather unfortunately, the audience of 'alternative' rock music and *chanson néo-réaliste* is overwhelmingly white, well-off and well-educated, just as that of 'quality' *chanson* was in the 1960s and 1970s (Bourdieu, 1979, p. 405; Looseley, 2003, p. 38; Donnat, 1998, p. 163). *Chanson néo-réaliste* is, as Chapter 5 underlines, enjoyed by a narrow section of the population in terms of age, and social and educational background. As a result, and although this does not constitute an intentional exclusion on the part of the artists in question, a large degree of social separation exists in the culture of *chanson néo-réaliste*, which affects ethnic representation. Because ethnic divisions form along socio-economic fault lines, and are reflected in cultural consumption, debating the potential (even if unintentional) reactionarism of *chanson néo-réaliste* remains a valid question to raise.

Moreover, with its critical ambitions, *chanson néo-réaliste* attempts to establish a vanguard culture whose 'protest nostalgia' requires a high level of cultural knowledge. This is most evident in the groups' literariness. The name of the band La Tordue, in addition to its cabaret connotations, echoes the name of a character in *Antigone*, a play by Jean Anouilh (1946), while the band Casse-Pipe refers to the author Louis-Ferdinand Céline. In interviews, the saxophonist of Têtes Raides, Grégoire Simon, quotes the somewhat 'difficult' poets Fernando Pessoa and Philippe Soupault as sources of inspiration.[27] In addition, the eclecticism of these artists, who can often play several instruments, write lyrics and compose music,

---

26 In the absence of French statistics on the ethnic origins of popular music consumers, the report by INSEE (Institut National de la Statistique) reveals the economic and cultural exclusion of French Maghrebis: www.insee.fr/fr/ffc/chifcle_fiche.asp?ref_id=NATCCI03308&tab_id=439&souspop=4, last accessed 21 March 2009.

27 Interview for the cultural magazine *L'Internaute*, February 2006: www.linternaute.com/musique/interview/chat/tetes-raides/tetes-raides-retranscription.shtml, last accessed 21 March 2009. The lyrics of Têtes Raides have been qualified as 'abstruse' and 'labyrinthine'

and frequently contribute to various artistic side projects, signals their 'higher level of artistic ambition' (Looseley, 2003, p. 49). For instance, the lead singer of La Tordue, Benoît Morel, and that of Têtes Raides, Christian Olivier, along with a third member, initially trained as graphic designers and, as the designer team Les Chats Pelés, have illustrated all the album sleeves of both bands, as well as many children's books.

Still, specific research into the reception of *chanson néo-réaliste* among audiences of immigrant origin, particularly North African, would be needed to evaluate the question of 'exclusion' more appropriately, and the following chapters make some steps in this direction. To conclude here, however, the question remains of knowing who can access the cultural capital necessary to 'read' the composite elements that form the cultural richness of *néo-réaliste* nostalgia. Anecdotal evidence would seem to suggest that it is impossible to draw a blanket conclusion on this point. One informant of Moroccan extraction, Rachida, acknowledged that some of Têtes Raides's music sounded 'retro', but emphasized immediately that she liked the band for that very reason. For her, the accordion did not exclusively connote 'Frenchness' anyway, since she used to hear it played by Gypsies in her home town of Avignon. When pressed about the question of a potential exclusion, Rachida replied that it was an 'absurd' notion, which could never be implied from Têtes Raides's well-known commitment to the disenfranchised (illegal immigrants, the homeless, etc). Although she did not describe herself as a fan, and admitted that buying a *néo-réaliste* album would never be her priority, she did not feel excluded, as a second-generation French-Maghrebi, from the pleasure of its retro identity.

Rachida's remarks follow Drake's point, cited above, about the vicarious pleasure one can derive from representations of experience, and her appreciation of Têtes Raides differs little from that of the bulk of contemporary *chanson néo-réaliste* audiences, who were not living in Parisian working-class districts between the two world wars either. Nonetheless, as will be seen in Chapter 5, Rachida's socio-cultural profile is unrepresentative of that of many North African minorities in France, as she is a highly educated middle-class woman, who holds an MA and not one but two teaching qualifications, and teaches English in a French secondary school. By her own admission, most of her friends are well-off white French teachers, and her music tastes differ from those of her less highly educated siblings. Rachida conceded that cultural and musical tastes were dependent on education, but refused to draw a link between her own cultural accumulation and her fondness for retro rock artists. Given the virtual absence of French Maghrebi artists in *chanson néo-réaliste*, and of *beur* fans for that matter, it would seem, however, that she constituted an exception in the overall trend of *chanson néo-réaliste* as an elite music genre.

(Pantchenko, 2004, p. 96 and p. 101), not the kind of 'simple' lyrics one might find in a pop song, then.

This chapter has shown that *chanson néo-réaliste* artists establish an intentional connection with the past in order to express their dissatisfaction with the present, the latter being, in their often simplistic views as idealist leftists, a time when individualism, consumerism, conformity and dehumanization have triumphed. By contrast, the realist song of the inter-war period equips them with tools of contestation, being (or being reconstructed as) a genre that embodies notions of marginality, hardship, but also of conviviality and inter-social compassion. In this polarized view, the apparent lack of modernity of *chanson néo-réaliste* is constituent of its protest identity today, and, more crucially, its engagement with representations of social inequalities and instances of human destabilization aims to challenge the (supposed) comfort and sentimentality prevalent in 'pure' entertainment. Meanwhile, the 'protest nostalgia' at work here is contradictory insofar as it appropriates a 'popular' culture in a highly sophisticated manner, excluding from its 'pleasure of recognition' large segments of the French population. Finally, the insistent homage of *chanson néo-réaliste* to a song genre situated in the inter-war period problematizes the relationship of its artists to multi-ethnicity in post-colonial France. The following chapter investigates this issue further.

Chapter 3
Hybridity, Arabness and Cultural Legitimacy in *Rock Métis*

Rock métis is another offshoot of *rock alternatif* that grew in parallel with *chanson néo-réaliste* during the 1990s. It has, like *chanson néo-réaliste*, been characterized by its commitment to left-wing causes and rejection of mainstream music codes, but it differs in the music style chosen to convey this. *Rock métis* (the phrase was coined in 1987 by the journalist Paul Moreira) is a genre fusing rock music with instruments, rhythms and languages drawn from non-Western, non-white genres, and often performed by French artists of migrant origin, whose parents usually, but not exclusively, hailed from France's ex-colonies. This genre is versed in musical and linguistic hybridity, a technique which the French term *métissage*, and this chapter examines the ways in which *métissage* has been used as a vehicle of protest by *rock métis* artists, at once against the dominant format of pop, and more specifically against the dominant discourse that insists on a neutral, non-ethnically marked definition of national identity.

This chapter examines the protest value of *rock métis* with specific reference to French North African, 'Arab' performers, often referred to, in many ways problematically, as *beurs*.[1] We shall see that, on the one hand, these *rock métis* artists have managed to move away from the connotations of exoticism that previously characterized an 'Arab' presence in French popular music, using the genre to mix together Western and Maghrebi influences in a critically acclaimed and innovative whole, which also appears to contest, more or less radically, the universalist understanding of French republicanism. On the other hand, *rock métis* has, spurred by the growth of so-called world music, become an increasingly popular genre over the last two decades, and its success has problematized its

---

1   I am using the word 'Arab' here, as Ursula Mathis-Moser (2003, p. 131) does, with caution, because of its multiple meanings. In the French context, 'Arab' is a catch-all term used to refer almost exclusively to Maghrebis and French Maghrebis of non-Jewish extraction. The term is thus at once specific and indiscriminate, bypassing the ethnic diversity of the North African population (Berber, Kabyl, Arab, but also Muslim, Jew, Christian, and so on). Because it reveals the prejudice of the dominant white French population, and is the usage prevalent in the French language, 'Arab' will be used here, with inverted commas. The notion of Arabness will also be used in the sense of those cultural elements that connote, both for Maghrebis and non-Maghrebi French, an origin in North Africa. The term *beur*, explained below, refers to the descendants of the (ex-)colonial migrants from North Africa, usually born in France (French Maghrebis). See Tarr (2005).

claims of radicality. Significantly, this success also paralleled the expansion of *métissage* as a catchphrase in left-wing discourse, the term referring to cultural and ethnic mixing in what the French believe to be a politically correct way, without having to mention the word 'ethnicity'.

In order to examine these tensions, and their role in shaping a *métis* form of protest in French popular music, this chapter provides a summary of the conceptual debates surrounding notions of identity in post-colonial France, introduces the development of *rock métis* in general terms, and charts the dominant representations of Arabness prevalent in French popular music up to the 1980s. The innovative yet fragile power of *rock métis* is then treated in greater detail with reference to Zebda (1988–2003), a group led by *beur* artists. While the main tendency in French popular music studies is to insist on rap music and its role in providing a meaningful platform for the cultural expression of French Maghrebis, this case-study challenges this consensus by locating Zebda firmly within France's rock and post-*rock alternatif* culture. However, as will be shown, gaining access to the more privileged rock milieu, with its politically active and anti-mainstream ethos, has thrown up its own problems for ethnic-minority youth.

Republicanism, *Métissage* and *Rock Métis*

In 1987, Paul Moreira published *Rock métis en France*, a book surveying the birth of a new music genre characterized by French rock groups singing primarily in French, but mixing Anglo-American rock music with North African, Latin and Afro-Caribbean influences. This was innovative in the French soundscape of the 1980s but, equally importantly, all the artists in this genre came from an immigrant and often post-colonial background. While it may sound reductive to locate an artist's process of artistic creation in their parental background, the fact remains that this new generation of artists was intentionally borrowing the rhythms, melodies, instruments and languages prevalent in the cultures of their migrant parents. In so doing, they explored the ambiguity of their own hybrid identities, being at once French nationals and visible 'others', projecting onto their music their special 'doubleness' (Gilroy, 1993, p. 30). Harlem Désir, the then-president of the anti-racist organization SOS Racisme, prefaced Moreira's book, and identified *rock métis* as 'an unheard-of hybrid that is radically original' (in Moreira, 1987, p. 9).[2] The radical power of the genre, it seemed to him, came from the artists' ability to reflect the contemporary multi-ethnicity of French society, and through this to challenge the official ideology of republicanism.

It is worth summarizing some of the tenets of republicanism, the prevailing political and structural system that channels and, in many ways, controls, national cohesion in France. French republicanism is based on the fundamental idea that the nation is 'one and indivisible', and that all individuals must be integrated within it,

---

2   'Un alliage inédit radicalement original' (Harlem Désir in Moreira, 1987, p. 9).

regardless of personal differences (sex, religion, language, skin colour, etc.). This principle seeks to guarantee democratic equality by distinguishing, artificially as it turns out, between the so-called 'private' and 'public' spheres. Only in the private sphere can social, sexual, racial or cultural characteristics be referred to, as the state considers that the public claiming of such individual differences can only lead to an atomization of identities (Silverman, 1995; Hargreaves, 1997). Dreading the fragmentation of national unity, into what the French call *le communautarisme*, the state considers that being 'French' is the sole admissible formulation of identity within the public sphere, where particularisms do not feature, individuals are purely citizens, and the democratic objective of equality is achieved. Although this understanding of what constitutes French national identity is relatively recent (it was only in 1905 that the separation between Church and State was officialized, and republicanism suffered a serious set-back during the Vichy regime), it is now indisputably dominant (Cole, 1998, p. 225). Of course, the relationship between republicanism and the expression of ethnicity is highly problematic, given the former's normative and rather inflexible insistence that national identity can only be an abstract, neutral and exclusively legal definition. Indeed, republicanism dismisses the ways in which one's sense of sexual, geographical, linguistic or ethnic belonging affects allegiance to the nation, and social behaviours more generally. Thus, especially since decolonization and the gradual realization that 'the end of colonialism presents the colonizer as much as the colonized with a problem of identity' (Dirlik, 1994, p. 337), debates have arisen in France around the relevance or otherwise of republicanism as a model of unity for a post-colonial society.

Métissage has been one of the most useful linguistic and conceptual tools for mediating this questioning of universalism. The noun 'métis' in French refers to the child of a mixed-race relationship. As an adjective, applied to music as in *rock métis*, it identifies the fusion of elements previously thought of as disparate. *Métissage* is the process through which this fusion takes place: it is a multicultural encounter, a cross-fertilization. From the first coining of the term in the 1830s in scientific circles, where biologists argued about the supposed 'degeneration' arising from racial mixing, to the present, when it mainly applies to the cultural domain and generally carries positive overtones, the meaning of *métissage* has evolved dramatically (Yee, 2003). Since the 1970s and 1980s, and partly thanks to the rise of the Parti Socialiste as an anti-conservative force in government, *métissage* has emerged as a notion challenging the shortcomings of republican universalism precisely because it signalled hybridity (Hargreaves, 1997, p. 192). Sometimes formulated as the 'right to difference', and basically functioning as a French form of multiculturalism, *métissage* recognizes the possibility of plural identities, and welcomes the visibility of particularisms as well as the merging of private 'differences' with the public sphere.

In *rock métis*, the enthusiasm for hybridity was immediately obvious in the artists' chosen pseudonyms, which all emphasized particularisms that connected their identities with (post-colonial) migration and non-Western 'otherness'. In the mid-1980s, when Moreira was researching *rock métis* acts, he identified two types of band, 'Arab' and 'Latin' respectively, and these two, often overlapping, articulations of 'otherness' would also dominate French popular music in the 1990s. In the 'Latin' camp were the Hispanic-sounding Mano Negra, Massilia Sound System, Lo'Jo, La Ruda Salska, Sinsémilia, Général Alcazar and Sergent Garcia among others. In the 'Arab' camp, the bands Zebda, Gnawa or Zen Zila all favoured the use of Arabic-inspired names. Gnawa payed homage to the ritual music of nomadic Maghrebi tribes, Zen Zila translated as 'earthquake', and Zebda meant 'butter', a pun on the French word *beur* explained below. These foreign or pluri-lingual *noms de scène* echoed the artists' desire to reach beyond the confines of the French language, and by extension those of French national identity. This process of self-othering, however, is far from rare in French popular music, the vogue of Anglo-American pseudonyms having been a regular feature of the twentieth century, from Max Dearly and his impersonations of English gentlemen in the 1900s, to Mistinguett' ('la Miss') in the 1920s, and, most notoriously perhaps since the 1960s, Johnny Hallyday, the alias of Jean-Philippe Smet. With *rock métis*, however, there were identifiable borrowings from Hispanic and North African cultural systems, which is to say from implicitly 'Third World' and ex-colonial locations. The sheer number of French bands ready to claim these influences, and to take them out of their previously 'exotic' confines, signalled a shift in mentalities. In relation to Arabness, these artists marked an evolution in French culture, from the silence or reticence vis-à-vis the North African 'other' throughout the twentieth century, to its integration and celebration in the 1980s and 1990s.

The enthusiasm of *rock métis* artists for hybridity was also evident in their music, and in the terms used to describe it. Overall, artists used electric guitars, bass and drums as in any rock music package, but fused that well-known punk-rock sound with influences from the Maghreb (châabi, gnawa, raï...), Latin America (salsa, cha-cha, tango, mambo, bossa...) and the Caribbean (ska, reggae and raggamuffin). Moreira's term of *rock métis* was a convenient umbrella for identifying like-minded artists, yet the phrase never really caught on in French discourse. Instead, journalists, producers and artists preferred to use lengthy, convoluted compounds, which precisely detailed the innovative qualities of the fusion realized by each band, and implied, by the impossibility or refusal to name the music in a simple, definite way, the ideological tensions at stake in its creation. For instance, one of the precursors of this style, Négresses Vertes, were described as playing 'popular waltzing tunes, java and world-music' (H.M., 1992b, p. 79). Mano Negra mixed 'rap, reggae, 1960s rock, Hispanic musics, Hendrix-like feedback, ska and Middle-Eastern song' (Saka and Plougastel, 1999, p. 315). Other groups were presented as playing 'French-rock-oriental-groove compositions' (Zen Zila), and as having 'an original sound, mixing ragga, rock, and Arab singing' (Gnawa).[3] Zebda was a 'grooving machine swinging between oriental tones, Occitan reggae and post-Négresses Vertes accordion' (Renault, 1999, p. 31). The band Lo'Jo

---

3   *Libération*, 19 February 2000, p. 41; *Dauphiné Libéré*, January 1999.

was introduced as 'chanson, ballade, châabi, accordian lunacy and dub fusionists from France'.[4] Occasionally, neologisms were forged to qualify these new results. Manu Chao, the lead singer of Mano Negra, invented the term 'patchanka' to describe his band's music, a mix of 'electric musette, Apache [Parisian] lyrics and a chorizo spirit' (in Barbot and Sorg, 2001, p. 72). The band Sergent Garcia, led by an ex-member of the *rock alternatif* group Ludwig Von 88, proclaimed itself as a 'salsamuffin' group, mixing salsa with raggamuffin.

Rock Métis and Protest Identities

Not only was *rock métis* a new music genre in the late 1980s and 1990s, but by also showcasing ethnic difference and cultural diversity in post-colonial France, it posed a stylistic and political challenge to the status quo. Firstly, in a manner akin to the development of world music (itself a contested term) in the 1980s, *rock métis* evolved around 'the tactic of deliberately and provocatively disrupting the commercial compartmentalizing that ... has seen world music confined to a musical and ethnic ghetto' (Warne, 1997, p. 147). As a product that was not inscribed in any single musical or linguistic tradition, it asserted its non-mainstream identity. Mano Negra was admired for its intentional 'scrambling' of genres ['brouiller les pistes'] (H.M., 1991b, p. 42). In their song 'Toulouse' (1995), Zebda claimed that living from their fusion of 'raï, rock and musette' allowed them to stand, proudly, on the periphery of mainstream TV success (this was before their hugely successful hit of 1999).[5] A journalist agreed that Zebda's force resided in their ability to bridge the previously separated genres of rock, rap and *chanson* (H.M., 1992d, p. 33). The band P18, featuring an ex-member of Mano Negra, was introduced as a lively answer to the 'deadly nothingness of mainstream radio pap'.[6] In a special issue of *Les Inrockuptibles* on French music (July 1999), almost every article referred to a need to go beyond the apparent simplifications of single definitions. Critics in general were concerned with disrupting the conventional and all-too-frequent compartmentalization of genres (Norot, 1999, p. 42).[7] It is clear, then, that musical hybridity was highly regarded by the profession as a welcome challenge to traditional conventions, in contrast to the supposed standardization of *variété*. Of course, these declarations were rather out of touch with the more complex workings of the music industry, since the majors have always thrived on originality to a certain extent, and even 'mainstream' acts regularly incorporate 'foreign' influences (Negus, 1999, pp. 152–72). Nonetheless, they helped those

---

4   Flyer announcing Lo'Jo's concert at Queen Elizabeth Hall, London, 14 November 2001.

5   '... à la périphérie des succès cathodiques'.

6   '... la dissolution mortifère dans la grande marmite FM', Von Badaboum (1999).

7   '... tordre le cou à ces a-priori qui cloisonnent encore trop souvent les genres'.

who made them to assert their own alternative identity, and authenticate their personal rebellion against perceived conventions.

Secondly, *rock métis* achieved a seemingly radical and long-awaited repositioning of national identity by taking French music outside its usual confines of a white, Western European ethnicity. For the journalist of *Rock & Folk* (H.M., 1992a and 1992b), Négresses Vertes represented a 'colourful touch of vibrant colour in the French musical landscape', and Mano Negra brought a welcome degree of originality and cosmopolitan warmth to the French scene. His positive descriptions implied that, roughly until the mid-1980s, French popular music had seemed disappointingly bland and cold, unable to engage dynamically with 'others', a view that was widespread among French critics at the time (Yonnet, 1985, p. 193; Looseley, 2003b, p. 38). Following the colour analogy, Paul Garapon (1999, p. 112) considered that the many *rock métis* bands of the 1990s reconfigured what it meant to compose and play French music: 'Now parts of our common language, African music, raï and rap contribute, alongside all the other colours of the world's musical palette now possessed by the artist, to shaping the new face of French popular music'.[8] In their song 'Le mélange sans appel' (1999), Zen Zila eulogized cultural inter-mixing ('I always recommend a cultural melting-pot'), while using diglossia in French and Arabic to home in on the idea that 'mixing' ['le mélange'] was a good way forward.

These positive appreciations of *métissage*, coming from artists and journalists alike, fitted into the broader context of a celebration of mixity in popular culture. In film, literature and political discourse, *métissage* was, throughout the 1980s and 1990s, hailed as a new definition of national cohesion, especially on the left, and potentially as the panacea to racism and segregation. From the Ministry of Culture under the Socialists, which was particularly ready to sponsor works of art that seemed to present a form of unexpected hybridity, to the conservative President of the Republic Jacques Chirac who, in 1998, praised the victory of a multiracial 'black, blanc, beur' football team at the World Cup, a consensus emerged that enthusiastically anticipated the collapse of traditional republicanism, or at least welcomed its 'mellowing' (Pinto, 1988). Indeed, these enthusiastic comments about *rock métis* were due to the critics' perception that *métissage* was new to France, constituted a radical change from past attitudes and could only lead towards greater tolerance. They also implied that France had well and truly shed its unease vis-à-vis ethnic difference and its paternalist aura as a colonial power. Ironically, by taking France outside of its traditional self, *métissage* gave reasons to be proud of being French.

Another aspect of the high value attributed to *métissage* in relation to national identity was the way in which it was systematically seen as a means of opposition to the rise of the Front National (FN), which was achieving its strongest electoral

---

8   'Devenues parties du langage commun, musique africaine, raï, rap contribuent, avec toutes les autres couleurs de la palette musicale planétaire dont dispose désormais le chanteur, à façonner le nouveau visage de la chanson française' (Garapon, 1999, p. 112).

results at this time. Openly racist, the FN was the first party in the 1980s to engage in debates about a redefinition of republicanism and national identity, albeit recommending greater separatism between 'native' French and foreigners, rather than less partitioning between private and public spheres. The fact that the FN vocally appropriated the concept of 'national identity', giving it connotations of racial exclusion, apparently made it difficult for mainstream parties to tackle the same topic (McMurray, 1997, p. 35). For Peter Fysh (1998, p. 21), this hesitation on the part of the left to confront the FN on this issue was 'rather specious', but the fact remains that anti-racist movements in late twentieth-century France, in and outside established parties, stopped short of questioning republicanism's assimilationist core, reverting instead to the catch-all term of *métissage* to praise the multi-cultural reality of society.

As a notion describing and accepting the inter-mingling of different elements, *métissage* thus stood out as a cultural, rather than political, possibility, and the term in fact became something of a buzzword, hiding the profound social dissatisfactions affecting ethnic minorities in France. As right-wing and centre-right parties moved towards an increasingly exclusionary understanding of national identity during this period (see below), so praising cultural *métissage* could imply the questioning of the status quo – if not its total rejection. The release of Négresses Vertes's first album (*Mlah*, 1987), for instance, was greeted as a powerful message of resistance to Le Pen: 'the real java, the popular java of the streets, threatens Le Pen more than any political discourse' (Vandel and Rambali, 1988, p. 105).[9] This being said, targeting the FN in songs was never the preserve of left-wing 'protest' artists. Many mainstream singers with prime-time exposure have also attacked racism, even if this was done in less hybrid music genres or with less vindictive lyrics (Vignol, 2007). For this reason, the notion of *métissage* is by no means a guarantee of radical protest, and equating it with a dramatic reconfiguration of inter-ethnic relationships in French society is idealist and naïve. In fact, *métissage* is a highly problematic notion that demands further qualification.

The Limits of *Métissage*

A contradiction sits at the heart of its formulation, since *métissage* seeks to reach beyond the 'archaism' of national confines, while at the same time hoping to establish new roots in a specific geographical and cultural space (Wolton, 2003, p. 31). This was the dilemma facing *rock métis*, a genre apparently taking France and French music beyond traditional confines, while relocating a sense of pride within national boundaries. When Garapon enthused, in his celebration of *rock métis* quoted above, about the 'new face' of French music, he certainly referred to a new, multicultural identity, yet this identity was also single, specific and

---

9   '… la vraie java, la java populo et gouailleuse, menace plus Le Pen que tous les discours politiques'.

ultimately French rather than trans- or non-national. Touring with Négresses Vertes in Switzerland, the journalist H.M. (1992b, p. 57) remarked that, for the Swiss, Italians and Germans who composed their foreign audience, the band epitomized France, and the French capacity to achieve a musical melting-pot.[10] Carte de Séjour, similarly, found that when touring abroad, foreigners would think of them as French ('we were French rockers, at least we were introduced as such. We might be denied this here, but outside it's quite clear', in Moreira, 1987, p. 32).[11] Stéphane Jarno (1999), a *Télérama* rock critic, considered that the 'salsamuffin' of Sergent Garcia demonstrated the innovative approach and remarkable skills of French artists, who could compose a believable salsa and make a foreign genre 'truly' theirs ('the French rockers have a secret recipe').[12] Jarno dubbed Sergent Garcia and P18 'Parisian *gringos*' ['les gringos parigots'], a playful rhyming of French slang with Hispanic connotations that went along the same lines as the description of Manu Chao, the lead singer of Mano Negra, as 'our smart little Spanish guy' ['notre titi espingouin'] (Barbot and Sorg, 2001, p. 72). Both appellations signalled the journalists' pleasure at realizing that some French artists could sing credibly in Spanish, and compose what they deemed to be good music influenced by Latin sounds. A certain sense of national pride seeped through, with the ultimate and affectionate grounding of the artists' prowess in a Parisian location (a 'titi' is a Parisian street urchin).

If the success of 'world' and *métis* forms of music in France, in the 1980s and 1990s, can be read as the enthusiastic projection of France as 'modern, dynamic and multicultural' and, importantly, as providing a welcoming ground for foreign music professionals (Looseley, 2003, p. 54), then championing *rock métis* also reproduces, in many ways, a series of traditional expectations of what constitutes national identity. These journalists still wanted to pin down the national identity of the musicians, and to fix them in a specific (French) territorial system. In another way, too, praising France's assimilation of, and tolerance towards, non-Western 'differences' is far from disruptive of republicanism, since it follows the aim of transnational fraternity that republicanism holds at its core. Having gone full circle therefore, *métissage* is as much a mode of national authentification as it is a means of national disruption (Looseley, 2003, p. 53).

Another limitation of *métissage* lies in its insistently upbeat joyfulness. Mano Negra were described as playing a 'happily *métis* alternative rock' ['un rock alternatif joyeusement métissé'] (Loupias, 2001, p. 124), Zebda embodied 'joyous contestation' ['la contestation festive'] (Leclère, 1999, p. 31), Sergent Garcia and P18 showed their 'celebratory ethos' ['un credo festif'] (Jarno, 1999),

---

10 'Les Négresses Vertes, c'est la France ... car ils renvoient une certaine image mythique de l'Hexagone ... le brassage musical' (H.M., 1992e, p. 57).

11 'Cette année on a tourné dans toute l'Europe. ... Nous étions des rockers français. En tous cas présentés comme tels. Ici on nous le nie, mais à l'extérieur c'est très clair' (Rachid Taha of Carte de Séjour).

12 '... les french [sic] rockers ont leur recette'.

with a widespread use of the French adjective 'festif/ve'. The assignation of 'fun' feelings to musical *métissage* was extremely widespread in the 1990s but, for several critics, would constitute the notion's main shortcoming. By celebrating inter-ethnic encounters through the central emotion of joy, cultural *métissage* grew at the expense of a consciousness of the real and unpleasant inequalities that develop, in France as elsewhere, along racial lines (Bhattacharyya, Gabriel and Small, 2002). Focusing on France, Hargreaves and McKinney (1997, p. 15) noticed 'the tendency to indiscriminately celebrate the post-modern play of hybrid difference', and underlined that *métissage* could never be a 'real' force of social transformation. Jennifer Yee (2003, p. 422) warned against the enthusiastic mixophilia of the 1980s and 1990s in France, precisely because of the ambiguous colonialist antecedents of the term, and its false promise of an end to race conflicts. A few music professionals also noted how *métissage* had become a new orthodoxy. For H.M. (1992d, p. 33), the first success of Zebda's music was down to the widespread fashion for an 'ethnic mix' in the early 1990s. For Fred Chichin, the late composer of the rock duo Rita Mitsouko, the 1990s were a period of dictatorial 'musical correctness', as artists, including himself, felt the pressure to compose with previously 'distant' genres. Interestingly, Chichin dismissed the material that his band released in that period, believing that he was always at his best as a composer when he followed his first passion for 'pure' rock music (in Cassavetti, 2007a, p. 14).

If *métissage* is at once a radical possibility and a type of musical correctness, an anti-racist statement and a form of neo-universalism, an expression of meaningful festivity and a naive celebration, then the ambivalence of the term becomes most salient when observed in relation to the place of Arabness within French society. 'Arab' music and the Arabic language compose one facet of *rock métis*'s hybridity. This is perhaps one of its most original and transgressive declarations of identity, yet one that also reveals most brutally the limits of *métissage* as a positive recasting of Frenchness. Basically, if *métissage* became a celebrated notion during the 1980s and 1990s, this was most certainly not the case for the presence of Arabness in France, and for *beur* identities in particular. The analysis of the rise to success of the group Zebda, as well as their rather bitter split, illustrates this point. Before this, however, it will be useful to survey the dominant representations of Arabness in French popular music in the twentieth century, as a backdrop for the innovative inclusion of 'Arab' elements in *rock métis* later on.

'Arabs' and Representations of Arabness in French Popular Music

Despite the view expressed by some that France has, in the twentieth century, enjoyed 'a century of mixed French music' (Hakem, 1999, p. 40), and that there is 'an extraordinary plenitude of all things Arab in French popular culture' (McMurray, 1997, 33), expressing Arabness in France has always been a problematic proposition. In fact, since 1830 and the first 'modern' contacts between

France and Algeria, courtesy of the French invasion, representations of 'Arabs' in French popular music have been virtually non-existent (Liauzu and Liauzu, 2002, p. 25; Mathis-Moser, 2003, p. 133). In the nineteenth century, the conquest of Algeria was mainly referred to in popular song from the perspective of conscripts and settlers, lamenting their exile or boasting of their good fortune overseas. Between 1880 and 1930, when the French colonial project was in full swing and song-making was becoming an increasingly popular form of entertainment, the colonies and the colonized were treated overall in a comical and/or exoticizing mode (Liauzu and Liauzu, 2002, p. 85). It was, however, the many Asiatic and black African characters of songs who were the butt of openly racist jokes, and not 'Arabs' (Liauzu and Liauzu, p. 97).[13]

This makes popular music rather unrepresentative of broader tendencies in French popular culture at the time, since many illustrations, postcards and, later, films, stereotyped the 'Arab' as a threatening colonial subject (Rosello, 1998b). While there is no scope to explain this difference of treatment here, the very absence of the 'Arab' from French song is noteworthy for it signifies a certain unease towards the depiction of North Africans. This unease carried on after 1962, with the independence of Algeria (the last French colony), although a few songs started to reflect the new economic relations between the ex-colonial power, France, and her ex-colonial subjects, many of whom were now migrant workers resident in mainland France. In the 1970s, some white French (metropolitan) artists, usually situated on the political far-left, composed songs sympathetic to what they saw as the plight of North African immigrants, and attacked the prevalent representations of 'Arabs' in the French media at the time.[14] Nonetheless, even when they were well intentioned and respectful of 'Arabs', these non-Arabs (the *chanson* artists Serge Reggiani, Renaud and Colette Magny for instance) would often represent Maghrebis as male immigrants, vulnerable yet aggressively proud, thereby forging a new kind of stereotype (Mathis-Moser, 2003, p. 139).

In parallel to this, throughout colonization and until the 1980s, no 'Arab' music performers in France reached any significant degree of recognition. There were, after the First World War, a handful of Maghrebi musicians in Paris, who followed the first wave of emigration and played in the cafés of immigrant districts, notably Barbès, for an 'Arab' clientele (Gastaut, 2006, p. 108). Despite evidence of some success, especially after the Second World War when the Maghrebi population increased, and the creation of a distinct 'Arab popular music' section in the catalogue of France's largest record label (Gastaut, 2006, p. 111), these artists

---

13   Liauzu and Liauzu (2002, p. 27) note three exceptions in a corpus of over 1,000 songs, all to do with the figure of Abd-el-Kader, the leader of Algerian resistance in the 1830s, and praising his military exploits.

14   Chris Tinker (2005, pp. 155–7) notes that Léo Ferré, with his support for the petitioners against France's conduct during the Algeria war, provides a rare yet distant engagement with anti-colonial criticism, in keeping with 'the long tradition of writing songs that oppose nationalism and militarism' only in general, symbolic terms.

never reached a mainstream audience. After the independence of Algeria, around 1 million French settlers, or *pieds-noirs*, were repatriated, and this set the scene for the success of non-'Arab' artists from North Africa, including many Maghrebi Jews. Most famously, the singer-songwriter Enrico Macias, born in 1938 in Constantine (Algeria), would provide early examples of a *métissage* between French lyrics and evocations of North Africa. His songs, however, mostly lamented the uprooting of Algerian colonists, and enthused about fraternity beyond racial divides (Dicale, 2006, p. 638), two themes that guaranteed his success among the large *pied-noir* community, and more generally among a French audience nostalgic for the loss of Algeria as a French possession, or indifferent to questions of the moral status of colonialism (Saka and Plougastel, 1999, p. 312). During the 1960s and 1970s, then, it was mainly Algerian Jews who carried echoes of Maghrebi music for the French audience, while many *pieds-noirs* threw themselves into the mainstream pop wave of *yéyé* music, in groups such as the highly successful Les Chaussettes Noires, whose four musicians were born in Algeria and Tunisia (Dicale, 2006, p. 193; Verlant, 2000, p. 54). Overall, the absence of any successful 'Arab' artists in France at that time signalled, quite dramatically, the lack of avenues for artists from this minority to reach a large audience.[15]

This brief overview is necessary to understand the shift that *rock métis* represented from the mid-1980s onwards, giving as it did a voice to a generation of, by then, *beur* artists, and allowing them to evoke, in more complex and personalized ways in their songs, the place of 'Arabs' and Maghrebi minorities in France. The term *beur* has often been contested, especially by those it denotes, yet its permanence in the French language and in academic studies of post-colonial France justifies its use here. The *beurs* are the descendants of 'Arab' (non-Jewish) North African immigrants who, by right of birth and/or residency on French soil, have French nationality. Given that the main wave of 'Arab' emigration occurred after the Second World War, the first generation of *beurs* reached adulthood at the turn of the 1980s, and this period marked the beginning of a conflictual relationship between French republicanism and the hybrid identity of these individuals, who were at once French nationals and 'visible' others (Cole, 1998, p. 226). The *beurs* are arguably 'the most visible, the most stigmatised and the most dynamic ethnic minority in postcolonial France' (Tarr, 2005, p. 3). Unfortunately, they became associated in the media and public consciousness with aggression, as a series of urban riots erupted in 1981 in the *banlieue* of Lyons, and in which some *beurs* took part. The image of the *beur* as unassimilable delinquent became widespread

---

15   Dalida, perhaps the most successful female performer of the 1970s in France, was born in Egypt, but only her Italian origins were emphasized in her early songs ('Ciao ciao bambina', 'Romantica', 'Bambino'). Besides, it was only in the late 1970s and early 1980s that she gradually recorded a few songs in vernacular Egyptian and Lebanese, taking diction lessons to 're-learn' a language she never fully mastered (Barnel, 2005, p. 166 and p. 194), and the success of her Arabic output was mainly limited to the Arabic-speaking world. She is not, in that sense, an example of a French 'Arab' performer.

(Rosello, 1998b, p. 2), and as the far-right seized on these events to advance its own racist agenda, even mainstream parties focused their efforts on reinforcing 'security' and facilitating exclusion.

This led, for instance, to a proposal for the limitation of access to nationality for French-born foreigners in 1986–8, and to the official recommendation after the first 'Headscarf Affair' (1989) that the secular, neutral and supposedly universal values of the Enlightenment should be upheld against the perceived threat of multiculturalism (Hargreaves, 1997, pp. 184–5). This culminated in 2004 in the highly idiosyncratic exclusion of 'ostensible religious signs' from state-run schools, a ban which sought to re-affirm the importance of republican universalism, but was particularly detrimental to, and some have argued intentionally discriminatory against, France's Muslim minority (Hargreaves, 2007, p. 111). Other instances of political unease with the presence of ethnic 'difference' in France characterized the 1990s, with the official denunciation of the dangers of *communautarisme*, and the violent expulsion of illegal immigrants (*sans-papiers*) throughout the decade (Cole, 1998; Balibar et al., 1999). In November 2005, new riots in French suburbs shook the country and triggered yet more antagonism between the expression of ethnic particularism on the one hand, and the supposed cohesion of republican universalism on the other (Mucchielli, 2006).

This dishearteningly repetitive history of social exclusion, from the early 1980s to the 2000s, forms the backdrop to the rise of *métissage* as a possibly radical, and hopefully more tolerant, way to envisage allegiance to French identity. It was also the context in which 'Arabs' in France, most of them *beurs* and French nationals by then, became successful musicians and performers for the first time. The extent to which their success led to durable changes in the perceptions and representations of 'Arabs' and French Maghrebis is debatable, however, and examining the rise and fall from grace of Zebda in the 1990s and early 2000s will help to build a picture of the ambivalence of French society towards *beurs* in that period, and of the role that *rock métis* played in channelling their attempts to establish a hybrid and 'protest' identity.

Zebda: *Métissage* and Success in the 1990s

Zebda was a *rock métis* band of the 1990s (they split in 2003), from Toulouse, which gained a high degree of commercial success and critical acclaim. Despite being composed of a majority of non-*beurs*, and in spite of the conflicts that arose within the group about whether or not to project Arabness (Marx-Scouras, 2005, p. 117), Zebda did construct their identity around a *beur* specificity. The three frontmen, Magyd Cherfi (lead singer, lyricist) and the Amokrane brothers, Hakim and Moustapha (chorists and dancers), were of Algerian origin, and it was Cherfi and Moustapha Amokrane who most frequently gave interviews. Zebda's *beur* members were therefore the band's main spokepersons, and the band's name played on the Arabic for 'butter' (زبدة), the French word for butter being *beurre*, which is an exact homophone of *beur*. This inter-linguistic pun expressed the group's concern with post-colonial identities, and many of their songs' protagonists were North African migrants and second-generation *beurs* ('Arabadub', 1992; 'Toulouse', 1995; 'Ça va pas être possible', 1998; 'J'y suis, j'y reste', 1998).

This 'Arab' element has led a number of critics to compare Zebda with an earlier *beur* band, Carte de Séjour. Carte de Séjour, a rock band formed in 1981 in Lyons by three musicians of Algerian origin, the most famous being the band's lead singer Rachid Taha, is often held as the first example of a French-Arab rock group, representative of a vibrant, empowered *beur* identity (Liperi, 1988, p. 248; Meouak and Aguadé, 1996; Breatnach and Sterenfeld, 2000, p. 253; Looseley, 2003, pp. 51–2; Howarth and Varouxakis, 2003, p. 150; Huq, 2006, p. 76). For the *Télérama* rock critic Philippe Barbot (2002, p. 30), Carte de Séjour paved the way for the possibility of Zebda's success in the 1990s, allowing *beur* artists to participate in the genre of protest rock music, and triggered a degree of enthusiasm among the public for their kind of musical hybridity. The major Universal Music, which still produces the solo music of Rachid Taha, connects the two groups on its website, with Taha's page offering a link to that of Zebda (also produced by Barclay/Universal).[16] Nonetheless, Carte de Séjour did not make a lasting impression on French culture. They rose to national fame in 1986 with a controversial cover version of Charles Trenet's 'Douce France', and split, largely unnoticed, in 1989. Carte de Séjour's expressions of Arabness were often brash and boastful, in line with Taha's own belligerent personality (Moreira, 1987, p. 34), and the brevity of their success signalled the presence of obstacles to the full acceptance of *beurs* as 'authentic' artists in the cultural sphere in the 1980s.

By contrast, Zebda presented a tentative, more despondent articulation of Arabness, befitting the introspective style of the lyricist Magyd Cherfi, and their active participation in left-wing activism earned them the praise of the elite press, as we shall see. Zebda first became famous in 1995 with 'Le bruit et l'odeur', a song targeting the racism of Jacques Chirac, and later reached media omnipresence in 1998–9 with 'Tomber la chemise', an inoffensive piece of fun which was the best-selling single of 1999. Generally speaking, the band benefited from a much longer 'shelf life' than Carte de Séjour, being together from 1988 to 2003 and releasing four studio albums, one live double album, two side projects under the names of 100% Collègues and Motivés, and taking part in various tribute albums and compilations. This larger output suggests that, in the 1990s, a *beur* group could achieve greater economic success than had been possible in the previous decade. Zebda also became culturally integrated, indeed an exponent of 'high' culture. They took part in all three of the tribute albums paying homage to the holy trinity of 'authentic' *chanson* artists, Jacques Brel (*Aux suivants*, 1999), Georges Brassens (*Les oiseaux de passage*, 2001) and Léo Ferré (*Avec Léo*, 2003). The only *beur* band alongside white artists, including the 'alternative' rock groups

---

16   www.universalmusic.fr/servlet/FrontCreatorServlet?action=biography&artiste_id=3784, last accessed 21 March 2009.

Têtes Raides and Noir Désir, Zebda proved that French Maghrebis could, at the turn of the twenty-first century, be constituent elements of France's national and musical heritage. Unlike Carte de Séjour's pastiche of Trenet, these cover versions were intentional homages to older, established singer-songwriters. Over the years, Zebda also became the object of several academic studies, articles and books published in English and French, testament to a recognition of their significant contribution to French popular music (Seery, 2001; Lin, 2001; Lebrun 2002 and 2007; Marx-Scouras, 2004 and 2005; Ervine, 2008).

Zebda's success raises the question of the place of Arabness in French popular music, since it would seem that only by appearing to follow the cultural norm (paying homage to *chanson*, participating in right-on political events), and thus assimilating into the model of left-wing 'authenticity', could French Maghrebis hope to gain artistic recognition. However, departing from the argument prevalent in most accounts of Zebda's career, namely that their success heralded the articulation of a 'vibrant and dynamic' *beur* identity (e.g. Ervine, 2008, p. 200), It is important to focus instead on the fragility of the process of cultural validation, and examine the contradictions in the group's trajectory towards success and cultural legitimacy as a *rock métis* act. Indeed, the evolution of Zebda from *beur* outcasts in Toulouse, to the status of national superstars from 1999 onwards, was as much a story of bitterness and compromise as it was a story of empowerment. As the word 'integration' suggests, becoming part of dominant society is imbued with inner conflicts as personal characteristics get lost along the way. As we shall see, Zebda shed the most obvious signs of their Arabness when they became a 'national' group, and lost some of their credentials as a protest group when they found commercial mediatization and fame.

Reluctant Arabness and bitter-sweet métissage

Magyd Cherfi, the lead singer and lyricist for the group, was born in Toulouse in 1963. Unlike Rachid Taha of Carte de Séjour, who wrote and sung mostly in Arabic, Cherfi primarily wrote his lyrics in French, although the occasional Arabic words cropped up ('Oulalaradime', 1998; 'Sheitan', 2002). From a purely linguistic perspective, then, Zebda would appear more 'integrated' than Carte de Séjour, and less ready, or less able, to contest the dominant model of linguistic integration. This conformist aspect of their identity was also evident in most of Zebda's songs, which emphasized the legal Frenchness of *beurs* in lyrics such as: 'I'm French, I've got the documents to prove it, I'm well integrated, I stand within the French norm', or 'I am secular and republican'.[17] In interviews, Cherfi often elaborated on the profound soundness of the republican principle separating the private and public spheres of identity, considering that the future of Arabness

17   '… moi je suis Français, j'ai tous mes papiers, je suis bien intégré, je suis dans la norme française' ('France 2', 1995); 'je suis laïc et républicain' ('Le Bruit et l'odeur', 1995).

was to disappear as a term of self-identification as it would as a term of othering: '*Beur* is a rather nice word ... . A transition. We were Arab, then *beurs* before becoming French. That's the positive evolution of society' (Aubel, 1999, p. 64).[18] These declarations contrasted with Taha's rejection of 'beur' as a meaningless compartmentalization (Moreira, 1987, p. 51). Moreover, when he worked as a social worker, Cherfi always tried to convince second-generation immigrants of the suitability of the French identity model: 'we kept repeating to the lads that they should integrate into a democratic framework, a French identity, their identity' (Aubel, p. 65).[19] As a teenager, Cherfi was ashamed of his working-class Algerian family and illiterate mother, and retrospectively considered that acculturation was the best thing that had happened to him, going to school, meeting French friends and having 'enlightened' role-models (Sorgue, 1998; Renault, 1999, p. 32). For Cherfi, mastering the French language brought refinement to his intellectual thought, coherence to his political beliefs, and general access to French culture (Marx-Scouras, 2005, p. 116; also Lebrun, 2007). Taha would probably identify this desire to 'fit in' as compliance, and Cherfi's declarations contrasted with the fact that he and his band derived credibility from being presented as outcasts, as social, ethnic and even regional marginals.

Similarly, in declarations the group often seemed to exemplify a certain strand of officially sanctioned republicanism. In interviews and song lyrics, Cherfi always extolled the virtues of the Enlightenment, stressing the theoretical righteousness of republicanism and the validity of its humanist foundations. In the face of reactionary tendencies and anti-Arab prejudice, for instance, he considered that '[liberty, equality, fraternity], that's the real driving anger, the real struggle, that of maturity' (Sorgue, 1998, p. 15).[20] Nonetheless, Zebda's desire for Frenchness and 'normalcy' was always contextualized in the existence of widespread prejudice against *beurs* in France, and Cherfi found that the centring of republicanism on abstract citizenship was not only one of the fairest political ideas, but also the perfect radical discourse with which to oppose the French state's day-to-day detachment from its own morally irreproachable objective.

As a result, Cherfi's affirmations of Frenchness in interviews, such as 'we are French, secular and republican' (Leclère, 1999, 32), or in songs as in 'Le bruit et l'odeur' ('I am secular and republican'), were not simple signs of compliance with the system, because the system simply did not work. Instead, they were in equal part provocations against France's hypocrisy and injustice, and appeals for the revival of France's philosophical tradition of human justice. Consequently, rather than being unequivocal expressions of empowerment and pride (Marx-Scouras, 2004;

18   'Beur, c'est un mot sympa .... Une transition. Nous étions arabes, puis beurs avant de devenir français. C'est l'aspect positif de la société'.

19   '... on se croyait à dire aux mômes d'intégrer un repère démocratique, une identité française, la leur'.

20   '[Liberté, égalité, fraternité] voilà la vraie colère, le vrai combat, celui de la maturité', Sorgue (1998).

Ervine, 2008), Zebda's declarations of identity often reached an ideological impasse, as *beurs* found themselves at a destabilizing crossroads between self-assertion, rejection and integration. In 'Je suis' (1999), one line goes 'I wasn't born the day I was born / I became myself when I realized I was different',[21] which conveys the idea that being a French 'Arab' in France is a tiresome process of self-awareness, due to the white population's tendency to other the 'visible' offspring of post-colonial migrants.[22] In 'Le bruit et l'odeur' (1995), this distress is also expressed: 'When I understood the law, I understood I was lost. "Integrate", it said, but that was already done'.[23] And again in 'Quinze ans' (1999), the following line becomes a repetitive chant: 'I am integrated, where's the solution? I am integrated, where's the solution?'[24] Such calls for help showed the gap between the theory of equality and the practice of discrimination in France, and were certainly not affirmative expressions of identity.

Although avoiding miserabilism (Seery, 2001, 22), Zebda's songs expressed Cherfi's ambivalence towards *beur* identity by portraying *beurs* as at once powerful protest figures, and victims of socio-economic constraints and racial prejudice. The song 'Toulouse' (1995) epitomizes this duality. A self-introductory song, opening the band's second album *Le bruit et l'odeur*, 'Toulouse' presents the mixed identity of the group by stressing their French origins, implanted in Toulouse, and praising the virtues of a 'vie métisse' ['hybrid life']. The lyrics talk of mixing spices, eating tagine and cassoulet, having roots at once in France, in a Mediterranean culture and further afield. Musically, it starts with a sample of a slow Arabic prayer, before kicking off with a fast raggamuffin beat, played with the usual instruments of rock music while acoustic percussions sustain the North African feel. Cherfi sings rapidly in French while the backing singers intervene one after the other on every other line, with a strong Toulouse accent. This fast delivery of words and music gives the song something of a confused air, conveying the idea that *métissage* challenges received wisdoms about the stability and tranquillity of national identity, and introduces Zebda as a lively band, hard to pin down.

This message is reinforced by the intentional contrast of this 'Toulouse' with the version, more famous in France, by Claude Nougaro (1929–2004), a singer-songwriter born in Toulouse who released, in 1966, a song of the same title. Nougaro carved out a career as an exponent of musical *métissage*, his inspirations coming from Afro-American and Brazilian music. He was famous for French cover versions of blues and samba numbers, including 'Armstrong' (1965) after a traditional gospel, and 'Bidonville' (1965), a cover of Baden Powell's 'Berimbau' (1963).

---

21   'Je suis pas né le jour de ma naissance / je suis né lorsque j'ai compris ma différence'.

22   On the 'oriental other' as non-assimilable, and Islam as the ongoing threat to Christian Europe, see Hargreaves and McKinney (1997, p. 17).

23   'Quand j'ai compris la loi j'ai compris ma défaite: "intégrez-vous" disait-elle, mais c'était chose faite'.

24   '… intégré je le suis où est la solution, intégré je le suis où est la solution...?'

Nougaro always encouraged the experience of 'difference', and the lyrics of his 'Toulouse' referred to the town's Spanish diaspora with delight. Nonetheless, Nougaro's 'Toulouse' was a slow-paced, oratorio-like song, accompanied by a symphonic orchestra and sprinkled with the jazz accents of a piano and horn section. The dominant tone was nostalgic, the narrator proclaiming his love for his hometown and retracing his happy childhood in a warm community. Not unlike Carte de Séjour's cover version of 'Douce France', therefore, Zebda's 'Toulouse' contrasted with this initial and well-known song. The first stanza nodded to Nougaro ('mon cher Claude'), but the whole song turned against his pleasant account of the city by depicting it as socially and geographically segregated, with the tramps clustering around the train station, North Africans bustling about in the poorer districts, and middle-class engineers relaxing in the city-centre cafés. In Zebda's representation of Toulouse, ethnic pluralism did not lead to joyfulness, and musical *métissage* accompanied a rather perplexed understanding of identity. Equally, the singers' quick-fire vocal delivery, and the splintering of identities via the three voices, brought dynamism as much as confusion. With their 'Toulouse', Zebda introduced themselves as disruptive towards national heritage (the supposed unity of Toulouse, the cultural prestige of Nougaro), but also problematized the situation of *beurs* and post-colonial migrants in France by refusing to use *métissage* as a straightforward expression of happiness.

In all their albums, Zebda have developed a rather embittered criticism of the habitually 'fun' connotations of *métissage*. In 'Le bruit et l'odeur' ['The Noise and the Smell'] (1995), Cherfi reformulated a line from Nougaro's song 'Armstrong', in which he wished to be black and sing like Louis Armstrong. Speaking this time from the standpoint of post-colonial migrants who had experienced racial prejudice, Zebda attacked the absurdity of this wish: 'to those who regret not being black, there's only one answer, guys, and that's you're bloody lucky'.[25] This statement was highlighted by a break in the music, and turned Nougaro's rather racialist argument around, suggesting that belonging to an ethnic minority was rarely an opportunity to be proud, at least as long as anti-Arab and anti-Black racism existed. This criticism of Western fondness for non-Western difference echoed theoretical debates on post-colonialism (Gilroy, 1993) and cosmopolitanism (Wolton, 2002), and revealed Zebda's complex, slightly defeatist account of hybridity in France, at the same time as their music resulted in inter-ethnic cross-encounters.

The imbrication of *métissage* within a deeper questioning of the global conditions of mass-migration has extended to Zebda's visual presentation. The cover of their last album, *Utopie d'occase* [Second-Hand Utopia] (2002), is a mise-en-scène of the group's concerns with worldwide economic disparities. In the outdoor setting of an African village, a young black child is photographed wearing the black cape, mask and hat of Zorro, the legendary Mexican righter of wrongs. The juxtaposition of Africa with Mexico sets the tone for a denunciation

---

25   '... si certains regrettent de ne pas être noir de peau / je n'ai qu'une réponse, les gars, vous avez du pot!'

of poverty in African and Latin American countries, an idea reinforced by the small print across the picture which describes the functioning of Human Development Indicators (HDIs). HDIs are a calculation system accepted by the UN to measure a country's level of development, using criteria of life expectancy, literacy and standard of living. As Zebda's record sleeve implies, at the time of this release in 2002, the bottom ten countries in this classification were all in Africa, while none of the Central or Latin American countries featured in the 30 wealthiest countries.[26] This awareness of global inequalities underlines Zebda's participation in the anti-globalization movement (the relationship of this international coalition with French popular music is analyzed in the next chapter, through the involvement of fellow *rock métis* performer Manu Chao). It also, via the presence of the large letter 'Z' on the child's cape (Z for Zorro and Zebda), asserts the group's protest identity, as they themselves adopt the role of dispensers of justice. The band's recourse to children's stories and to utopianism could elicit accusations of naivety, and in interviews Cherfi has often appeared something of a dreamer, considering music as the means to realize a 'society [that would be] just, fraternal' (in Barbot, 2002, p. 30). The band's projection of themselves as Zorro figures also contrasts with Taha's refusal to act as spokesperson for general unfairness (Moreira, 1987, p. 39). Nonetheless, Zebda have grounded their political discourse in a concrete, evidence-based knowledge of world migration, and showed their ability to discern between the illusions of *métissage* and the socio-economic reality of displacement.

Political and national integration

The level of intellectual sophistication shown by Zebda is one reason behind the band's important place in France's national culture, but another is their systematic and intentional political commitment, usually taken to be an outward sign of 'authenticity' in France. Carte de Séjour only had irregular and somewhat chaotic relationships with various anti-racist organizations in the 1980s, and Rachid Taha sharply rejected what he considered to be the moroseness and strictness of left-wing militants (Moreira, 1987, p. 51; Pascaud, 2007, p. 16). By contrast, Zebda have frequently and systematically supported left-wing organizations, parties and causes, ultimately appearing as some of the most 'committed' artists of the period. For example, Zebda created Tactikollectif, an anti-fascist organization aiming to help disaffected Maghrebi youths (Reijasse, 2002, p. 83). In 1997, they released an album of 'protest songs' with the sponsor of the radical far-left party, the Ligue Communiste Révolutionnaire, which covered well-known French and foreign revolutionary hymns, including 'La Cucaracha', 'Bella Ciao' and the Resistance song 'Le Chant des Partisans'.[27] In 2001, during the Toulouse municipal elections, some

---

26 'Human Development Reports', http://hdr.undp/org/en/statistics, last accessed 24 March 2009.

27 In this album, Zebda covered 'Hasta siempre', Carlos Puebla's 1965 homage to Che Guevara. At exactly the same time (Winter 1997–8), the French actress Nathalie

members of the band launched a 'citizen-centred' electoral roll, the Motivé-e-s, which won 12 per cent of votes in the first round. Zebda have also played in support of José Bové, the leader of the Confédération Paysanne, are vocal opponents of globalization, and have participated in various charity concerts, supporting factory strikers in Toulouse, illegal immigrants (*sans-papiers*), and taking part in actions against the repatriation of foreign convicts (*double peine*). Engaged in local and global politics, then, and always taking the side of the 'oppressed', Zebda have, more systematically than Carte de Séjour, demonstrated their rigorous 'protest' identity and strong left-wing allegiance.

As a result, Zebda have been recognized as a 'French' group by critics. They were held to be 'real representatives of French rock' ['une réalité du rock français'] (H.M., 1992d, p. 32), and considered to have composed, with 'Tomber la chemise', 'a song to which the whole French population danced during the summer of 1999' (Marx-Scouras, 2005, p. 96).[28] They have been compared to a winning goal by Zidane, the Tour de France and 14 July, all symbols of national pride, for their capacity to unite the French population (Monnin, 2000). In the press, the dominant approach in assessing Zebda's place in French popular music has been to acknowledge their role as an authentic rebel group, with such qualifiers as 'honest', 'useful', 'brave', 'radical', 'refined' and 'impeccable'.[29] This all-round positive appreciation suggests that Zebda have acquired the cultural credibility

---

Cardone also released a version of this song (arr. by Laurent Boutonnat, collaborator of Mylène Farmer), which she interpreted in a less politicized manner. The video of the song showed Nathalie wandering in a sun-drenched landscape, in a floaty and slightly ripped dress, sweat pearling down her cleavage and her long black hair sexily tousled. In the chorus, she danced in the mud, under heavy rain, her dress totally torn, while photos of Che were interspersed. This rather raunchy pop video was broadcast on prime-time TV, where Cardone also made several appearances, and her single sold 500,000 copies (http://nathaliecardone.malibuprod.com, last accessed 24 March 2009), therefore faring much better than Zebda's album (150,000 according to Reijasse, 2002, 61). There was no video for the Motivés, no prime-time TV exposure, and their 'non-mainstream' identity, which had 'nothing to do with M6's prime-time TV Che' ['rien à voir avec le Che sauce M6'] (Aubel, 1999, p. 65) was asserted at the time in contrast to this other product.

28   '… cette chanson sur laquelle toute la France a dansé pendant l'été 1999'.

29   See the highly positive reviews by Mortaigne (1998), Renault (1999), Leclère (1999), Monnin (2000), Verlant (2000, 161), Barbot (2002) and Santolaria (2002). By contrast, one disparaging review is worth mentioning, even if it comes from the unreliable source of www.amazon.com, and takes the form of a message posted by a certain Austin C. Beeman from Ohio, USA (6 June 2001). Beeman considers that *Essence Ordinaire* was only worth buying for 'Tomber la chemise', the best-selling single: 'The rest of the album is awful Arab rap with depressing lyrics and unimaginative rhythms. Zebda is completely a one-hit wonder.' His remark interestingly goes against the grain of French reviews, which considered that this song remained an embarrassing, out-of-character foray into purely 'fun' and mainstream pop.

that Carte de Séjour never possessed and, by extension, become a 'legitimate' national product worthy of, and validated by, the intellectual (left-wing) elite.

Indeed, Zebda's ambivalent positioning vis-à-vis republicanism associated them with 'authentic' left-wing protest artists. The band's utopianism, its attachment to universalism, its political commitment and calls for electoral participation, were all features of a typical protest discourse *à la française*, strictly in line with the evolution of the left. Zebda clearly asserted their broad left-wing support: 'from the Socialists to the far-left, there is a lot of scope for us to get involved'.[30] Asked to elaborate on the meanings of his participation in the Toulouse electoral list, Cherfi explained that his aspiration was to 'revive politics, seriousness and commitment', while the main route to achieving this was to 'stir things up'.[31] His insistence on maturity and seriousness reflected the French tendency to consider intellectual reflection as the best way to achieve political destabilization. The leap from seriousness to unruliness is characteristic of the modalities of existence of the French Republic, which originated in revolutionary upheavals, yet owes its resilience to order and control. In France, the Revolution, and by extension any idea of transformation and contestation, has remained 'a constant inspiration and call to action wherever injustice and exploitation were present' (Gildea, 1994, p. 16). Seeking to disrupt the Republic, in order to attain yet more justice, is exactly what republicanism seeks. If, in France, to transgress is somehow to fit in, then Zebda proved that they were French to the core, as they combined dissidence, in their criticism of injustice, with assent, in their validation of the Republic's foundations.

Cultural Integration and Exclusion

Finally, if Zebda's commercial success and enthusiasm for republicanism made them French, their intellectual and cultural sophistication also associated them with the French cultural elite. Cherfi never hid his aspiration to belong to the more articulate and educated segment of the French population, and often sought to use his politicized songs as a means to attain recognition in this area (Marx-Scouras, 2005, p. 74; Lebrun, 2007, p. 334). His lyrics, for instance, showed off his 'high' cultural capital by their frequent references to France's most revered novelists (Voltaire, Hugo, Saint-Exupéry), even paying homage to that most emblematic of French books, the *Robert* dictionary (Seery, 2001, p. 22). Unlike Rachid Taha, who parodied *chanson* artists, Zebda willingly paid homage to 'quality' singer-songwriters, including Georges Brassens and Nougaro. Although Cherfi disagreed with Nougaro on certain points (see above), he referred to him as the artist he

---

30   '... des socialistes à l'extrême-gauche, il y a un vaste terrain sur lequel on peut s'impliquer' (in Cyran, 2000, p. 11).

31   '... renouer avec la politique, le sérieux et l'engagement' and 'foutre le bordel', interviewed by Daniel Mermet for 'Là-bas si j'y suis', *France Inter*, 5 December 2000.

would most like to emulate, as the epitome of musical and poetic refinement (Aubel, 1999, p. 64). Nougaro himself sought to use poetry to 'open up people's intelligence', and his song lyrics were published in the same 'Today's Poets' collection as Brassens, by the editor Seghers in 1974.[32] This, as Looseley (2003, p. 38) demonstrated, was one of the most evident signs of the inclusion of French music artists within an 'authentic' and prestigious national cannon. Zebda pursued this traditional form of legitimation, and certainly since releasing solo albums and publishing collections of short stories, Cherfi has become considered as a serious, successful poet (Jordana, 2004; Dahan, 2004).

The access of Zebda to an established form of popular culture was also evident in their choice of playing, and affirmation that they played, rock music ('we're evolving within a rock culture, ... I am not a rapper', Cherfi in H.M., 1992d, 33).[33] As we will demonstrate later (Chapter 5), a taste for rock music is, in France, typically the prerogative of a well-educated middle class, and *beurs* playing rock music are something of an anomaly. Because *beurs* tend to come from the least educated, least privileged sections of society, only a few of them actually developed a taste for or the inclination towards playing this music – and when they did, this was usually through friendships with non-*beurs*, as was the case for Cherfi. In the 1980s, it was common for *beurs* to be refused entry to white nightclubs, where pop and rock music were predominantly played, so they would attend 'alternative' clubs run by blacks and Antillais, where funk music, disco and later rap music, were played (Moreira, 1987, p. 40). As a result, many ethnic minority French ended up playing in rap groups, while only a few *beurs* 'integrated' into France's rock music culture. Taha and Cherfi both epitomized the exception to this tendency, their participation in a rock rather than raï or rap music culture signalling their access to the cultural tastes of the ethnic majority.

There is obviously no harm in this as such, and this trajectory is in fact typical of the most 'successful' cases of post-colonial integration in contemporary France. However, the problem here is that, in joining the club of French rockers, the group became caught up in the 'messiness' of maintaining a sense of authenticity, which was doubly complicated by their desire to also maintain a sense of ethnic difference. This ambiguity was harshly felt with the success of the single 'Tomber la chemise' ('Take your shirt off') in 1999. This song, by far Zebda's least political track, and originally appearing on a generally gloomy album (Marx-Scouras, 2005, p. 95), was a rock-steady number about dancing and having simple, physical fun. It was released as a single just before the summer, with the agreement of the artists, and its repetitive music and simple lyrics were excellently timed for a summer hit. To promote it, Zebda appeared on many prime-time TV shows, the song was broadcast on commercial radio, and it very quickly became number one,

---

32   Froissart and de Gaudemar (2004).

33   'On évolue dans le circuit rock, ... je ne suis pas un rapper'.

selling over 1.5 million copies (Santolaria, 2002, p. 9) and receiving the NRJ Music Award for Best Francophone Single in 2000.[34]

Rock music, as we have seen, thrives on its opposition to mainstream mediatization and 'pure' entertainment (Chapter 1), and Zebda's conflictual relationship with this code was demonstrated in their handling of the success of 'Tomber la chemise'. By contrast to the 'popular' authenticity sought by *néo-réaliste* artists, the kind of popularity Zebda achieved from 1999 onwards was not associated with working-class fraternity, cultural 'authenticity' or protest politics. Rather, since it resulted from an entertaining, non-political song, in which the group's habitual questioning of the place of ethnicity in France was markedly absent, and was broadcast relentlessly on all commercial media, the group lost their credibility for their existing 'serious' fans. Zebda's success suddenly affiliated them with 'mere' entertainers of *variété*, with conservative pop music. For the left-wing press that had, up until then, enthused about the political credentials of Zebda, the widespread success of 'Tomber la chemise' suddenly marked their downfall as serious artists, and commentators gradually rejected the group as 'chavvy' ['beaufisant'] (Renault, 1999, p. 31), narrow-minded and populist ['franchouillard'] (Barbot, 2002, p. 30).

Reluctantly, the members of Zebda were drawn into a debate about the potential loss of their 'authenticity'. The satirical radical-left weekly *Charlie Hebdo* ran a whole interview premised on the idea that mainstream exposure corrupted political integrity (Cyran, 2000). Elsewhere, the artists were asked to explain how they dealt with this misrepresentation of their protest identity on a mainstream and national scale (Renault, 1999, p. 32; Santolaria, 2002, p. 14; Barbot, 2002, p. 30). If, in these interviews, the journalists revealed their cultural prejudices as members of an intellectual elite, the artists' answers to these questions were interestingly subtle. On the one hand, they agreed that finding fame had crowned their aspiration to 'make it' and was a recompense for the many years spent struggling financially (Cyran, 2000, p. 10; Barbot, 2002, p. 30). They also considered that inflexible positions against mediatization were untenable, given that they had chosen to become professional musicians: 'As soon as one decides to play music within a commercial framework, it would be incoherent to reject all forms of television advertising' (Cherfi in Cyran, 2000, p. 10).[35] On the other hand, they sought to re-establish their original, broader political credentials, admitting for instance that their commitment in this song was 'not very far-reaching' (Renault, 1999, p. 32).[36] They also commented on its unrepresentative genesis: 'This song, we almost didn't record it. We didn't

---

34 The album from which it was taken, *Essence Ordinaire*, also fared well with over 600,000 copies sold (Barbot, 2002, p. 30), and Zebda received the Victoires de la Musique Award for Best Group in 2000.

35 'Dès lors qu'on accepte de faire de la musique dans un cadre marchand, ce serait incohérent de refuser la télé en bloc'.

36 'Sur cette chanson, notre démarche ne va pas très loin'.

like it', said the keyboard player Rémi Sanchez (Barbot, 2002, p. 30).[37] Zebda also insisted that the rest of their album was much darker, and found solace in the fact that it also sold well (Renault, 1999, p. 32; Barbot, 2002, p. 30). These remarks, elicited by journalists who implied that Zebda's authenticity had become diluted by fame, sounded like apologies at times, and revealed that Zebda suffered from rock culture's dominant, purist belief that commerce corrupts thought.

At the same time, the way Zebda dealt with their *beur* ethnicity also became problematic, since the group's only large-scale national success had been a song in which ethnicity was irrelevant. The unproblematic insistence of 'Tomber la chemise' on singing and dancing, delivered with a heavy Toulouse accent, now followed the superficial celebration of *métissage*, as the perception of ethnic minority for the public was now only present, and unquestioned, in the name of the band and the faces of its singers. This also confirmed Cherfi's dreaded perception that 'Arabs' could only be tolerated and successfully mediatized in France if they 'sang about the desert and exoticism' (Sorgue, 1998).[38] By contrast, all the other politicized songs of Zebda, which reflected on integration and Arabness in sophisticated terms, had failed to reach no.1 and to make a profound impact on France's mainstream culture. In a 2002 interview for the state-sponsored radio station France Inter, Cherfi and Moustapha Amokrane explained that they had aspired to be at once 'popular and refined' ['large et fin'], and to stand at the junction between 'consensus and anger' ['consensus et colère'].[39] This subtle approach to popular music, however, had proven impossible to achieve. Managing mainstream success ultimately proved impossible for Zebda, and a few months later they split.

Zebda's access to national success is thus a complex story, and not simply a symbol of empowerment. On the one hand, the group demonstrated that French mentalities had changed since, at last, at the very end of the twentieth century, 'Arab' artists could achieve visibility in the media and commercial success on a large scale. Their success was certainly noteworthy in the sense that it went beyond that afforded to *beur* artists within rap music. None of the biggest stars of French rap in the 1990s, including MC Solaar, NTM or the frontmen of IAM, were *beurs*.[40] On the other hand, it sadly confirmed the ossified state of cultural and political conventions in the country. Zebda's mainstream success of 1999 only

---

37   'Cette chanson, on a failli ne jamais l'enregistrer ... . Elle ne nous plaisait pas'.

38   '... un pays qui tolère les Arabes lorsqu'ils chantent le désert et l'exotisme'.

39   Interview by Pascale Clark for 'Tam Tam Etcetera', *France Inter*, 2 October 2002.

40   The mainstream success of raï stars in France, such as Khaled, Cheb Mami and Faudel, only serves to confirm Cherfi's perception that 'Arabs' are only tolerated if they sing 'Arab' (in this case, Algerian) music, thereby reinforcing existing cultural stereotypes. Faudel's endorsement of conservative politics was also evident in 2007, when he attended the concert organized in support of the election of the new right-wing President Sarkozy (see Chapter 5).

seemed possible because this was a group of *beur* artists showing their compliance with republicanism's general rule of assimilationism. In the group's only number one hit, 'Tomber la chemise', their Arabness had become completely invisible. Besides, their sudden access to mainstream mediatization also revealed the sharp intransigence of the rock music sector, for whom a momentary lapse in the group's commitment to politically conscious music, through the release of just one 'fun' song, constituted an unforgivable transgression. Zebda were certainly a longer-lasting group than Carte de Séjour, although not on account of their hybridity, Arabness or contestatory power, and participation in France's 'authentic' popular music culture was denied to them in the long-term. The following chapter continues the examination of these difficulties, this time looking at what happens when French 'protest' music encounters commercial success abroad.

Chapter 4

Manu Chao, Anti-Globalization Protest and International Success

The previous chapter showed how the notion of *métissage* or cross-fertilization was sometimes used by artists from ethnic-minority backgrounds to criticize the artificial neutrality of republican identity.[1] *Métissage* also emerges as an important marker of 'resistance' in the context of anti-globalization politics, with artists employing hybrid music styles showcasing minority musical influences in what is often presented as a challenge to the global domination of Western cultural and economic power. A key figure in this protest culture is Manu Chao, a French-born artist who first reached fame in France in 1988 with his *rock alternatif* band Mano Negra, and has since gained international success as a solo artist, with acoustic ballads sung mainly in Spanish. In his solo work, Chao's use of *métissage* is audible in compositions that blend together various 'national' genres (Jamaican reggae, Cuban rumba, American blues, French *chanson…*), a technique that parallels his concerns with processes of deterritorialization and the displacement of migrants. In this context, Chao has emerged as a spokesperson linked to the loose coalition of anti-globalization campaigns, whose critique of Western economic domination advocates open frontiers and free migration. However, his active role within this international movement, alongside the hybrid character of his music, has complicated his reception in France as a 'national' protest hero.

Chao has also achieved a significant degree of commercial success. His first solo album, *Clandestino* (1998), topped the charts in France, Spain and Italy, and sold over 3 million copies worldwide. This success was repeated in 2001 with the release of his second solo project, *Proxima Estación: Esperanza*, which also sold around 3 million copies, won the Best World Music *Victoire* Award in France, and saw its various singles go gold and silver.[2] In the UK, Chao's concerts

---

1   Extracts of this chapter appeared in an earlier form in Barbara Lebrun, 'Banging on the Wall of Fortress France: Music for *Sans-Papiers* in the Republic', *Third Text*, 20/6 (November 2006): 709–19.

2   *Clandestino* sold 1.3 million copies in France and 1.2 million copies abroad (mainly in Spain and Italy); *Próxima Estación* sold 950,000 copies in France and more than 1.5 million abroad the year of its release (Belhaddad, 2003, p. 73 and p. 76). See the statistics compiled by the SNEP (Société Nationale de l'Edition Phonographique) in the 2001 archives of www.disqueenfrance.com (access through 'dossiers', then 'archives', then 'Bilan économique de l'année 2001', and click on two different documents: 'Les certificats de l'année 2001', and 'Les performances à l'export').

have sold out immediately, with tickets reaching up to £80 on the black market in 2002, leading a *Guardian* journalist to sum up wryly: 'This is Manu Chao, anti-globalization folk hero and France's most successful music export' (Forrest, 2002, p. 37). Indeed, while Chao does not rank with the top best-sellers of all time, his modest but steady success, in France and abroad, signals France's capacity to produce an artist of international scope, and demonstrates the global appeal of his politically conscious, 'protest' music that has its roots in France. To understand this success and its impact in France (and to a lesser extent outside France), this chapter examines Chao's music through its use of *métissage* as a tool of protest, and discusses the added impact his music derives from his support for *sans-papiers* (clandestine immigrants) in the context of anti-globalization resistance. Through a wider discussion of the commodity value of *rock métis*, whose global reach parallels the success of so-called world music, the ambivalent articulation of anti-globalization protest to the Western music industry is scrutinized, as are Chao's timely compositions in that style.

Métissage, Festivity and Cosmopolitanism

Manu Chao was born in Sèvres near Paris in 1961, and is a French citizen. His parents came from Spain, and his artistic trajectory as the son of an *émigré* in post-colonial France epitomizes the development of *rock métis* artists, as identified by Paul Moreira (Chapter 3).[3] Unlike the many *beur* artists of *rock métis* who often came from under-privileged backgrounds, however, Chao grew up in an artistically gifted, middle-class family, his father Ramón coming to France to study music at the Paris Conservatoire, and his mother Felisa being a keen artist. Ramón Chao trained as a classical pianist before embarking on a career as a sound engineer, radio journalist and novelist writing in French and Spanish (Gustave, 2003). At home, Manu grew up surrounded by intellectual and political discussion, as his parents regularly mixed with Latin American expatriates and refugees (Manche, 2004, pp. 127–8). Although Chao's musical influences extend beyond the origins of his family, he grew up bilingual in French and Spanish, and his trademark has been to incorporate Spanish in his lyrics and to pepper his compositions with Latin American influences. After his band Mano Negra split up in 1994 (see Chapter 1), Chao pursued his interest in Hispanic cultures by travelling extensively in Central and South America, and in 1998 released his first solo album, *Clandestino*, which was mainly sung in Spanish. In 2002, his second solo album was released, and in 2007, having honoured his contract with the major EMI, he released the self-produced *La Radiolina*.

---

3   Among the 'Latin' bands that Moreira (1987) lists is Los Carayos, one of the early formations of Manu Chao, in which François Hadji-Lazaro, the producer of the indie label Boucherie, also played.

Chao's musical influences are diverse, and his solo output echoes the *métis* mix already prevalent in Mano Negra. *Clandestino* (and the two albums that followed it) is characterized by a wide selection of acoustic Afro-Latin rhythms that include reggae, rumba, mambo, cha-cha and blues. Linguistically, Chao switches easily from Spanish to French and English, and individual songs incorporate lyrics from all of these languages to achieve a hybrid effect of 'Franglais' and 'Spanglish'. In *Proxima Estación*, Arabic and Brazilian Portuguese also feature. Furthermore, his solo albums expand this musical hybridity by being, in technical terms, the result of an assemblage of voice-overs, street sounds, recorded media (radio and TV programmes), fragments of political speech recorded during his South American travels, and the voices of other singers. This mixing, sampling and overdubbing adds to the already multi-faceted feel of the music, and the overall character of the albums, at once transient and plural, has generated an overwhelmingly positive reception, not least in France. His music is for instance praised as 'the ideal soundtrack to a well-deserved summer' (Barbot and Sorg, 2001, p. 74), 'a huge party, with a few sunburns in the bargain' (Deschamps, 2002b, p. 46), and as 'colourful and imaginative songs' (Loupias, 2001, p. 124).[4] In the UK too, his music is considered 'defiant, slippery and downright catchy', and 'captivating' (Spencer, 2007).

In these reviews, the notion of *métissage* is presented as inseparable from that of joyfulness, a positive appreciation that recalls the impact of so-called world music on Western audiences. World music, or the popular music genre inspired by Third World traditions and successfully marketed in the West since the early 1980s, arguably provides 'a glimpse of briefly realized solidarities between musicians and listeners stretched out across the globe' (Negus, 1999, p. 168). Forging an emotional bond between listeners and performers is probably the aim of any music piece, but the argument here is that the distance and foreignness of non-Western music styles expands the 'geographical imagination' of Western audiences, confronting them with references taken from outside Europe (Morley and Robins, 1995, p. 26 and p. 38). In their study of television audiences, David Morley and Kevin Robins (1995) have similarly underlined the sense of vertigo and pleasure that audiences feel when boundaries seem to fall, when bearings appear lost. Because Chao intentionally copies non-Western styles such as reggae and rumba, he establishes a direct, if somewhat vague, affiliation between his mainly European listeners and the 'Southern' cultures being showcased. In interviews, conducted in French festivals in summer 1999, audiences enthused about Manu Chao's music precisely because it connoted 'otherness':

---

4   Respectively 'la bande-son idéale d'un été qu'on n'a pas volé', 'une fête énorme, avec des coups de soleil en plus' and 'des chansons pleines de couleur et de fantaisie'.

I love it, it doesn't really sound French at all, there are lots of different languages. ... you don't really know if it's French or what, anyhow it's really cool.[5]

For this speaker, and for the many journalists who have reviewed Chao's music, the impossibility of attributing a fixed national origin to the music seemed the fundamental premise of their enjoyment.

Many critics have also highlighted the fact that Chao has 'really' travelled abroad for many years, visiting and touring a lot in Latin America, and pointed out the supposedly 'universal' message of his music inherent in its lack of specific localization. Chao is thus frequently described as a 'globe-singer' (Barbot and Sorg, 2001, p. 72), his songs bearing 'the accents of a universal anthem' ('des accents d'hymne universel', Belhaddad, 2003, p. 74). Chao himself, reflecting upon his travelling, has expressed a fascination for his own ubiquity, comparing himself jestingly to an international mail delivery service, able to give concerts in different places and adapting well to new situations (Manche, 2004, p. 135). Often, too, his audience appears confused about his origin, and Chao has underlined his ability to 'morph' into different nationalities: 'I am proud that in Rio, locals tell me "you're at home here", and that others say the same thing in Tijuana or in Mexico' (quoted in Pinsard, 2001).[6] A Brazilian student I met in Manchester in 2005 thought that he was Columbian or Mexican, and a Catalan student thought he was Castilian. For an Argentinian journalist, who omitted the fact that he was French from her review, the appeal of Chao's music resided in its reach beyond frontiers and nationalities: 'It doesn't matter if tomorrow he plays in Chiapas or in Paris, the message that underlies his work is that it is "One and for all"' (Belén Luaces, 2003).[7] Even for Spanish speakers, therefore, his music remains impossible to pin down, stylistically transnational and seemingly capable, for this very reason, of going beyond fixed and implicitly constraining notions of national identity. Chao's 'universal' appeal thus generates disorientation and pleasure, in a direct echo of the optimistic re-evaluation of the notion of *métissage* in contemporary France at the turn of the twenty-first century discussed in the previous chapter.

Immigration, Deterritorialization and 'Protest'

The positive appreciation of *métissage* in Chao's music derives added 'authenticity' from the fact that his songs deal, directly and indirectly, with processes of migration. His lyrics recurrently describe transnational population movements (including

---

5   '... j'aime bien ça fait pas trop français, y'a plein de langues différentes. ... on sait pas trop si c'est français à l'origine ou quoi, en tous cas c'est super'.

6   'Je suis fier qu'à Rio, on me dise que je suis chez moi, et qu'on me dise la même chose à Tijuana ou à Mexico.'

7   'No importa que mañana toque en Chiapas o en Paris, el mensaje que subyace a todo su trabajo es Uno y es de todos.'

reflections on his own movement as a travelling singer), and adopt the voice of representatives of the Third World. This theme is quite explicit in 'Clandestino', the title song of his eponymous first solo album (1998), which narrates, in Spanish, the journey of different immigrants from their native 'South' to the 'West'. Overall, this song uses musical *métissage* not as a conscious trigger for joyfulness, but as a mode of transposition for the evocation of deterritorialization. For instance, the lyrics use passive constructions to objectify the clandestine protagonist in the eyes of Western authorities 'they say I am a clandestine' ['me dicen el clandestino'], and this establishes a critical platform from which to scrutinize anti-migration policies. The lyrics also mention various nationalities in different stanzas ('Boliviano', 'Peruano', 'Nigeriano', 'Algerino' and so on), and this accumulation of references to potential migrants from the Third World illustrates Chao's exasperation with the economic poverty of these areas. Musically, the song's minor mode (F# minor) creates an impression of sadness, reinforced by a repetitive melody which almost resembles a lullaby. The melancholy tone suggests that migrants are primarily vulnerable people, leaving home against their wishes, and this positions the song as critical of the conditions of border regulation by Western states. The video accompanying it (directed by François Bergeron) unequivocally argues for freedom of circulation. On each utterance of the word 'clandestino', Chao's arm emphatically draws a cross in mid-air, symbolizing the official rejection of immigrants in the West, and the negation of their identity. On the key word 'illegal', repeated during the chorus, Chao points his index finger directly to camera, in an accusatory gesture that questions the judicial system that engenders illegality. Overall, then, the song's musical hybridity, lyrics and visual effects convey an impression of 'protest', since Chao attempts to represent, in this three-minute format, the confused identities of unwanted migrants who try their luck in the West, and this challenges the official (European) line on migration today.

In interviews, Chao has explained that his travels in Southern countries have led him to consider the creation of national borders as 'the biggest problem of the end of the [twentieth] century', alongside poverty in the Third World (quoted in Kun, 2004, p. 338). As a result, he has chosen to compose music by borrowing styles from Latin American and Afro-Caribbean cultures, whose historical connotations as places of colonial rule symbolically question current inequalities. Chao's choice to sing mainly in Spanish only reinforces this symbolic contestation of Western and especially Anglo-American hegemony in popular music (see Robecchi, 2002, p. 37). Despite being a European country, Spain still is not a G8 member, and the Spanish language reaches outside Europe to encompass connections with Latin America, where no country belongs to the Top 30 of 'developed' nations according to the UN.[8] The Hispanic feel of Chao's music thus sides, superficially perhaps, yet

---

8   As of the time of writing (2008). The Human Development Indicators (HDIs) are used by the UN to operate this classification; http://hdr.undp/org/en/statistics, last accessed 25 March 2009.

convincingly so for a number of people, with the 'oppressed' of the world – Chao's favouring of a Jamaican accent when singing in English similarly positions him as the implicit victim of colonialism and globalization.

The only published academic study of Chao's music so far is by Josh Kun, a specialist of US Latin rock. For Kun, Chao's music is 'a migratory song-mix born from placelessness, a song-mix that explores the racialization of Europe's and America's displaced others' (Kun, 2004, p. 336). Chao himself is introduced as 'one of globalization's most eloquent voices of protest, an artist who participates in the workings of global capitalism ... as a vehicle of giving voice to globalization's underbelly' (p. 337). This analysis chimes with the comments of many journalists to the effect that musical cross-fertilization has not only the capacity to shape new sounds, but also to achieve a powerful criticism of Western centrism. Kun stresses that Chao is a subversive musician, a 'global rebel' (p. 335), who succeeds in giving a voice to the 'subaltern' (p. 337) through his criticism of enforced legal borders. This interpretation of musical *métissage* as an effective tool of political protest follows the argument developed by Timothy Murphy and Daniel Smith, who, adapting Gilles Deleuze and Félix Guattari's concept of the rhizome, define 'resistant' pop music as a rhizomatic (rootless, placeless) cultural production, 'an inventive and intensive usage of the heterogeneous elements of different sonorous territories', with the capacity to resist an oppressive world order (Murphy and Smith, 2001, p. 6). Murphy and Smith do not refer specifically to the Spanish-speaking French artist but, for Kun, it is clear that this argument could apply to Chao. The heterogeneous nature of his compositions represents the process of deterritorialization, and since he borrows from genres associated with subaltern identities, a seemingly dissident soundscape, forcefully challenging Western regulations, arises. In France, the many positive reviews already quoted demonstrate that the general consensus around Chao seems to be, indeed, that he is an 'authentic' protest artist. A number of political organizations have endorsed this view, sensing in his music the perfect illustration of the many problems affecting the world today. The group Le doigt qui montre la Lune ('The Finger Pointing to the Moon' – a reference to utopianism), which campaigns for 'collective citizenship' and the attribution of residency rights for all immigrants, has chosen the song 'Clandestino' as music background for their website.[9]

The Movement for *Sans-Papiers* and the Anti-Globalization Campaign

Manu Chao's efforts to criticize the artificiality of borders and the glaring disparities of wealth between North and South are certainly morally irreproachable. Nonetheless, the analyses referred to above are perhaps simplistic in their readiness to equate *métissage*, and a sometimes basic commentary on injustice, with real, effective rebellion. The fact is that, when trying to understand why Chao's music

---

9   http://ledoigt.free.fr/sanspapier.htm, last accessed 22 March 2009.

has been so enthusiastically received, its context of production and circulation must be borne in mind. In a 2001 interview, Chao admitted to being bewildered by the impact of his songs: 'I am totally unable to analyze why 1 million French people bought *Clandestino*. I cannot understand what moved them' (in Deschamps, 2001, p. 43).[10] This humility may work in his favour, but the release of his solo albums must be relocated in a context that was highly favourable for an 'anti-global' *rock métis*, as the success of the anti-globalization campaign in the late 1990s, and that of Spanish-influenced popular music at the same time, paved the way for his positive reception among left-wing Western audiences.

Indeed, arguing for free migration flows and sympathizing with clandestine immigrants is at once an increasingly polemical position to uphold nowadays, in the face of nationalist legislation, and an increasingly attractive one for the 'radical' fringes of the Left. This is especially true in France, where violent expulsions of illegal migrants have taken place throughout the 1990s, but also where non-mainstream left-wing parties and organizations have enjoyed high levels of membership in recent years. Firstly, as briefly outlined in the previous chapter, the recent history of France's political and legal system shows that the state's conception of national identity has been shifting towards an exclusive, rather than inclusive, understanding of 'the nation'. After two centuries of free migratory traffic and decades of government-sponsored recruitment of a European, then colonial workforce, France is now, like most Western European countries, characterized by a defensive attitude towards migrants (Silverman, 1995; Hargreaves, 2007). Since 1974, it has closed its borders to non-European immigration, regularly banned the regrouping of family members, increased limitations on access to French nationality, and enforced rigid secular laws that are detrimental to some religious minorities. In the 1990s, moreover, France increased the number of asylum-seekers it deported, and was noted as one of the worst places in Europe for the detention of migrants (Schuster, 2004, p. 8). Due to a series of administrative complications introduced to restrict access to nationality, illegal or 'undocumented' immigrants (*sans-papiers* as they are known in France), are arguably the most vulnerable group of people to be caught in anti-migration policies today (Pellerin, 2003, p. 181).

In this context, what has become known in France as the 'movement for the *sans-papiers*' has vocally responded to the toughening of legislation, and generally encouraged the visibility of ethnic minorities in the public sphere, advocating *métissage* in response to the apparent inflexibility of the Republic. This movement gathered momentum in the mid-1990s, with famous French actors and film-makers making declarations against the heavy-handed expulsions of Malians from a Paris Church in 1996 (Powrie, 1999, pp. 10–16). Well-established academics have also criticized the Jospin reforms on *régularisation* (Balibar, Chemillier-Gendreau, Costa-Lacoux and Terray, 1999), while sectors of the press and television began to cover the life stories of illegal workers in a gradually more nuanced and

10   'Je suis incapable d'analyser pourquoi il y a un million de Français qui ont acheté *Clandestino*. Je n'arrive pas à comprendre ce qui les a touchés.'

sympathetic manner (Rosello, 1998a). In the field of popular music, certain French artists have supported this movement in a variety of ways, especially within the politically active milieu of alternative rock (Lebrun, 2005a and 2006a). With his overt focus on clandestines and *métissage*, Manu Chao simply joined an already-existing cohort of formal and informal supporters of free migration flows.

Indeed, Chao's success as a 'protest' artist is not so surprising if we consider that left-wing protest movements, in particular those opposing economic globalization and the social discrepancies arising from it, have grown throughout the 1990s, and particularly so in France. Chao is a well-known member of ATTAC, the French-based organization which proposes to alleviate global economic disparities by taxing international financial transactions. ATTAC was launched in 1998, the same year *Clandestino* was released, and in just a few years it was attracting 'soaring levels of support' (Waters, 2006, p. 151). The vitality of its radical agenda was matched by that of the Confédération Paysanne (CP), another French-based protest movement whose demands for the implementation of farming regulations and trade barriers Chao also supports, and which has enjoyed an 'unexpected' degree of success and mediatization since 1999 (Bruneau, 2006, p. 234). In August 2003, Chao performed for free in Millau during one of the organization's rallies, having already been nicknamed 'the José Bové of pop music' (Belhaddad, 2003, p. 78), and 'a singing José Bové' (Barbot and Sorg 2001, p. 72) after the CP's notorious leader. Juxtaposing Chao's skills as a musician with his ideological commitment, such sobriquets authenticate his credentials as a 'protest' artist who is also a politically active citizen. In France, this is an essential prerequisite for achieving cultural credibility, as the previous chapters have showed. Nonetheless, the success of both ATTAC and the CP were, in France at the beginning of the twenty-first century, part of a wider repositioning of left-wing activism, in reaction to the perceived shortcomings of mainstream political parties, particularly the Parti Socialiste, and signs of what has been seen as a new left-wing consensus (Waters, 2006).

Outside France, direct echoes of this trend could be found in the work, for instance, of the theorists Michael Hardt and Antonio Negri (2000), who argued that today's global order, or 'Empire', is characterized 'fundamentally by a lack of boundaries' (p. xiv). For them, this situation corresponds to the demands of global trade but creates conditions of poverty in the Third World. They also consider that this process of deterritorialization leads to the uprooting of workers, their transformation into migrants and their suffering as an 'illegal' workforce in the West (pp. 397–8). However, Hardt and Negri also suggest that deterritorialization can be used to shape a movement of resistance to 'unfair' profit-driven economies, thus paving the way for 'an alternative political organisation of global flows and exchanges' (p. xv). Manu Chao, as the composer of songs that illustrate, sonically and thematically, this very process of migration, followed this new trend in French and international politics. Because he is a public figure and singer, Chao has been hailed as the proponent of an anti-Western 'resistance'. For critics, Chao is the uncontested 'anti-globalization folk hero' (Forrest, 2002, p. 37), the 'great anti-global activist',[11] and the 'anti-globalist world-music superstar [that] is huge outside the English-speaking world' (Anon., 2007).

Chao's participation in left-wing political movements has extended to other domains. In France, he has taken part in various anti-racist initiatives. He wrote a song entitled 'Dans mon jardin' for a compilation produced by the anti-fascist organization Ras l'Front (*Les oreilles loin du front*, 2004). In April 2002, when the Front National candidate reached the second round of the presidential elections, Chao's music could be heard in the street during the anti-Le Pen gathering, a testament to its symbolic power as a tool of 'protest'.[12] He has, moreover, been dubbed 'Subcommandante Manu' (Kun, 2004, p. 332) for his support for Subcommander Marcos, the leader of the Zapatista army in Chiapas, Mexico. Chao has said of Marcos that 'he's done a wonderful job in his own neighbourhood. ... back then, he was one of the few beacons of hope that I could see in the world' (in Loupias, 2001, p. 126),[13] and he dedicated *Clandestino* to the EZLN, Marcos's army, and to the dispossessed Indians of Chiapas. In August 2001, Chao supported the anti-G8 demonstration in Genoa, and made various public declarations that echoed the claims of the anti-globalization campaign (e.g. Manche, 2004, pp. 55–6 and p. 97). The fact that Naomi Klein, the famous author of *No Logo* (2001) and one of the most high-profile anti-globalization activists, also interviewed Marcos and repeatedly criticized the G8, places Chao in the loose web of left-wing 'alternative' dissenters, his *métis* music playing a central role in accompanying the emergence of this international 'resistant' consciousness.

Fads and Fashion: The Success of 'World Music'

Just as Chao's ideological commitment to anti-globalization fitted into a left-wing trend in the late 1990s and early 2000s, so his chosen music style followed, to an extent, an established and already successful formula. The previous chapter demonstrated that *rock métis* was in full swing in this period in France. Paris is sometimes referred to as the world capital of world music (Warne, 1997, p. 137), and it is perhaps no accident that Chao's music, with its mix of foreign influences, should have emerged and become primarily successful in France. More broadly speaking however, France fits into the general Western trend for non-Western music genres. In particular, if the Latin American and Afro-Caribbean styles that Chao so enjoys (reggae, rumba and blues) have something in common, it is the fact that they are some the most familiar and best-selling music genres in the

---

11   'Manu Chao', www.rfimusique.com/siteFr/biographie/biographie_8981.asp (article from July 2003), last accessed 22 March 2009.

12   'Paris: contre Le Pen et avec les sans-papiers', http://hns-info.net/article.php3?id_article=976, last accessed 22 |March 2009.

13   '... il a fait un travail fabuleux au niveau de son quartier. ... à l'époque c'était une des rares lumières que je voyais dans le monde'.

developed world after rock, since at least the 1960s (Connell and Gibson, 2003, p. 160). These non-Western genres are also all variations on the acoustic ballad, a style which constitutes an established 'international repertoire' sought after by major record companies for its capacity to transcend national contexts, being 'less easily located and much more open to local appropriation' (Negus, 1999, p. 165). In other words, even if a *métis* genre might appear radical in its ability to challenge 'the notion of cores and peripheries in music' (Connell and Gibson, 2003, p. 187), it nonetheless potentially constitutes an ideal product for the music industry. Keith Negus (1999) proved this point with reference to salsa music, a Cuban-born style which has gradually broken free of its national anchorage to find fame abroad, as illustrated in 1997 by the highly successful release of the album *Buena Vista Social Club*.

It is perhaps significant, then, that *Clandestino* became highly successful around 1998, only a year after *Buena Vista*, as Chao's nonchalant and predominantly reggae style, as well as his lyrics in Spanish, in many ways paralleled the ubiquitous model of salsa. In 1999, both *Clandestino* and *Buena Vista* stood within the Top 20 album charts for France (and so did Zebda with *Essence Ordinaire*).[14] The simultaneous success of these groups points to the fashion at the time, at least in France, of musical hybridity, and Chao's compositions in that style were a godsend for his company Virgin/EMI, which had sensed the commercial potential of *rock métis* back in 1989 when it bought Mano Negra's contract from Boucherie (see Chapter 1). After 1998 and the (unexpected) success of his first solo album, Virgin decided to make Chao a 'priority for global release' ['une priorité mondiale'], giving him the necessary logistical and financial back-up to perform, be broadcast and have his records sold on an international scale (Belhaddad, 2003, p. 76).

It is important to emphasize, too, that Chao's music, while a hotchpotch of languages and genres, is also overwhelmingly reggae-based, and that the mellow up-tempo ballad style of reggae is 'by far the most familiar diasporic music' in the world today (Connell and Gibson, 2003, p. 174). Chao is a big fan of Bob Marley, whom he argues was the only real 'world music' artist (Belhaddad, 2003, p. 64). Like blues before it, reggae symbolizes black people's struggle against oppression and has been linked to the rejection of consumerism in the capitalist world, otherwise known as 'Babylon' (King, 2006). Chao's lyrics are peppered with such references, from the songs 'Mr Bobby' and 'Merry blues' which pay a direct homage to the Jamaican artist, to *Casa Babylon* and *Babylonia en Guagua*, respectively the titles of Mano Negra's last album (1994) and a DVD released in 2003. These associations with reggae music and Rastafarianism (Chao's lyrics often convey banal incantations to dope-smoking) also help explain the consistent reception of his music as a symbol of anti-Western protest. It should also be noted that there was, in France at the turn of the twenty-first century, quite a large reggae music scene, with numerous bands, including PierPolJak, Sinsemilia, Massilia Sound System, Tryo and Baobab, all reaching comfortable positions

---

14   See www.ifop.com/europe/sondages/discannu/albums99.stm

in the national charts. The place of reggae music in contemporary France lies beyond the scope of this research, but this favourable ground is arguably another contributing factor in Chao's positive reception in the country at this time (see Dicale, 2006, pp. 370–71 for a brief outline).

Finally, it has been noted that repetition and simplicity are further characteristics of Chao's songs. While this might seem surprising given his reception as a politically sophisticated artist, these attributes can be taken to connote sincerity and authenticity, as is the case here. For one critic, Chao's music is enjoyable precisely for its capacity to 'convey the impression of listening to a collection of familiar classics' (Belhaddad, 2003, p. 76).[15] His rather undemanding lyrics, with catchphrases in Spanish, English and French that sometimes seem lifted from a Berlitz phrasebook ('corazón' rhyming with 'Babylón', 'mon amour' with 'tous les jours'; 'long way from home', 'it's a long, long night', etc), are praised precisely for their charming naivety. This, according to some, makes Chao's music particularly popular among young children (Manche, 2004, p. 42), but also gives it a fraternal, inter-generational appeal (Belhaddad, 2002, 76). This crossover echoes the positive values attached to humanism and old age by the equally leftist genre of *chanson néo-réaliste* (Chapter 2). It is hardly surprising, too, that one of the reasons why Manu Chao likes Bob Marley is because of the alleged limpidity of his lyrics ('Bob Marley is a master of simplicity. His songs are very basic but they manage to touch people's hearts', in Pinsard, 2001).[16] Simplicity in this context becomes a synonym for timelessness and a raw, direct emotion. Given these overwhelmingly glowing reviews, and the impressive degree of his commercial success (for a French artist), it seems that Chao has, albeit on a lesser scale than Marley, achieved the goal of 'touching people's hearts'.

The Cosmopolitan and the Clandestine

The only area where Chao has attracted some negative criticism is in relation to his commercial success. Thanks to the sales of his solo albums, Chao is now a 'multimillionaire' (Belhaddad, 2003, p. 78), and this rankles with certain critics. In 2003, a French anarchist newspaper sneered at Chao in a scathing article.

> For another world to be possible, it's really easy. Just pick up some strong convictions, a minimum of ten words of vocabulary, like Manu Chao does ... . Then, you need to stick

---

15   'l'impression d'écouter une collection de standards familiers'

16   'Marley ... est un maître de simplicité. Ses chansons sont ultra-simples mais elles touchent le cœur des gens'.

a Peruvian hat on your head and have a bank account with several million Euros in it.
Bouledogue Rouge, 2003[17]

With an allusion to ATTAC's slogan, the author of this critique stressed Chao's lack of nuance, his tendency to repeat himself, and his complacency in posing as a 'marginal' (with his trademark Peruvian woolly hat, which associates him with deprived Indians), when he is in fact rich. Some music journalists have similarly tried to expose Chao with 'embarrassing questions' relating to his income (Deschamps, 2002b, p. 49). Even when their reviews were ultimately positive, they sometimes moderated their enthusiasm with references to Chao's personal wealth. For Deschamps (2002b, p. 46), 'on the surface, [Chao] doesn't look his age (41 years old), nor does he look his bank balance (a figure with lots of zeros after it)'.[18] In a TV documentary, the question of Chao's *compte en banque* was a recurrent concern (Lorton, Ciron and Charriéras, 2002). In 2003, the French rock group Les Wampas released a single entitled 'Manu Chao', whose lyrics focused on the size of the wallet of the artist. The song poked fun at Chao and fellow 'alternative' band Louise Attaque (see Chapter 1), suggesting that this artist and that group had not only become wealthy as a result of their mainstream success, but also lost their protest credentials by the same token. The song's chorus was more ironic than critical, however, especially coming from a band which had risen to fame, like Mano Negra, in the *rock alternatif* movement of the late 1980s. Besides, the added irony was that Les Wampas had their first major national hit with it in more than ten years.

Nonetheless, the success of Les Wampas, like the comments above, points to the wider resonance, among French critics and audiences, of the assumption that success is incompatible with sincerity. The obvious discrepancy between Chao's discourse on behalf of the 'oppressed', and his personal position as a successful artist, remains a troubling concern for many, who appear unable to see that the two go hand in hand. This prejudice is the legacy of a widespread left-wing idealism in France that has proved extremely resilient in the discourse surrounding French popular music, as we have seen. The group Zebda, for instance, came under fire in 1999 for releasing their song 'Tomber la chemise' that had the 'tastelessness' to reach number one (Chapter 3). This ideological pressure ultimately contributed to the band's split. For most Anglo-American academics however, this conundrum is not only obsolete but irrelevant, since the question of the credibility of a 'protest' artist is seen as being necessarily marred in paradox, caught in the 'messiness' of combining a pragmatic political agenda with the utopianism of transcending the

---

17 'Pour qu'un autre monde soit possible, c'est pas compliqué. Il faut s'armer de convictions fortes et d'au moins dix mots de vocabulaire, comme Manu Chao ... . Ensuite, il faut s'enfiler sur la tête un bonnet péruvien et avoir sous la main un compte en banque de plusieurs dizaines de millions d'euros.'

18 '... à le voir, on ne lui donnerait pas son âge (41 ans) ni son compte bancaire (un chiffre et plein de zéros derrière)'.

very context (i.e. the music industry) that gives it a platform for expression (Shuker, 1998, p. 20). Besides, the simplistic view that being in contact with the music business or gaining fame would 'corrupt' the otherwise 'authentic' autonomy of an artist bypasses the complexities of the music industry's workings (Negus, 1999; Hesmondhalgh, 1999; see Chapter 1).

In contrast to Zebda's ultimate implosion, it is refreshing to note here that Chao himself is not overly distraught by his success, and rather takes it in his stride with satisfaction and self-awareness at the same time. On the whole, Chao regrets that many journalists' questions deal with the topic of his income (Barbot and Sorg, 2001, p. 74), and expresses a certain exasperation at having to 'admit', as if standing in a trial, that he has made money out of his music. 'Of course I do alright...' ['ben ouais j'commerce...'], he replied wearily to a TV journalist prodding him on this topic (Lorton, Ciron and Charriéras, 2002). Upon the release of *Proxima Estacion*, whose musical feel was very similar to that of *Clandestino*, Chao also had to fend off accusations of facility. Responding to criticism of his recycling of musical gimmicks from album to album, he underlined that his intention had always been to make saleable music, and repeatedly dismissed the 'dictatorship of novelty' (Loupias, 2001, p. 126; Deschamps, 2001, p. 40; Manche, 2004, p. 61). This statement, which insists that musical originality, political protest, personal sincerity and commercial success can be compatible, follows the flexible understanding of 'alternativity' already encountered with the independent record producer Hadji-Lazaro, for instance (see Chapter 1). It also suggests that Chao is a level-headed businessman, able to question the prevailing purist ethos of the indie rock music culture, even as he claims allegiance to it. Therefore, even if Chao sometimes 'justifies' his current financial stability with reference to the many years spent struggling before (Manche, 2004, p. 133), he is very much aware of his own privileged position, and does not hesitate to discuss, quite lucidly, the material comfort afforded him by his recent success (Deschamps, 2001, p. 42 and 2002b, p. 46).

This self-awareness is evident in relation to his support for clandestines, too. In the video of 'Clandestino', he positions himself ambiguously, with the crowd of migrants being shot in medium close shot in the background, while he stands in the foreground, slightly off-centre and shot in close-up, mouthing the lyrics of the song. This difference of treatment establishes a distance between the migrants and the singer, between the clandestine characters of the lyrics and Chao the 'real' artist, who does not pretend to be 'one of them'. His disassociation from the song's migrant narrator reveals his awareness, as a visible and successful artist, of his incapacity to fully represent the invisible 'subaltern'. It also acts as a critical commentary on the supposed radical power of *métissage*, supporting the view that simply celebrating *métissage*, instead of questioning it, constitutes a Western fantasy which fulfils social needs of distinction (see Chapter 3; also Wolton 2003, p. 50).

Indeed, critics have noted that white audiences often enthuse about ethnic 'mixity' and the music of artists from minority backgrounds, but rarely mix socially with people from these groups. Whether looking at the white Quebec audiences of black rap artists (Chamberland, 2002), the UK audience of Asian bhangra (Hutnyk, 2000, p. 132), the US public of 'Gypsy' festivals (Silverman, 2007, p. 343), or that of Cuban salsa (Negus, 1999, p. 150), many agree that musical *métissage* provides pleasant feelings of disorientation for its audience, but mainly in 'safe', culturally mediated situations, such as concerts. Chao, by contrast, attempts to deflect this reality by commenting, quite self-critically, on the networks in which his music circulates. He has pointed out that his commercial success was due to the purchasing audiences of Western Europe: 'One thing is sure, I'm not making millions off the back of the Third World, but from the buyers in Europe' (Lorton, Ciron and Charriéras, 2002).[19] Journalists back this up (Forrest, 2002; Deschamps, 2001; Cassavetti, 2007b), as do personal observations in concerts in France and the UK, where his performances are predominantly attended by a middle-class university crowd. The fact that the vast majority of the members of ATTAC, the organization that Chao supports, also come from 'educated, well-paid groups employed in the liberal professions such as teaching or civil service' (Waters, 2006, p. 151), highlights the gap between, on the one hand, the vulnerability of the fictional characters of Chao's songs, or that of the real migrants whose welfare is at the heart of organizations such as ATTAC, and, on the other hand, the privileged position of the 'real' audiences who enjoy these songs and participate in related political mobilization. The socio-economic profile of the audience of France's 'protest' music culture is developed in the next chapter, yet it is already clear that, unlike many of his reviewers and audience members, Chao is sharply aware of the tensions shaping a 'protest' identity in French (and Western) popular music, and never takes for granted the expression of 'authenticity' in this music culture. Rather than simply celebrating *métissage*, or the cultural, musical and linguistic encounter with the non-European 'other', he carefully considers the economic and social conditions that have made these encounters possible.

The example of Manu Chao as a French 'protest' artist is thus revealing of the many tensions shaping France's 'alternative' music culture. It shows, firstly, that *rock métis* is a highly acclaimed music genre in early twenty-first-century France, although accounts vary as to why this is so. While many critics and audiences see Chao's music as the powerful expression of an opposition to exclusivist conceptions of the nation, others, including Chao himself, are more tentative in their interpretation of this success. Chao, for one, remains sharply aware of the personal and economic privilege that has shaped his political awareness of inequalities, namely his coming from an educated milieu, holding a French passport, having the legal right to cross frontiers, and benefiting from financial security and fame. Secondly, the example of Chao's commercial success reveals that, despite being praised by some critics as an example of 'authentic' protest, his music could be seen in a different light. While undoubtedly the result of personal sincerity and a degree

---

19 'Une chose sûre, les millions, c'est pas sur le dos du Tiers-Monde que je me les fais, c'est grâce aux acheteurs en Europe.'

of artistic originality, it is also the product of a very specific historical juncture, at which (and this is especially evident in France) the renewal of left-wing ideology, influenced by anti-globalization concerns, met the trend for songs sung in Spanish and composed to reggae tunes. These contingencies do not cancel out the fact that *rock métis* in general, and Chao's music in particular, accompany the morally irreproachable formulation of a more flexible understanding of French (and of other) identities, especially in times of increasingly stringent nationality laws. However, they help bring out a more nuanced and accurate picture of the success of *rock métis* in contemporary France. Chao's success also shows how 'protest' music can at once challenge dominant views (in this case, the closing down of frontiers) and be part of the 'system' by becoming commercially successful, while also being perceived as 'authentic' by many, even when it is historically, politically and socially constructed, and to this extent artificial. The place and power of this 'protest' music culture in French society can further by gauged by its influence on audiences, and the uses they make of it, an aspect which the next and final two chapters develop.

PART III
Participation, Audiences and Festivals

Chapter 5
Audience Reception and 'Alternative' Identities in Contemporary France

In this and the following chapter, we will move our attention away from the modes of production of popular music in France, in order to examine the modes of its consumption through an analysis of audiences' reception of French 'alternative' acts, and participation in a French 'alternative' culture. In traditional research in this area, the music tastes of the French have been evaluated through surveys which, based as they are upon a set of answer choices, fail to assess the variety of meanings that audiences attribute to artists, genres and their own identities as consumers. For instance, a 1997 state-funded survey and a 1998 survey run by SACEM (France's copyright agency) both drew up their questionnaires in such a way that the terms 'variété' and 'chanson' were made to appear interchangeable, while a separate category of 'rock and pop' only applied to Anglo-American music.[1] Such imposed definitions are unrepresentative of consumption patterns and musical meanings in contemporary France, for, as we have seen, many artists, producers and journalists discriminate between *chanson* and *variété*, and consider French rock music to be a distinct musical and ideological category – the creation in the mid-1990s of specialist 'rock français' aisles in Fnac shops is a further indication of how widespread this perception is. It is therefore necessary to develop a more nuanced understanding of audiences' engagement with generic categories and, further, of what music means to the French and how music tastes are experienced and expressed in France. Audience research, with its emphasis on qualitative data and 'letting people speak', is one of the best ways to achieve this.

Outside France, the study of popular music has paid increasingly serious attention to the practices and discourses of audiences. The empirical work this involves, however, has only been carried out by a handful of scholars, such as Robert Walser (1993) with heavy metal listeners, Sarah Thornton (1995) with the UK club scene and Daniel Cavicchi (1998) with Bruce Springsteen fans. The lack of wider engagement with audiences can, perhaps, be attributed to the time-consuming nature of ethnographic work. This trend in Anglo-American popular music scholarship is even more pronounced in the field of French and francophone music studies, where, whether in contributions written in English or French, the very consideration of audience reception, let alone its empirical analysis, remains problematic. In recent years, three key texts about popular music in France have ignored audience research altogether, although their authors partly acknowledge

---

1   Donnat (1998); 'Les goûts musicaux des Français', publication SACEM, 1999.

this omission (Hawkins, 2000; Dauncey and Cannon, 2003; Looseley, 2003). Others have followed ethnomusicological methods in their analysis of French rap concerts (Pecqueux, 2002) and zouk music gatherings in Martinique (Berrian, 2000), yet without engaging with audiences as such. Using methods derived from ethnography, Jean-Marie Seca (2001) carried out interviews and participant observation in the French rock milieu, but focused on artists and practitioners, not the public. Anne-Marie Green (1997), in her work on the music tastes of French *lycée* students, interestingly emphasized the notion of 'hyper-conformity', which is of use to the present study, although she relied exclusively on questionnaires with ready-made answers for collecting her data, therefore bypassing the advantages of qualitative research. In the same volume, Laurent Brunstein (1997) relies heavily on Seca and, despite a welcome attempt at conducting 'open' audience interviews with a crowd of rock music practitioners, never questions the meanings placed by interviewees upon the notions of 'purism', 'authenticity' and 'anti-mainstream' identity.

The work of Antoine Hennion and his collaborators (2000), on the fluctuations in the moods and practices of classical music *amateurs*, stands out for this reason. Hennion is perhaps France's most Anglo-American music sociologist, equally critical of the aesthetic tradition according to which the value of music resides in the music itself, and of the sociology of tastes, which regards tastes as deriving exclusively from socio-economic structures. Focusing on classical music lovers, he highlights the complex and unpredictable situations in which musical emotions are born, whether in domestic settings, in shops or during the collective practice of concert-going. This is the kind of field sociology that the present chapter seeks to reproduce, while modestly challenging the Anglo-American centredness of previous studies on rock.

In response to Martin Barker's call for audience researchers to be 'ambitious' (see Barker, 2006), this single chapter cannot hope to fully re-evaluate the application of audience research methodologies in the area of (French) popular music studies. Rather, given its focus on self-defined 'alternative' audiences of French popular music, its principal concern is to understand the ways in which these individuals negotiate their social identities in relation to their constructions and articulations of the concepts of the 'mainstream' and 'alternative'. Following the example set by a number of colleagues who, working in and outside popular music studies, have noted the pleasure that audiences take from their cultural practices, while stressing their contradictions and regressive tendencies (Moores, 1993, p. 131; Plummer, 1995, p. 178; Thornton, 1995, p. 24; Auslander, 1999, p. 70; Cameron, 2001, p. 14; Austin, 2002, p. 80), this chapter is concerned with laying bare the social and cultural constructedness of 'protest', 'non-mainstream', 'alternative' or 'resistant' identities in 1990s and early 2000s France. While this approach ultimately stresses the constructedness and ordinariness of this music culture, it also takes seriously the enthusiasm of contemporary listeners for oppositional stances, seeking to explain the significance of these positions in their lives. Overall, then, through the use of group and individual interviews, this small-scale investigation constitutes a so far unique attempt at conducting nuanced audience research in the area of French popular music.

Accordingly, the fieldwork carried out among French audiences is examined from two related vantage points. Firstly, the strong socio-economic parallels between the data collected here and Pierre Bourdieu's postulation of the vanguard will contribute to debates about the resilience of left-wing ideologies in contemporary France. Secondly, the study will move into more psychological terrain by analyzing interview material using a combination of discourse, conversation and narrative analyses, revealing the anxieties and 'conflicting priorities' that audiences have to juggle as they attempt to define themselves as 'alternative' within consumer society (MacDonald, Miell and Wilson, 2005, p. 337).

Presentation of Fieldwork

The fieldwork cited here was carried out at rock concerts and popular music festivals in France, in the summers of 1998, 1999 and 2000. The festivals I attended were Les Francofolies in La Rochelle, La Route du Rock in Saint-Malo, Un Eté à Saint-Nolff (in Saint-Nolff), and Les Vieilles Charrues in Carhaix, all in Western France. I also attended the Paléofestival in Nyon in French-speaking Switzerland, and various one-off concerts in North-West France. A representative selection of 'alternative' French artists performed at these festivals, including Zebda, Manu Chao, Têtes Raides, Louise Attaque, La Tordue and others. Following the approach developed in semi-guided interviews, I spoke with audiences face to face, asking them open questions and avoiding the use of visible research tools such as notepads (Mason, 1996). Typically, I would engage someone in conversation about the venue, as casually as possible and almost always using the informal 'tu'. After this initial contact, I would ask whether my interviewee would agree to answer further questions and to have our conversation tape-recorded. Audiences were interviewed at random, both individually and in clusters of 'ready-gathered' groups of friends. I also carried out one interview in the home of participants in Rouen, one unplanned interview in a bar in Le Havre, and one telephone conversation. Interviews at festivals varied in length from five minutes to an hour, often taking place during the intervals between bands. The events I attended ranged from small-scale concerts (audiences of fewer than 200 people, ticket prices as low as 40 francs), to France's largest popular music festival to date, Les Vieilles Charrues, with around 200,000 people over three days, tickets selling at 320 francs in 2000 and reaching over 600 francs on the black market. The variety of venue sizes provided a diversity of impressions about live music events, and a large range of answers from people from different backgrounds and age groups. Having said this, among those interviewees claiming a 'non-mainstream' identity for themselves and their peers, a clear socio-economic and cultural pattern emerged, as will be seen below. Overall, around 100 people were interviewed, with a more or less equal male:female ratio, totalling 16 hours of recording.

Interviewing people is problematic. An interview is an artificial situation created in order to generate 'authentic and credible data' (Mason, 1996, p. 39), and the risk of 'over-interpretation' of data has long been recognized (Cavicchi, 1998, p. 185; Hesmondhalgh, 2002, p. 125; Austin, 2002, p. 64). Bearing these caveats in mind, it is nonetheless informative to let cultural participants express themselves, and a number of analytical theories are available which allow us to make sense of the recorded interviews. The present research combines models drawn from discourse and conversation analyses (Flick, 1998), and narrative analysis (Coffey and Atkinson, 1996). This allows the factual knowledge that audiences have about music to be assessed, revealing both the social dynamics within groups of friends, and how individuals sometimes shape their cultural identities through patterns of story-telling. It is also a fact of life that music audiences, and most cultural participants for that matter, seek to construct their sense of self by avoiding 'identification with less desirable groups' (MacDonald, Miell and Wilson, 2005, p. 322). Studies of musical identities have shown that to cast one's tastes, and by extension, oneself, as unusual, is a remarkably common impulse. In rock music studies, distinction from less desirable groups, such as mainstream pop listeners, revolves around a rejection of heavily mediatized, commercially successful music, and an attribution of positive, 'authentic' values to the music which seems to bypass the profit-driven strategies of the industry (Cavicchi, 1998, p. 89; Auslander, 1999, p. 69; Hesmondhalgh, 2002, p. 126).

In other taste groups, a similar concern for avoiding the mainstream is also visible, as has been demonstrated with reference to classical music (Hennion, Maisonneuve and Gomart, 2000), rap music (Huq, 2006) and rave culture (Thornton, 1995). Of course, because the conditions of popular music production cannot be reduced to a neat opposition between commercial and non-commercial categories, elaborating one's 'alternative' identity (in the broad category of French rock, for instance) is an inherently fluid process. This identity is at once based on, and experienced as, a simplified version of the complex workings of the industry, and is constantly being redefined, repositioned, negotiated. French 'alternative' audiences are, in this respect, little different from other taste and national groups. Nonetheless, 'alternative' identities also bear national characteristics, and this chapter pursues its investigation of the particularity of non-mainstream music tastes in France by relating the resilience of the anti-mainstream bias there to the wider sense of crisis in left-wing intellectual circles, where the fear of neo-liberalism and mass mediatization has remained a perhaps anomalous yet persistent feature (Cornick, 1998). The pages that follow will therefore stress the significance as well as the banality of alternative identities in popular music, while signalling the 'Frenchness' of their articulation in France when appropriate.

The Sociology of Taste and the Cultural Vanguard

Bourdieu's sociological analysis of cultural preferences has been criticized for its over-determinism (Hennion, Maisonneuve and Gomart, 2000), yet his comprehensive exposition of the mechanisms of socio-economic distinction remains, to a surprisingly large extent, relevant to the context of alternative music identities in contemporary France. Bourdieu engaged with popular music only sporadically, describing how different professional categories, for instance the intellectual elite, tended to prefer text-based *chanson* at the expense of 'dancing' or 'unpretentious' music (1979, for instance p. 16 and p. 420). In the 1960s, when the fieldwork for *La Distinction* was first carried out, the music tastes of the French middle class already seemed to be shaped according to a binary system opposing quality to commerce, and *chanson* to *variété* (esp. p. 406 and p. 413). This classification system is obviously more flexible at an individual level, as this chapter also underlines, but as a broad trend, it has remained deeply entrenched in France, and the opinions expressed by the majority of audiences interviewed for this fieldwork bear this out. With their rejection of the profit-driven codes of the music industry, their attachment to various left-wing causes and their high cultural capital, the participants in this research displayed, in general, the characteristics of what Bourdieu called the cultural vanguard (pp. 305–6 and p. 332).

The vanguard is the segment of the lower-middle class (*petite bourgeoisie*) which, unlike the traditional bourgeoisie whose power is based on economic capital, is a newer, up-and-coming middle class, mainly consisting of educated people, university students, teachers, intellectuals and artists (Bourdieu, 1979, p. 333). The traditional bourgeoisie, which Bourdieu compared to the British upper-middle class, is economically dominant. It derives its authority from close relationships with non-political institutions such as the church, the school and the family, and owes its longevity to the transmission of financial possessions to following generations. It is a class which reproduces itself, and is essentially conservative (Pinçon and Pinçon-Charlot, 2000, p. 30). The vanguard, by contrast, belongs to an 'ascending' bourgeoisie. Its cultural capital is higher than its economic capital (Bourdieu, 1979, p. 326), its members claim to be anti-conservative, to favour risk-taking (p. 321) and 'quality' in music (p. 419), and despise both the upper classes' financial wealth, and the economically and culturally dominated position of the lower classes (characterized in the derogatory terminology of today as *beaufs*).

This trend is present in the personal backgrounds of some French 'alternative' rock artists, including Manu Chao (Chapter 4) and Magyd Cherfi of the group Zebda (Lebrun, 2007). It is also indisputably the case that the majority of my informants were mainly, in economic and educational terms, highly educated young adults, teachers and artists. For instance, Isabella was a university student already holding one *Licence* (Degree), and about to embark upon another.[2] Yannick, Cécile,

---

2   Higher Education in France is state-sponsored and university students benefit from accommodation grants and much lower fees than their UK counterparts for instance.

Gaëtan and Loïc were at various stages of completing their *Licences* (Degrees) and *Maîtrises* (Masters) in Arts subjects. Léonore was an undergraduate, as were Anne, Julie, Manue, Benoît and Jérôme. Marie was a newly qualified teacher and Rachida, already introduced in Chapter 2, had not one but two teaching qualifications. Those who worked tended to be teachers, social workers and artists (*intermittents*), linked in many cases to the ever-present French public sector. A few were educated people without a guarantee of continuous employment, benefiting from temporary 'solidarity' contracts such as the minimum wage and young persons' job schemes. Many were also active in various artistic fields (music, dance, street theatre). Those under 18 were all *lycée* students. The few exceptions to this model included a mechanic in his early twenties and a young school drop-out claiming to be a petty drug dealer. These young men tended to confirm Bourdieu's model, however, since they did not follow the anti-mainstream bias of most of the other interviewees. Finally, not all interviewees gave information about their parental background, so that identifying class belonging, in the strict Bourdieusian sense, was not always possible. Among those who answered regarding their parents' professions, the variety of patterns actually weakened the validity of Bourdieu's system, since manual workers, businessmen, teachers in the state sector and highly paid professionals (architect, psychiatrist) were all mentioned. These differences suggest that non-mainstream tastes in this instance were not, or not always, purely 'class-based' or linked to parental background, but rather an emanation of the interviewees' personal educational and cultural trajectories.

The informants' taste for rock music and festivals also confirmed their overall belonging to France's more well-off classes. All surveys show that, in France at least (but this is a broader tendency in the West, see Frith, 1981, p. 190), the genre of rock music tends to be preferred by the better educated. In 1988, among the population of 15- to 24-year-olds regularly attending rock music concerts, the bulk (46 per cent) came from a 'superior intellectual background' ['professions intellectuelles supérieures'], versus 24 per cent coming from 'lower-class backgrounds' ['ménages populaires'] (Teillet, 1993, p. 74). In the 1990s, attendance figures for the Printemps de Bourges festival showed that 81 per cent of participants had received a secondary education, and 50 per cent were or had been in higher education (Davet and Tenaille, 1996, p. 101). In 2001, the most represented socio-cultural group at the Francofolies festival of La Rochelle were university students, who made up 35 per cent of spectators.[3] A survey for La Route du Rock (1999) similarly underlined the fact that the 'superior intellectual professions' were by far the most represented. More generally, this follows the evidence that, since the 1970s, the well-off and educated middle classes have participated the most in cultural activities (Dirn, 1998, p. 41; Donnat, 1998, p. 109; Mermet, 2000, p. 397).

---

3   Personal communication with Maryse Bessaguet, Public Relations Department for the Francofolies festival, 15 April 2002 (email).

Moreover, when respondents detailed their busy consumption habits of cross-checking information, drawing up lists, spending time in shops, discussing values and genres with friends and so on, they demonstrated their inclination towards spending a large amount of time on their cultural activities. This financially non-productive 'free time', during which one engages in an accumulation of cultural knowledge referred to as *thésaurisation* or 'cultural saving' by Bourdieu (1979, p. 320), is another central criterion in identifying the vanguard (p. 336). Finally, the audiences' taste for destabilization, repeatedly demonstrated in their celebration of the need to take risks and the value they attach to the out-of-the-ordinary, is also characteristic of the vanguard segment (p. 35). These trends demonstrate that members of the more intellectual section of the (lower-) middle class, while forging an oppositional, alternative identity, are at the same time fully integrated, economically and culturally, in society. Torn between their left-wing criticism of capitalism and their full access to consumption, and between their aspiration to marginality and their membership of a culturally dominant group, alternative audiences shape their identities through a series of ambivalences, which these interviews clearly exposed.

Anti-Mainstream 'Protest' in Everyday Life

While not necessarily sharing the same tastes in groups and artists, and thus not constituting a distinct subculture, many informants positioned themselves against the continuing commercial success of *variété* in France (see Chapter 1), and constructed similar mental images of the mainstream media and mainstream music they claimed to reject. In July and August 1999, out of 19 group interviews conducted during the Francofolies and Route du Rock festivals, 17 groups of respondents insisted that they did not listen to any *variété française*, or any kind of 'commercial' music. In July 2000, out of 32 interviews conducted in the festivals of Saint-Nolff and Carhaix, an average of 80 per cent of respondents claimed that they did not listen to *variété*, repeating comments such as 'I like a bit of everything, except mainstream'.[4]

Music festivals traditionally attract a crowd critical of the dominant radio and TV media (see Chapter 6), and no doubt because of this the responses tended to follow the exclusionary pattern of the 'rock prejudice' (Auslander, 1999, p. 70; Negus, 1992, p. 61). Indeed, audiences dismissed the triad of mass mediatization, quick profits and short-term career development, with statements such as: 'mainstream pop, that's just guys wanting to make money', 'mainstream pop means nothing, it's commercial, a one-hit-wonder and you don't see them again', or 'we don't like ready-made music, all the French artists on TV and that, they're all doing the same

---

4   'J'écoute de tout sauf de la varièt'!'.

thing'.[5] More often than not, audiences expressed their musical identities in the negative, defining themselves through what they were not. The statements above implied, for instance, that in opposition to the dominance of repetition, brevity, money-making and the absence of reflection, there existed a cultural practice characterized by originality, longevity, parsimony and intellectual substance. In one rare definition in the affirmative, a female informant considered that 'quality' principally entailed 'open-mindedness', reprising the discourse of authenticity already developed with regard to *chanson* and its supposed intellectual stimulation (see Introduction).[6] Respondents placed great emphasis on the restricted, specialist appeal of the acts they followed, and reacted strongly to any perceived loss of exclusiveness. This was evident in their comments regarding the artists performing at these festivals. Manu Chao, Zebda and Louise Attaque, among others, attracted their share of disappointed fans during the time of the fieldwork because of their transfer from the 'alternative' fringes to the mainstream, between 1998 and 2000.

> The fact that everybody knew them pissed me off really quickly [about Zebda]; we've had enough of listening to them everywhere, in shops and all that [Zebda again]; at first we used to listen to them, but then they became famous and now we don't listen to them anymore [Louise Attaque]; it's not what I would call ready-made music but I'm not really into it… You know, [Manu Chao] had a huge success and that's crucial because I don't really like that sort of thing.[7]

These statements showed that the knowledge of a cultural artefact or artistic trend prior to its wider dissemination, or the possession of 'cultural antecedence', was central to the speakers' assertions of prestige (Bourdieu, 1979, p. 79 and p. 419). Their social distinction took the form of a claimed knowledge of music artists 'before' mainstream mediatization, and they systematically rejected those other audience members who, unlike them, had 'just' discovered the same acts through the mass media.

The primacy of cultural antecedence in asserting one's alternative identity was obvious during the group interview conducted in Rouen (January 1999), among a panel composed of Arts students. The interviewees discussed the initial merit and

---

5 'La variété c'est vraiment des mecs qui veulent faire du fric', 'la variété ça veut rien dire, c'est commercial, un tube et on les revoit plus', 'nous on n'aime pas la musique préfabriquée, tous les artistes français qui passent à la télé, ils font tous la même chose'.

6 'La qualité, euh … c'est ce qui m'ouvre l'esprit'.

7 'Le fait que ça soit connu ça m'a vite fait chier'; 'on en a eu ras le bol de l'écouter partout, dans les magasins et tout'; 'au début on écoutait et puis c'est devenu célèbre, alors on n'écoute plus'; 'ça fait partie des musiques pas fabriquées, mais j'ai un peu de mal… et puis, [Chao] a eu un succès énorme, ça joue dans la mesure où j'aime pas trop ça'. Such comments are extremely common among a certain group of young music listeners. See MacDonald, Miell and Wilson (2005, p. 326) for the reflection by a teenager, John, who stopped listening to the 'indie' US group Nirvana: 'Everyone else started listening to it so I just felt like "everyone else is listening to it – I'm going to stop listening to it"…'.

gradual loss of prestige of the retro rock band Louise Attaque, a group perceived as 'alternative' in 1996–7 due to its original music style and semi-independent production, but which gained vast commercial success in 1998 (see Chapter 1). Loïc, a 23-year-old male informant with a *Licence* in French Studies, commented thus: 'the first time, I had never heard anything like it, I thought this is brilliant, it's really pacey and weird. But after three or four months, you could even hear them at the supermarket, and just knowing that you could hear them everywhere, I stopped listening to them.'[8] He added that he would even change radio channels at home when the group was on, in order to avoid listening to them. At first, Loïc had enjoyed Louise Attaque's outlandishness ('weird' equated to 'brilliant'), establishing his taste for destabilization by using a vocabulary of novelty and potential risk, already encountered among rock artists and independent label producers, and typical of the vanguard according to Bourdieu (1979, p. 35). Gradually, however, his enthusiasm for Louise Attaque dwindled as the band's fame increased.

For Bourdieu, consumers with a strong sense of cultural antecedence usually hold on to their exclusivity over products that overlap traditional taste divides by enjoying them 'differently' from mass consumers (Bourdieu, 1979, p. 321). In this case, Louise Attaque came to straddle the traditional divide between alternative and mainstream tastes, releasing singles and being broadcast on commercial radio. However, Loïc stopped listening to the band altogether, feeling that the sense of prestige he had previously attached to them was irretrievably lost. It is striking, for instance, that even in the secrecy of his own home, he still would not listen to the group anymore, such was the power of their newly debased status. This anecdote confirms Barker's observation that individual audience members can adopt collective positions even when they are alone (Barker, 2006, p. 28), and reveals that the pleasure one has in listening to music does not necessarily reside in the music itself, nor is it directly determined by one's socio-economic background (Hennion, Maisonneuve and Gomart, 2000, p. 160). Loïc's attitude towards Louise Attaque changed throughout 1997–9, whereas the music stayed exactly the same (only one album was released in this period), as did his socio-economic background. Furthermore, his membership of the cultural vanguard, by virtue of being an educated young man with a taste for non-mainstream rock music, could not fully account for his deep, physical reluctance to listen to the group's music again. The sociology of taste is therefore not enough on its own to explain the unexpected, intimate moments when musical emotions arise (Hennion, Maisonneuve and Gomart, 2000, p. 243) – and when they cease.

In the same interview, Loïc's friends explained why they had been fans of Louise Attaque until the band's 1998 success. Gaëtan (*Maîtrise* in English Studies, 25) stated that he had known the band prior to their nationwide success ('the CD

---

8   'La première fois j'avais jamais entendu ça, je me suis dit c'est bien, ça bouge et c'est bizarre. Mais après trois-quatre mois, on l'entendait même au supermarché, et de savoir que ça s'entendait partout, j'ai arrêté de l'écouter.'

was out long before it became successful'), and considered that they had achieved fame 'in the old-style way, by touring a lot'.[9] Yannick (*Maîtrise* in English Studies, 24) qualified Louise Attaque as 'indie guys, they had a sense of ethics'.[10] Both young men activated a classic conception of rock authenticity, associating nostalgia with a strong sense of morality, and opposing these values to their perception of the media and major companies as immoral bullies. They were, as Chapter 1 showed, actually ill informed about Louise Attaque's career (not quite indie, contracted to Sony for the distribution) and the music industry more generally (live performance has cohabited with mediatization since the late nineteenth century). Nonetheless, they shared the same conception of authenticity, by valuing an imaginary pre-modern period, idealizing the group's anti-corporate stance as ethical, and asserting their own prestige through cultural antecedence. As friends, through this conversation, they actualized their participation in the same cultural identity, invoking common values and making similar simplifications.

Discussions about music reveal how individuals shape their musical identities in respect to others (MacDonald, Miell and Wilson, 2005), and this conversation particularly highlighted the power relations among the participants, with some individuals emerging as 'taste leaders' over others (Flick, 1998, p. 117 and p. 124). A female respondent, Cécile (*Licence* in German Studies, 24) waited until the interview had finished and the tape-recorder was off to clarify a point about her music tastes. Sheepishly, she confessed to me, and for the first time to the rest of the group, that she liked listening to Jane Birkin and Gérald De Palmas, two artists considered somewhat 'mainstream' in France. As the ex-wife of France's *enfant terrible* Serge Gainsbourg, Jane Birkin actually benefits from a semi-cult status, despite being 'merely' an interpreter. Similarly, De Palmas crosses various taste zones since he is at once a singer-songwriter and a serial chart-topper since his first release in 1995. The artists mentioned by Cécile were therefore not obviously 'mainstream', yet mainstream enough for her to have kept her preferences quiet so far, for fear of receiving unfavourable comments ('or else I'll have the piss taken out of me').[11] In fact, nobody seemed to judge her badly, everyone replying sweetly that her tastes were 'fair enough'. Cécile's remark emphasized, however, that social anxiety stood at the heart of her alternative identity, and that (the male) members of her group of friends inflicted, even unknowingly, taste constraints upon her. In a manner similar to that of Loïc who could no longer listen to Louise Attaque because of an invisible yet strongly felt socio-cultural pressure, Cécile enacted upon herself a form of self-censorship because of how she interpreted the reactions of others around her. In both cases, claiming or not claiming specific music tastes was guided by an anxiety to maintain cultural prestige.

---

9   'Le CD était sorti depuis longtemps avant que ça marche'; 'un succès à l'ancienne, en tournant beaucoup'.

10   'Des indépendants, ils avaient une certaine éthique.'

11   'Je vais me faire foutre de ma gueule, sinon.'

Social Distinction and Narratives of Anxiety

Fear of peer-pressure, a desire for exclusivity and a need for cultural distinction were also at the heart of a long one-to-one interview with a female student, Isabella, whom I met in July 2000 at the Saint-Nolff festival. Sitting alone at a bar table, her hair loose on her shoulders and wearing a colourful top, Isabella, 23, smoked a roll-up cigarette. She looked every bit as hippyish as any female festival-goer. Prompted about her likes and dislikes in music, she categorically rejected all forms of mainstream music, remarking: 'mainstream pop is for a less initiated audience, like, everyone has to like it, it's for the masses, you know'. She claimed that her approach was different: 'I try to escape the masses, they scare me a bit. Maybe because it's too easy, listening to the same stuff as everybody else, it's like being forced into the same... it's nice to tread a different path, you know.'[12] She considered that a homogeneous mass audience existed, which was given over to facility and conformity (the French expression she left unfinished refers to being forced in a 'mould'), and implicitly opposed this to a knowledgeable, experienced ('initiated') audience. Of course, Isabella's presence at the Saint-Nolff festival both reinforced her sense of belonging to a 'special' audience of festival-goers, and contradicted her declaration of exclusivity since some 3,000 people attended the event alongside her.

Lengthy individual interviews can be most usefully examined from the angle of narrative analysis theory, which considers that informants construct, as they speak, 'first-person accounts of experience' (Coffey and Atkinson, 1996, p. 54). These narratives, or personal interpretations of the socio-cultural reality that surrounds the locutors, are usually modelled on traditional patterns of story-telling, and can often be reduced to the plot sequence of a departure point, followed by a complication or obstacle, ending with a result or evaluation (Coffey and Atkinson, · p. 60). In terms of narrative analysis, Isabella's projection of an alternative identity onto a story-telling framework was transparent. The institutions of mass mediatization and mainstream music were the departure point of her personal trajectory, with threatening obstacles ('they scare me') leading to her fleeing away ('I try to escape'), and going elsewhere amounted to an ultimate resolution and her sense of satisfaction ('it's nice to tread a different path'). Isabella presented herself as an outcast, unwilling to submit to an oppressive system, in a discourse that revealed both its imaginary, naive force (the story of the all-powerful commercial system) and its real implications (she did avoid the mainstream media, she came to festivals, she despised *variété*, and so on).

Using a vocabulary of violent emotions (fear, escape), Isabella espoused the pattern observed by Auslander (1999, p. 7 and p. 83) among rock music fans in

---

12 'La variété c'est quand même pour un public moins initié, il faut que tout le monde aime ça, c'est la grosse masse, quoi'; 'je fuis un peu la grosse masse, ça me fait un peu peur. Peut-être parce que c'est trop facile, écouter la même chose que tout le monde, c'est aussi rentrer dans un certain... c'est bien d'aller dans d'autres sentiers, quoi'.

the US, whose sense of authenticity was a performative process based on just such feelings of oppression. The terms chosen by Isabella, including 'the masses', 'easy', 'initiated' and 'different paths', were also strikingly similar to those uttered by the French classical music buffs interviewed by Hennion, Maisonneuve and Gomart (2000, esp. p. 95, p. 100 and p. 102), and by the UK clubbers who posit themselves against 'chartpop disco' (Thornton, 1995, p. 99). This analogy between her self-representation as alternative, and that of American rock fans, French classical music *amateurs* and UK dance fans, suggests that anxieties about social distinction are a fact and a need of human life, rather than a generational affectation or a national, gendered or socio-economic phenomenon. Like Loïc, Isabella favoured taking risks (going elsewhere, setting off into the unknown) and, like so many others before her, she displayed the characteristics of the 'adventurer' (see Hennion, Maisonneuve and Gomart, 2000, p. 121) whose tastes and musical emotions emerge out of danger and destabilization.

In her statements of defensive individuality, Isabella also trod a thin line between self-satisfaction and snobbery. On the one hand, she appeared very tentative, modulating her discourse with hesitation markers ('like', 'you know'), aborting sentences, pausing frequently. On the other hand, this threw into sharper relief her central argument, namely that she had found a satisfactory resolution to the obstacles in her cultural life by pursuing individuality at all costs. She only had derogatory comments for 'others', those presumably not as daring as herself, and came across in this respect as rather dismissive. At an individual level, she exemplified the views of David Morley and Kevin Robins (1989, p. 15) on the reactionary formation of taste cultures, whereby 'the defense of a given "cultural identity" easily slips into the most hackneyed nationalism, or even racism, and the nationalist affirmation of the superiority of one group over another'. Without going so far as to brand as racist what remains a quite harmless cultural identity, it is nonetheless important to stress that narratives and expressions of self-worth, such as those produced by Isabella, can often be 'conservative and preservative, tapping into the dominant worldview' (Plummer, 1995, p. 178). It is equally true that there exist 'reactionary elements within popular culture' (Moores, 1993, p. 131). In this instance, while actually striving to avoid the dominant worldview, Isabella revealed that her agency as a cultural consumer was, as Thomas Austin (2002, p. 80) put it regarding Hollywood film viewers, 'not necessarily progressive'. Despite being a non-mainstream audience member, and thus being different on one level from the fans of US blockbusters observed by Austin, Isabella still displayed some simplistic and reactionary views that could be deemed characteristic of more conservative audiences. In particular, she showed rigidity in her tastes, contempt for commercially successful music and a misguided belief in the homogeneity of its audience. Such views ran contrary to her preference for sophistication and subtlety in her cultural life. These points must not take us away from the pleasure that individuals can feel when surrounded by music, but it is equally important to recognize that such emotions, because they serve to shape personal identities against imagined others, can entail a fair amount of defensiveness.

Another extract from Isabella's discourse revealed her deep-seated preoccupation with social distinction, even within 'alternative' circles. Elaborating on the music she liked and disliked, she picked the *chanson néo-réaliste* band La Tordue, who were performing at Saint-Nolff, as an example around which to situate her identity. As discussed in Chapter 2, La Tordue's preference for acoustic music and left-wing politics epitomizes their non-mainstream identity. Isabella, however, took a different approach:

> You know, La Tordue is a passing fad, it's a word-of-mouth fad alright, but all the people around me listen to them, and I just don't want to listen to the same stuff as they do. I decided that I wouldn't do the same thing as them [my friends], so I don't listen to that. ... Maybe I'm missing out, like, but you know.[13]

Acknowledging that the band's fame was due not to the mass media but to the more marginal network of word of mouth, she still discarded them on the grounds of fashion ('phénomène de mode'). Her repetitive remarks about 'not listening' established as an obstacle the possibility of taste-sharing with her acquaintances, so that even within her own circle of non-mainstream friends, she remained conscious of a certain conformity and consciously sought to avoid it. Strikingly, she admitted that she denied herself potential musical pleasure, purely out of stubbornness. Auditive pleasure, in her case, did not seem to be what her musical identity was about. Music was a means through which she asserted her defiance of any perceived form of consensus, and asserted her personal 'intrinsic quality' according to a set of imaginary criteria (Bourdieu, 1979, p. 320).

Such an extreme position raises the question of representativeness. Qualitative audience research always runs the risk of being anecdotal, and David Morley (2006, p. 268) has stressed that any consideration of audiences should open up onto processes of 'general applicability'. On the one hand, Isabella was unrepresentative of broader behaviours, being extremely self-conscious and more 'perverse' ('tordue'?) in her musical tastes than, for instance, the previous informants Loïc and Cécile. Loïc seemed to regret his change of heart about Louise Attaque, and Cécile felt the need to 'come clean' with her mainstream tastes. Isabella, however, actively created the conditions of her own dissatisfaction, isolating herself both from the dreaded 'masses' and from her like-minded peers. Not surprisingly, many of the acts performing at Saint-Nolff left her cold, including the British indie rock band Muse and the French singer-songwriter Tété. Nonetheless, even in her peremptory declarations, she echoed the general tendency of 'alternative' audiences to construct their cultural identities through polar opposites, staging the existence of fears and dangers in mainstream music, and activating stringent criteria

---

13 'Tu vois, La Tordue, c'est un phénomène de mode, c'est une mode de bouche à oreille mais tous les jeunes autour de moi ils écoutent ça, et j'ai pas envie d'écouter comme eux. J'ai décidé que je voulais pas faire comme eux alors j'écoute pas. ... Je passe à côté, ça se trouve, mais bon.'

of distinction, which might be imaginary, yet still have 'very real' implications in everyday life (Auslander, 1999, p. 70). Isabella's *cas-limite*, moreover, echoed other general patterns about the consumption of the music media in France. Like many interviewees, she rejected the mainstream media, and praised instead a handful of magazines, radio and TV programmes, which included *Télérama*, France Inter and Arte. All these outlets were also quoted frequently by other interviewees, and have established connections with 'high' quality, left-wing ideologies and the French intellectual elite. These specific tastes thus hinted at Isabella's inscription within a broader and definable cultural group.

Real Tactics and Imaginary Power

When asked about their media consumption, most audiences insisted on their selective appropriation of the press, the radio and television, cultivating an 'adventurous' approach to culture. Yannick asserted that he would rather 'go and find out about something I don't yet know'; Isabella wished to 'discover artists you've never heard of'.[14] They and others cross-checked information from select magazines, radio shows and TV programmes, distinguishing between overtly visible artists, and more original or 'secret' ones. 'I read reviews, I sort things out, I select stuff ... it's good to contrast opinion', said one; and another: 'yeah, I feel I'm active, lots of information overlaps and you can avoid commercial stuff'.[15] A sense of pride pervaded all these statements ('it's good', 'I'm active', 'I discover'), as informants explained that keeping on the look-out for new music not only permitted them to outwit the industry, but also to feel good about themselves.

Such declarations were reminiscent of the analysis of transgressive behaviours in everyday life by Michel de Certeau (1990, p. 60), who classified the various 'tactics' (at the individual level) and 'strategies' (at the institutional level) that could be deployed against oppressive structures. In this context, the mass media and mainstream music were cast as an abstract, ever-shifting entity, which interviewees sought to avoid through a series of tactics. The use of a vocabulary of 'traps' and 'tricks' was most evident in the narrative of Léonore, a 20-year-old student from La Rochelle, who admitted to being 'a big consumer of CDs' and thus facing a dilemma as an alternative person. She conceded that 'it's true, I can't say I'm outside the system, like'.[16] Aware of this ambiguity, she had developed her own ways of dealing with the omnipresent 'system':

---

14 '... aller voir plutôt autre chose que je connais pas'; 'découvrir des artistes qu'on connaît pas du tout'.

15 'Je lis les critiques, je fais des tris, des sélections ... c'est bien de recouper ces avis'; 'Ouais, j'ai l'impression d'être actif, plein d'infos se recoupent et t'évites le truc commercial'.

16 '... une grande consommatrice de CDs', 'c'est vrai, je peux pas dire que je l'évite, le système'.

They try to trap you, you know. You mustn't forget that it's for profits above all else. You have to be careful .... In record shops, I go to the 'independent' section. For instance in Fnac, I look at what's in the display sections, all those albums piled up by the dozen, but then there's something that there's only one copy of, well that's what I like best.[17]

Her danger narrative was transparent. The music industry and record shops were threats, which the impersonal turn of the sentences (quite obvious in the French original) presented as widespread. Her cultural life being dominated by a vague, ubiquitous enemy, she had put concrete avoiding tactics in place, which left her pleased with herself (the positive resolution of 'that's what I like').

Such frenetic activity should not, however, be mistaken for 'power' (Morley, 2006, p. 278). Even in his largely enthusiastic assessment of people's ruses and stratagems, de Certeau recognized that such alternative behaviours were actually 'an art of the weak' (1990, p. 61). Léonore's satisfactory resolution to her own danger narrative cannot be divorced from the fact that shop owners capitalize on a non-mainstream clientele, intentionally dividing taste zones within the shopping space (Hennion, Maisonneuve and Gomart, 2000, p. 85 and p. 111). Equally, record producers cater for alternative tastes with visual devices such as cardboard packaging and the absence of 'star' photographs (see Chapter 1). The French rock artists that Léonore quoted as some of her favourite included Négresses Vertes, La Tordue and Yann Tiersen, whose records were all displayed in both the indie-looking 'French rock' aisle and the more mainstream *variété* section of Fnac shops that very summer. Her sense of self as a cunning, empowered music consumer was therefore as real to her as it was misinformed, her alternative identity being at once invented and materialized through the strategies (rather than the tactics, this time) of record retailers. Moreover, as the section below highlights, even apparently 'non-commercial' and 'alternative' media work together to announce the release of the same artists, thereby comforting audiences in the importance of their tastes, in much the same way that more mainstream media showcase their own products. Rather than dwelling on the radical role played by 'alternative' tastes, then, it is more appropriate to recognize that, when faced with the real contradiction of being anti-consumerist consumers, Léonore and the others performed an 'imaginary resolution' to their dilemmas (Jameson, 1984, p. 77), a 'subjective definition' of the social world around them (Flick, 1998, p. 117).

---

17 'Y'a des pièges, quoi. Faut pas oublier que c'est pour le profit avant tout. Faut faire attention. ... chez les disquaires, je vais au rayon indépendant. Par exemple à la Fnac, je regarde ce qu'il y a en tête de gondole, tous les albums qui sont par dix ou par vingt, mais ceux qui sont en un exemplaire, bon bah je préfère.'

Distinction in Media Consumption

Studying music practices in the US, Auslander (1999, p. 10 and p. 92) claimed that popular music was nowadays primarily experienced through television, especially since the advent of the channel MTV in 1981, dedicated to music videos. Consequently, perceptions of 'authenticity' for all consumer groups were now defined through a televised experience of music. In France, however, this is not quite the case. Even though the channel M6 was launched in 1986 with the express purpose of competing with MTV (Hare, 2003, p. 71), and despite an overall increase in the number of hours spent watching television (Mermet, 2000, p. 389), the French public does not tend to consider television as an important means of music consumption. In fact, since the 1970s, the number of live rock concerts in France has greatly increased (Mermet, 2000, p. 395), and listening to music on the radio and with home-entertainment equipment, as opposed to watching it on TV, is the leisure practice that has increased the most (Mermet, 2000, p. 423).[18] In particular, figures for radio-listening are 'excellent' according to the profession, and the year 2007 was the country's all-time high for the number of radio listeners, across all types of stations (including those dedicated to music) and audience groups (Brocard, 2008). The French population therefore tends to be more old-fashioned, compared to the US, in its conception of what constitutes musical 'authenticity', often opposing it to TV broadcast and considering the radio as one of the main media through which it can be enjoyed.

Like the majority of my interviewees, Isabella both followed and differed from this national trend, as she rejected commercial radio stations in general but engaged with the radio often, if selectively. NRJ, France's most successful music station, was usually despised by respondents for its 'repetitiveness' and 'mechanical' character.[19] 'NRJ just plays music for making money, it's commercial',[20] one person said, summarizing fairly accurately the station's motto of broadcasting 'hit music only' in order to please its sponsors (see Chapter 1). By contrast, local and 'independent' radio stations were received positively, several interviewees mentioning Canal B in Rennes, Jet FM in Nantes and Cigale Mécanik in Toulouse as such examples of praiseworthy autonomy. The latter, for instance, boasted on its website its 'rebel' youth audience and 'rare' music selection, including the indie rock bands Mano Negra and Zebda as examples of its 'daring' playlist.[21] Many respondents also praised the music selection of France Inter, the state-funded generalist station whose playlist is not dependent on sponsors.

---

18   This research is not concerned with the Internet, whose intensive use started around the turn of the twenty-first century and did not affect the present study.
19   Hennion's audiences also tended to reject the radio (2000, p. 129).
20   'Sur NRJ, c'est que de la musique pour vendre, c'est commercial'.
21   '[Nous diffusons] l'univers du rock parallèle en France, celui qui n'est que peu diffusé, écouté par une jeunesse contestataire et différente, hors des sentiers du show-biz; le rock alternatif, le rock à tendance subversive, souterraine et hexagonale.'

For many, the press, radio and television could not be taken in isolation from one another, and the cultural values of one were often found in the format of another. In particular, France Inter was often perceived by respondents as being linked to the weekly cultural magazine *Télérama*. Marie, a newly qualified teacher of 24 interviewed in Carhaix, was particularly explicit in this respect: 'personally, I go for quality above all. In *Télérama* they have that sort of quality criteria, you know... and France Inter, well that's a bit more targeted, in the style of *Télérama*.'[22] The adjective 'targeted' ['ciblé'] echoed Isabella's preference for an 'initiated' audience, and implied that quality could only arise within a niche market. Meanwhile, the association of state-funded radio with 'coolness' confirmed the observations of Chapter 1 on the national and 'anti-commercial' authenticity of this publicly funded media.[23] *Télérama*'s music critics have regularly and favourably reviewed French 'alternative' rock artists over the years, including Têtes Raides, Zebda and Manu Chao. It is not incidental, in this respect, that when Manu Chao released his third solo album *La Radiolina* in 2007, he chose the studio of France Inter as the only venue for a live performance in France that year (on 29 September), while *Télérama* adorned its front cover with a picture of the artist, with a caption that underlined the 'ethics' of the artist ('Chao: fair-trade rock').[24] Such convergence of interests between different types of media is not unusual. Back in the 1960s, the radio station Europe 1 and the teenage magazine *Salut les copains* worked jointly (Tinker, 2007), while today the radio station NRJ and the commercial channels TF1 and M6 often create partnerships (see below). What is important to stress here, then, is that the same strategy applies to so-called 'alternative' networks too, giving them added weight as mediators of France's anti-mainstream and left-wing protest.

Another magazine mentioned by interviewees as an important source of alternative music information (albeit not solely on French groups) was *Les Inrockuptibles*. Initially launched as a music monthly in the late 1980s, *Les Inrocks* eventually came to share direct parallels with the media mentioned above, giving birth to an eponymous music programme on France Inter in 1990, and competing directly with *Télérama* when it adopted a weekly format including a TV guide in 1995 (Pires, 2003, p. 94). *Les Inrocks* has also been described as an austere, sophisticated magazine, whose designated cultural enemy, the *beauf*, grants its editors a 'new kind of legitimacy' as members of the vanguard (Andrews, 2000, p. 236 and p. 245).[25] The centrality of *Télérama*, *Les Inrockuptibles* and France Inter

---

22   'Moi, je fais un choix de qualité avant tout. ... dans *Télérama* y'a quand même un certain critère de qualité. ... sur France Inter, c'est déjà plus ciblé, genre *Télérama*'.

23   Hennion's classical music audiences also mentioned *Télérama* as a valuable source of information (2000, p. 136 and p. 139).

24   'Manu Chao: le rock équitable', front cover of *Télérama* no. 3007, 29 December 2007.

25   Andrews' analysis of the magazine uses a Bourdieusian framework, which also demonstrates the ongoing relevance of his sociology for today's cultural identities –

in the respondents' mediation of their alternative music knowledge reveals, ultimately, a central contradiction with regard to the formulation of their identities. The many references to these well-established media show that an anti-mainstream position vis-à-vis popular music can actually occupy the middle ground, while the audiences' sense of 'alternative' distinction is expressed and disseminated through some of the most popular and, for this reason, 'dominant', media in France. Before exploring this contradiction further, it is worth saying a word about music consumption on television.

Interviewees barely watched television, and usually not with the purpose of listening to music. Significantly, the channel M6, which broadcasts annually around 2,500 hours of music videos against an average of 300 for other channels (Hare, 2003, p. 72), was rejected as 'too commercial', pandering to advertisers ('faire de la pub') and discouraging musical originality. The few music programmes which received the interviewees' approval were *Tracks* and *Music Planet*, both broadcast on Arte. Arte is a publicly funded Franco-German channel, launched in 1991 and introduced as 'the cultural channel'. Arte does not have commercial breaks, uses subtitles rather than dubbing when broadcasting foreign programmes, and therefore unambiguously privileges 'high' culture. *Tracks*, which is broadcast once a week at the somewhat inaccessible hour of 11.30p.m. (with a repeat at 2.30a.m.), boasts its 'original and off-beat' identity.[26] This example clarifies the existence of a cultural dichotomy in TV viewing practices in France, with most respondents participating in a *de facto* 'non-mainstream' television experience because of the late broadcast (not prime-time), and the association of their favourite channel with state-sponsored intellectualism. Auslander (1999, p. 87) observed that American viewers watching music on MTV felt a sense of cultural distinction, but the state-sponsored nature of 'authenticity' and 'quality' in music programmes in France is a significant departure from his analysis. The officially sanctioned character of alternative tastes in France would seem to lend participants a greater degree of confidence than is the case for other national groups, and explain that popular music in France, as Looseley (2003, p. 6) stressed, is perhaps the most significant sector in recent years in which the process of cultural and national legitimation by the state can be seen in action.

Some respondents also mentioned watching the live music segment of *Nulle Part Ailleurs* (NPA), a general-interest programme broadcast on Canal +. NPA stopped in 2001 but had, over the years, become a staple of provocative, anti-establishment humour since its creation in 1987, and its daily live music sessions were associated with this anti-conservatism.[27] Antoine de Caunes, famous in the

---

and points to the old-fashionedness or, in Andrews's terms, the 'social ageing', of the French vanguard.

26 'Le magazine des musiques émergentes et décalées', www.arte.tv/fr, last accessed 23 March 2009.

27 Auslander (1999, fn. 41 p. 88) noted the links between the US satirical programme *Saturday Night Live* and a taste for alternative rock. The comic *quatuor* (later trio)

UK for fronting the comedy shows *Rapido* and *Eurotrash*, was NPA's long-time co-presenter. De Caunes actually started as a rock music journalist, hosting France's first rock music programme on TV, *Les Enfants du Rock*, in the early 1980s. *Les Enfants du Rock* also launched the career of Bernard Lenoir, who later hosted the radio show 'Les Inrockuptibles' on France Inter (relabelled 'C'est Lenoir' in the mid-1990s), presided over the creation of the eponymous music magazine, and co-founded the rock music festival La Route du Rock, where French 'indie' acts over the years have included Yann Tiersen and Rachid Taha (see Chapters 2 and 3). These connections expose the somewhat 'incestuous' relationships between the TV, the radio and the press in France, and the broad terrain over which the country's 'alternative' culture is mapped out.

This cultural mapping (and bordering – in the sense of excluding the mainstream) was further exemplified in July 2000 when an article in *Télérama* reviewed the place of rock music on French television.[28] Not surprisingly, *Télérama* highlighted *Tracks* and NPA as two welcome exceptions to French television's general reluctance to broadcast rock music, praising these programmes' trendy niche audience, their 'vanguard, curious and underground' image, and their overall 'counter-cultural' identity.[29] This flurry of high-brow qualifiers were reflected in the vocabulary used by interviewees, establishing clear parallels between *Télérama*'s journalists and music audiences in their discussion of what were, furthermore, the same programmes. On a linguistic and cultural level, a seemingly coherent 'alternative' identity thus existed in France in the late 1990s and early 2000s, which was mobilized through the same select range of media, vocabulary and cultural assumptions, and given national gravitas through its re-assertion in well-known, often state-funded media, by a number of high-profile journalists.

Marginality, Consensus and the Right–Left Divide

This non-mainstream music culture is far from being marginal, then, and the media that audiences referred to as sources of 'alternative' knowledge all in fact enjoy a high degree of popularity. When considered as a generalist weekly rather than a TV guide, *Télérama* is France's second best-selling cultural magazine, with around 2.7 million readers in 1999, after *Paris-Match* with just over 4 million (Mermet, 2000, p. 432). Despite its lower circulation figures as a specialist music magazine, *Les Inrockuptibles* has steadily increased its sales since the 1990s, with 34,500 copies in 1998 (*L'Année du Disque*, 1999, p. 139) and over 40,000 in 2001 (Mongeau, 2002). Among the generalists, France Inter is France's third

---

Les Nuls, which performed on NPA until the mid-1990s, explicitly based its sketches on SNL.

28 'Pas très rock'n'roll, la télé', *Télérama* no. 2636, 19 July 2000, pp. 52–4.

29 '… public branché et pointu', '[Tracks est] à contre-courants, … avant-gardiste, curieuse et friande d'underground'.

most-listened-to station with 10 per cent of the radio audience, behind the commercial stations RTL and Europe 1 (Mermet, 2000, p. 422). These statistics, coupled with the similarities in the discourse of journalists and audiences, illustrate the hold of non-mainstream tastes over the French media at the turn of the twenty-first century, and signal the somewhat conventional, predictable character of these tastes. 'Alternative' tastes might be about protesting against mainstream music and modes of production, but they are not necessarily, and indeed are rarely, surprising or subversive.

The numerical significance and cultural power enjoyed by these media do not alter the fact that they are, nevertheless, subordinate to, and indeed 'dominated' by, the most heavily consumed media. *Paris-Match* and RTL, assuming they are not usually read or listened to by the same people who consume *Télérama* and France Inter (although some overlapping certainly occurs), boast audience figures almost twice as high as the latter, and France Inter only fares well when compared with other generalist stations, whereas we might recall that the commercial music-specific NRJ is, by far, France's most popular radio station (Arteta, 2003; see Chapter 1). Moreover, these best-selling media are also associated with the symbolic and economic power of right-wing ideologies. *Paris-Match* is famous for its right-of-centre affiliation and sensationalist approach to news, publishing eye-catching photographs of celebrities and accidents (Provencher, 2003, p. 41). Meanwhile, the most popular show on the station RTL is 'Les Grosses Têtes', a crude, often homophobic and chauvinistic comedy programme (Mermet, 2000, p. 422). The radio station NRJ also has a deal with France's most popular television channel, TF1, for the retransmission of the NRJ Music Awards (Arteta, 2003), and TF1 is often presented as the flagship of neo-liberalism for its emphasis on audience share and the broadcasting of celebrity chat shows during prime-time (Mermet, 2000, p. 404).

Given their much higher audience and circulation rates, these media outlets (NRJ, *Paris-Match*, TF1) are statistically more mainstream, and more economically 'dominant', than their 'intellectual' counterparts. Their contents are also a far cry from *Télérama*'s wordy exposés of moral issues, France Inter's left-leaning tendencies and NPA's political satire, meaning that the latter become non-mainstream by virtue of their open contrast with the dominant presence of the former. In terms of media coverage and audience figures, therefore, mainstream music, commercial media and populist programmes do dominate France's cultural landscape. Consequently, and even if it does not constitute a rare, victimized or rebel identity, an alternative to this statistical domination does make sense, and engaging with culture in, literally, an other way, is highly significant for many.

The differences between these media also indicate that the cultural split between alternative and mainstream identities in France closely follows the divide between the political right and the left, with commercial success and mainstream exposure usually equated with the conservative values of the right. In 2000, a cartoon published in the radical left-wing satirical weekly *Charlie Hebdo* made this connection evident. The cartoon illustrated an interview with the band Zebda, and depicted a French couple watching the band on TV, wondering in unison: 'Are Zebda right-wing because they're appearing on TF1, or are TF1 left-wing because they're showing Zebda?'.[30] This caption referred to Zebda's relentless TV promotion around 1999, after years of small-scale success and anti-government claims that had brought them an initial reputation as authentic protest artists (Chapter 3). The cartoon's reference to a confusion of values was more than a joke, however. It touched on the fundamental perception that TF1, France's most-watched TV channel, propagated populist values, and that an artist's crossover to the mainstream irreversibly shifted their political identity to the right.

The uncontested association of TF1 with right-wing conservatism was also taken for granted by the left-wing, 'anti-liberal' (in the economic sense) magazine *Marianne* in July 2007. Assessing the two-month-old presidency of Nicolas Sarkozy, *Marianne* displayed on its front cover a picture of the rock veteran Johnny Hallyday, with a caption reading 'Sarkozy at the Elysée: why the values of TF1 have triumphed' (see illustration 5.1).[31] The mismatch between the photo and its caption (a picture of Hallyday, but a commentary on Sarkozy and TF1) established the unquestioned merging of *variétés* (Hallyday) with profit-making media (TF1) and reactionary politics (Sarkozy). By implication, the left-wing press (such as *Marianne*), 'serious' popular music and vanguard-thinking were diametrically opposed to these. Here, on the front page of a widely read magazine, was an overt sign of irreconcilable differences between the right and the left in the French cultural landscape, which affected discussions of popular music.

The perception of a neat cultural divide in France along mainstream/alternative music lines and right/left political positions does not just come from the left. In May 2007, a concert was organized on the Place de la Concorde to celebrate the new president's victory, and among those present were Johnny Hallyday, the *pied-noir* Enrico Macias and the prim Piaf copycat Mireille Mathieu. A few weeks after the concert, which was criticized by the left-wing opposition as a collection of 'fuddy-duddy ex-stars of the music-hall and TF1' (Le Vaillant, 2007),[32] Jean-Pierre Pasqualini, the director of France's self-declared *variété* magazine, *Platine*, wrote an angry editorial. In his paper, Pasqualini (2007) defended these apparently pro-Sarkozy stars against accusations of their implicit conservatism, by dismissing the view that singing for this President had to be a sign of commitment to the right. Instead, he argued, these artists were only there to congratulate the will of the majority, since the President had won the election. In any case, he added, popular music was 'simply meant to entertain', including entertaining the military and political elite. As a result, Pasqualini continued, participating in political events was neither a sign of 'being political', nor 'significant' in judging the quality of artists.

---

30   'Est-ce que Zebda est de droite parce qu'il passe sur TF1, ou bien TF1 de gauche parce qu'elle passe Zebda?', cartoon by Charb, in Cyran (2000, p. 10).

31   'Sarkozy à l'Elysée [the presidential palace]: pourquoi les valeurs de TF1 ont gagné', front cover of *Marianne* no. 535, 21 July 2007.

32   '[Les] vieilles gloires tartignolles du music-hall et de TF1 réunis'.

Illustration 5.1   Front page of the weekly magazine *Marianne*, no.535, 21–7 July
                    2007. Reproduced by kind permission of Aline Fayet, on behalf
                    of the publisher.

Finally, he also accused the left-leaning critics of *variété* of being 'intolerant', self-righteous and out of touch with 'real' people.[33]

Pasqualini had a point. By highlighting the contrast between the left's discourse of marginalisation, and the reality of its socio-economic privilege, he touched on the central contradiction of the French left, which has, at least since the creation of the SFIO in 1910 (later to evolve into the Parti Socialiste), declared itself a workers' party while receiving most of its support from teachers and the middle classes (Bell, 1997, p. 19). This trend only increased in the 1980s, as an affluent middle class interested in socialist issues grew, for which the neologism of *gauche caviar* (champagne socialists) was even forged (Reader, 1987). Moreover, Pasqualini's paper derided the snobbery of left-wing admonitions, partially deconsecrating the notion of political commitment as a sign of artistic authenticity. In so doing, he interestingly questioned the assumed links between the left, prestige and popular authenticity, denying the left the monopoly of 'quality' in music, and apparently exploding the binary discourse that had shaped the reception of popular music in France for decades.

Nevertheless, his argument as a whole contained key assumptions and contradictions which ultimately undermined it and re-inscribed it within the old polarization between *variété* as conservative, and non-*variété* as more progressive. Indeed, his very sensitivity to attacks against *variété* stars actually lent weight to the existence of both a distinct anti-*variété* campaign, and a *variété* victim group. Either way, he seemed to agree with his detractors about the existence of two clans being pitted against each other. After all, he was the creator of France's first and only magazine openly dedicated to *variété* ('Platine, le magazine de la variété'), a title that necessarily antagonizes whatever artists or genres might be considered as non-*variété*, and is the intentional mirror image of the older monthly *Chorus*, subtitled 'Les Cahiers de la chanson' ['*Chanson*'s Notebooks']. In addition, Pasqualini followed a line of reasoning that ran completely contrary to that already identified as left-wing and 'alternative', in particular by considering popular music as merely 'entertaining' (rather than, say, intellectually significant), and as non-committed (rather than anti-Establishment, for instance). His refusal to see a connection between the presence of specific artists at the presidential concert and commitment to the right was also rather dubious. For one, Hallyday, Mathieu and Macias were all decorated with the Légion d'Honneur by Jacques Chirac in 1997, 1999 and 2007 respectively, and if this did not necessarily prove their personal support for the right-wing Chirac, it still showed their willingness to accept these official honours from the hands of an arch-conservative. Moreover, it is well known in France that both Hallyday and Mathieu are personal friends of Chirac and Sarkozy

---

33   'Ces artistes ne peuvent-ils pas se réjouir ... de voir s'appliquer la volonté de la majorité du peuple? ... La chanson est faite pour distraire .... Les artistes ont toujours été essentiellement là pour animer les militaires ou les politiques .... Chanter lors d'une manifestation politique ne signifie rien ... nous avons voulu interviewer une "victime" de cette nouvelle intolérance.'

(Dicale, 2006, p. 211), while Macias has built his career as a *pied-noir* regretting his forced post-colonial exile – hardly a progressive attitude (Dicale, p. 368; see Chapter 3).[34] Despite Pasqualini's best efforts, then, playing at the concert which celebrated the victory of Sarkozy could hardly be a stronger sign of right-wing conservatism (or maybe of blind political apathy, but that may amount to the same). In either case, it only confirmed that conservative artists tended to belong to the genre of *variété*, and vice versa. Pasqualini therefore not only seemed unable to break the binary oppositions that qualify French popular music, but actually re-inscribed himself within the old polarization by openly defending *variété* artists (and not others), and their endorsement of reactionary politics.

This *querelle* about the potential political affiliation of artists signals how popular music in France is almost always ideologically loaded, even in the case of apolitical songs, and that music remains a catalyst for socio-cultural positioning within what is often considered and constructed as a hermetically sealed, mutually exclusive binary system. This example also underlines the fact that it is virtually impossible to speak of French popular music, in France, in neutral terms, given the 'baggage' that both *chanson* and *variété* carry. Simply translating the notion of 'French popular music' into 'musique populaire' would open itself up to many conflicts, because the adjective 'populaire' can have vastly different meanings, connoting on the one hand great commercial success, and thus being suspicious for the left-wing fringes, or on the other hand working-class bonding, and then eliciting either praise for its implied leftist fraternity, or rejection for its implied *beauf* crassness. As a result, the re-inscription of alternative audiences into a squarely left-wing social milieu is quite inevitable, as well, maybe, as being a mark of their 'Frenchness'.

Self-Representations and Self-Awareness

The ingrained yet quite transparent bi-polarization of French popular music along set political lines explains why interviewees would typically define their musical identities in, literally, counter-cultural terms. Unlike the members of a generic subculture who would take pride in their 'goth', 'rave' or 'gangsta' self-image, they principally defined their tastes simply through their antagonism toward *variété*. On one level, this 'tunnel vision' responded to the biased nature of this research, which looked for expressions of 'alternative' identity at the expense of other, less strict or more indifferent formulations of identity, and influenced the

---

34   On the relationships between Hallyday and the conservative Establishment, see Looseley (2005). On Mathieu as mainstream, conservative and catholic, see Leahy (2005). Macias modified the lyrics of a song he sang that night, in order to expressly celebrate Sarkozy's victory ('On est content pour Nicolas Sarkozy', to the tune of 'Enfants de tous pays'). The video of the concert was placed on Sarkozy's personal website: www.sarkozy. fr/video/index.php?intChannelId=2&intVideoId=1026, last accessed 23 March 2009.

data produced. This constitutes a serious methodological limitation that only a larger study could redress. However, the readiness of many audiences to claim their rejection of *variété* reveals the widespread character of such claims. Besides, not all respondents followed simplistic binaries in their positioning of themselves as a particular kind of audience member. Many, for instance, expressed a sense of unease about such loaded terms as 'alternative', 'authentic', 'rebel' or 'resistant'. Describing the music they liked, a substantial number of interviewees used the abbreviation *alterno* for *alternatif*, often in modulated phrases such as 'plutôt alterno' (rather alternative) or 'un peu alterno' (a bit alternative). This gentle diminutive brought a slight sense of derision to the adjective, and to their own musical identity. It seemed that these individuals had internalized the system of categorization described by the sociology of tastes, and anticipated accusations of elitism by downplaying, through this rhetorical device, their own cultural authority (Hennion, Maisonneuve and Gomart, 2000, p. 68).

The same pattern occurred during the conversation recorded in Rouen, when Cécile hesitated for a long time before attributing the adjective 'underground' (she used the English term) to the magazine *Télérama*. She had described the magazine thus: '... it's not mainstream like ..., it's kinda more... I don't know if you can say 'underground', but I discovered really fantastic stuff through their reviews.'[35] Understandably looking for a simple word to signify the bulk of her alternative aspirations (original, not mass-mediatized, meaningful, and so on), Cécile had stated her preference for non-mainstream acts ('fantastic' = 'underground'), and positioned *Télérama* as an important vehicle for her tastes. Yet, she had done so hesitantly and had only tentatively named what she really meant, therefore demonstrating her awareness of the social prestige to be derived by employing these terms, and her reluctance to use them without some sort of pre-emptive apology.

In relation to their avowed affiliation with cultural elitism and the left, many interviewees also acknowledged, truthfully and rather ashamedly, that they belonged to privileged backgrounds. Isabella, for instance, described her background as 'intellectual and leftie' ['un milieu intello-gauchiste'], using a compound phrase with, once again, an abbreviation (*intello* instead of *intellectuel*) that is commonly perceived to be pejorative in colloquial French. Other informants admitted to their middle-class background by using different distanciation techniques. Manue, the daughter of a bank clerk said 'well yeah, my parents are bourgeois', and Jérôme, the son of a teacher, concluded 'quite frankly, I know I am well-off' ['nanti'].[36] The terms 'bourgeois' and 'nanti' are rather derogatory in French and are used to refer to the affluent classes, especially in left-wing or radical left circles where declaring one's contempt for the bourgeoisie is *de rigueur*. Coupled with interjections and adverbs underlining the obviousness of the statements ('well yeah', 'frankly'), these terms suggested that the speakers were aware of their social privilege,

---

35 '[*Télérama*] c'est pas populo comme ..., c'est des trucs plus ... je sais pas si on peut dire underground, mais moi j'ai découvert des trucs géniaux grâce à leurs articles'.

36 '... bah oui, mes parents sont des bourgeois'; 'moi franchement, je suis nanti'.

and somewhat embarrassed by it. Similar declarations of self-awareness are also found in the music press, for instance with reference to the mainly affluent make-up of Manu Chao's audience (Chapter 4). Contrasting the artist's middle-class audience with the poorer public he met during his tour of Argentina, one *Inrockuptibles* journalist described his Western listeners thus: 'our lot, the privileged group of the Old World who can afford to buy CDs' (Deschamps, 2001, p. 39).[37]

Other respondents, upon acknowledging the ambivalence of their membership of an elite, reflected on their earlier declarations of alternative tastes and eventually softened their views against the mainstream. While still denying any affiliation to the right, they conceded that their disapproval of the mass media and mainstream music was too simplistic, unfair, or often pompous. In La Rochelle, Léonore remarked that her tastes mattered little in the grand scheme of things: 'but you know, everybody has different tastes'.[38] In Carhaix, another interviewee said:

> Well, personally I don't like *variété*, it pisses me off when people just listen to what they're fed, the stuff on television, all that shit. Maybe others are more careful with… but hey! In fact no, what I've just said is stupid, it sounds intolerant, each to their own and that's the end of it.[39]

Although he had started, like so many others, by opposing mass consumption to a small initiated group (those who are 'careful'), this young man's conclusion expressed a sense of exasperation with his own feeling of superiority, as he saw through the intolerance of criticizing mainstream tastes at all costs. Even Isabella, as she attempted to rate the small Saint-Nolff festival higher than the much larger, nearby event of Vieilles Charrues on her scale of good taste, eventually dropped this line of reasoning. Reconsidering her attempts at cultural distinction, she concluded by stating the need to keep a sense of balance: 'At the end of the day, everyone comes to a festival with who they are. Well, I suppose you could enjoy it [the Vieilles Charrues], but hey.'[40] Like the declarations above, her use of hesitation markers showed that she saw through her own elitism and felt uncomfortable with it. Finally, Loïc in the Rouen interview commented on his own preference and that of his peers for 'quality' by acknowledging, fatalistically but rightly so, that cultural identities were necessarily elaborated around processes of selection and exclusion: 'for sure, there's a taste for exclusivity, but that's just normal human snobbery'.[41] Loïc's conclusion interestingly relativized the process of identity construction, and

---

37   'Nous autres, les privilégiés du Vieux Monde qui peuvent [sic] se payer des CD'.
38   '… mais bon, c'est suivant les goûts et les couleurs'.
39   'Oh moi j'aime pas la variété, et puis ça m'énerve les gens qui écoutent que ce qu'on leur donne, ce qui passe à la télé. Y'en a d'autres qui font peut-être plus gaffe au… mais oh! En fait non, c'est con ce que je dis, ça fait intolérant, chacun ses goûts et merde.'
40   'Finalement, chacun aborde un festival à sa façon. Enfin, en même temps on peut être séduit, mais bon.'
41   'C'est sûr, y'a un goût de l'exclusif, mais c'est un snobisme humain!'

the significance of alternative denominations by the same token. He understood that cultural identities were necessarily established at the expense of others, and he expected others to dismiss his tastes just as he rejected theirs. An analyst of his own socio-cultural behaviour, Loïc found that his sense of superiority did not invalidate his tastes, although it did characterize them.

This brief foray into audience research raises a number of issues, which all point to the significance of expressions of 'alternative' music tastes in contemporary France. Firstly, audiences tended to engage with their cultural identities in negative terms (i.e. not mainstream), using vague and homogenizing definitions of the music genres and social groups they rejected (*variété*, *beaufs*), following the already well-analyzed pattern of the 'social logic of subcultural capital', which 'reveals itself most clearly by what it dislikes' (Thornton, 1995, p. 105). In particular, their cultural identity reinforced the perceived existence of a simplistic binary system, and produced and repeated its own set of conventions, in a manner contradicting its claims of marginality, contestation and destabilization. In this, they resembled other music groups observed before them, such as US rock fans, UK ravers or French classical music lovers, and probably mainstream music listeners, too, although research is unfortunately scarce in accounting for the practices and discourse of the (supposed) majority of music audiences (Thornton, 1995, p. 101; Morley, 2006, p. 274). At the same time, because a small number of commercial media outlets relentlessly broadcast a limited range of music which is often derivative and unsophisticated, defending an alternative to mainstream music consumption is meaningful and, overall, the sign of a healthy degree of democratic access to popular culture. In this sense, the fact that the French state still (but for how long?) subsidizes many radio stations, TV channels and, as the next chapter demonstrates, music festivals, with a view to disseminating an 'other', not so quickly profitable, type of music, is all the better for the French. The official recognition of 'alternative' music identities in France is thus at once a sign of their national specificity, their internal contradictions, and their sense of self-worth, for it undoubtedly gives participants more stability and resilience than is the case in other national contexts.

Chapter 6

Music Festivals as Sites of 'Alternative' Identities

In his 1998 edition of *Key Concepts in Popular Music*, Roy Shuker noted that, 'given their scale and significance', popular music festivals were curiously under-analyzed in academia (Shuker, 1998, p. 123). Some ten years later, the situation regarding studies on rock and pop music festivals has greatly improved, with a number of publications addressing such topics as the marketing of 'authenticity' in festivals, their media reception, networks of production, the audience's sense of local identity, and their sense of rupture from everyday life. Events covered include American rock festivals (Schowalter, 2000; Bennett, 2004), Canadian and Australian folk festivals (Hagen-Smith, 1995; Duffy, 2000), North American 'world music' festivals (Silverman, 2007), or the UK popular music festival of Glastonbury (McKay, 2000). Despite the evidence of an emerging trend for 'festival studies' in English-speaking academia, however, so far only one study has, to our knowledge, focused on France, a brief and somewhat outmoded discussion of the supposed 'conflict' between idealism and entrepreneurialism in the Brittany-based Route du Rock festival (Valéro, 2002). While the present chapter cannot aim to redress this imbalance, it suggests some further directions for the analysis of the meanings attached to music festivals in France by promoters, artists, journalists and, above all, audiences.

Following our exploration of 'alternative' music identities in contemporary France, this chapter considers the role of popular music festivals in the process of constructing 'anti-mainstream' discourses and practices. As live and collective events, which offer virtually non-stop music for several days and nights, often take place outdoors and tolerate public drink and drug consumption, music festivals are places that differ from people's everyday, home-bound and work-related routine, and from the dominant, individualized and mediatized mode of popular music consumption. Popular music festivals have also, at least since the late 1960s, been associated with left-wing politics, counter-culture, hippiedom and 'indie' music (Shuker, 1998, p. 123; McKay, 2000). They would therefore seem to provide an alternative environment to the channels of consumption of 'mainstream' music, and offer respite from the propagation of dominant ideologies. Audience interviews, based on the fieldwork described in the previous chapter, tend to confirm this, with festival-goers expressing their pleasure at the festival experience chiefly in terms of the destabilization of dominant media and dominant social conventions.

Nonetheless, when observing these spontaneous reactions, it is important to bear in mind the fact that live concerts are also a banal, widespread commodity, festivals in particular being imbricated within economic expectations that are themselves the result of local, national and international negotiations (Mazdon, 2007). Moreover, only a very low proportion of the population has never attended a live music show in their lives. Throughout the 1990s in France, a large proportion of the population regularly went to music concerts (Donnat, 1998, p. 248; Mermet, 2000, p. 449), and the participation in live music, including that of festivals, was systematically higher among the population most active in its engagement with mediatized music in the home (Donnat, 1998, p. 107). As a result, festival audiences tend to have a very high level of music consumption both at home and outside the home, meaning that festivals cannot really be seen to constitute an obvious 'disruption' of their cultural habits. The experience of festivals, for most audiences, involves a considerable degree of continuity and expectedness, which is the first contradiction that this chapter seeks to address. Furthermore, all accounts of festival experience reveal that the music bill is typically of secondary importance for the audience's sense of enjoyment of music festivals. By contrast, the atmosphere and collectivite character of these events are what primarily shape their pleasure of participation (McKay, 2000, p. 5; Laing, 2004, p. 7; GECE, 2007, p. 3). As a result, this chapter seeks to examine the physical characteristics of festival sites, including their insertion within a web of geographical, local and private concerns. This analysis reveals the tight regulatory system that codifies festivals, whose structural and economic rigidity is somewhat at odds with the experience of them by audiences (and artists and critics) as places of instability. Focusing on the French context, then, this chapter reconsiders the common perception that festivals are 'extra-ordinary' events, pointing out the inconsistencies on which the myth of a 'marginal' or 'alternative' authenticity is based.

Popular Music Festivals in France

Contemporary popular (pop and rock) music festivals are events organized over several days, often taking place outdoors, and showcasing the music of many different artists during a series of daytime, evening and night-time concerts (Shuker, 1998, p. 122). American and British rock cultures have provided, and to a large extent mythologized, the templates for such events, the names of the Woodstock festival (1969) and the Isle of Wight festival (1970) being frequently cited. It is perhaps surprising, therefore, to find that France is currently, at the start of the twenty-first century, the European leader in terms of the number of popular music festivals organized every year. In 2000, there were at least 1,000 music festivals registered in France, covering genres as diverse as rock, pop, classical, opera and jazz, while other arts festivals, including those for dance and theatre, were increasingly devoting parts of their programmes to multimedia performances featuring a strong musical component (Benito, 2001, p. 8 and p. 15).[1] The largest French music festival to date is the Festival Interceltique de Lorient, an 'ethnic' Celtic event launched in 1971 and held in Brittany, which attracted 325,000 participants in 2001 and upwards of 650,000 in 2006.[2] More broadly, France has, since the early 1990s, been the European leader in the number of themed outdoor cultural events, with over 5 million festival-goers ['festivaliers'] recorded in 1993, spread across a variety of music, dance, theatre, film and historical events (Delaroche, 1994, p. 48; Dicale 2006, p. 411). In the specific sphere of popular music, the number of festival-goers has increased 'exponentially' since the early 1980s (Benito, 2001, p. iii), pop and rock music festivals in France in 2006 boasting a combined audience of over 1.6 million people (Teillet, 2008, p. 28).

Among the most high-profile popular music festivals in France today is the Printemps de Bourges, which takes place in the town of Bourges in the Centre region south of Paris. It has taken place every year in April since 1977, and showcases a range of pop, rock, rap and electro acts from France and beyond. It attracted 100,000 participants in 1991, and had doubled in size by 1996 (Benito, 2001, p. 24). The Francofolies festival, set up in 1985 and taking place in July in the harbour and city centre of La Rochelle, is dedicated to popular music from France and French-speaking countries. Despite this restrictive bill, it drew in over 90,000 spectators in 1993 (Lupieri, 1994), and 101,000 in 2001 (Bessaguet, 2002). More impressive perhaps is the rapid growth of the Vieilles Charrues music festival, an outdoor rock and pop event launched in 1991 outside the town of Carhaix in Finistère (Western Brittany). This festival attracted a mere 500 participants in its first year, but pulled in an impressive 200,000 people in 1998, and has done so every year since.[3] Since the mid-1990s therefore, there have been at least four annual festivals of popular music in France attracting between 100,000 and 600,000 participants each. This compares interestingly with the UK, where the largest pop and rock festival to date, Glastonbury, peaked at an estimated 150,000 participants in 1999, and this figure has stagnated or fallen since (McKay, 2000, p. 39),[4] and with the US where the 1969 Woodstock festival registered around 450,000 participants in a country already far more populous than France is today (Bennett, 2004, p. xiv).

---

1   There were an estimated 600 music festivals in the UK and Ireland in 2007 (Walsh, 2008, p. 22).

2   Benito (2001, p. 24) and Festival Interceltique de Lorient, at www.festival-interceltique.com/?nav=D, last accessed 24 March 2009.

3   www.vieillescharrues.asso.fr/association/histor.php.

4   Glastonbury Festival, at www.glastonburyfestivals.co.uk/uploadedFiles/Information/Student_Information_Pack/5 per cent20Attendance per cent20Numbers.pdf, last accessed 24 March 2009.

State Decentralization and Commercial Profits

A number of factors can account for the popularity of music festivals in contemporary France, but the most important of these relates to the involvement of the state through public funding. France has been a fertile ground for other types of festival, especially film and theatre with the launch of the Cannes Film Festival in 1946 (initially planned for 1939), and the Avignon Theatre Festival in 1948. Both events were set up in the post-war era on the initiative of the state, in a bid to showcase high-quality French productions and to establish France as an important platform for the dissemination of international artists (Benito, 2001, p. 46; Crisp, 1997, p. 223). As underlined in Chapter 1, however, the state was much slower in considering popular music as an area of legitimate public spending, and music festivals were by and large non-existent in France until the late 1970s. A few did exist, and were established before public funds were available (including the highly successful Festival Interceltique de Lorient), but it was in the 1980s that the practice, production and consumption of popular music, including its 'live' form in concerts and festivals, boomed in France. The democratization policy of the Ministry of Cultural Affairs had had the effect of encouraging amateur music practices back in the 1960s and 1970s, but the richer, more youth-oriented, post-1981 Ministry of Culture triggered a surge in live music participation, providing distinct opportunities for the setting-up of local music events (Looseley, 1995, p. 108).

In the 1980s, the Socialists increased direct subsidies for the performing arts, while encouraging decentralization reforms which impacted on the local re-organization of cultural practices, and on the self-promotion of French regions as attractive tourist destinations. In particular, decentralization was instrumental in granting financial and decision-making powers to the local government levels of municipalities, departments and regions (see Chapter 1). Local governments started allocating funds for the development of local artistic activity, often with a view to enhancing, and in certain cases creating from scratch, cultural tourism in their areas. As a result, and as Philippe Teillet (2008, p. 28) has argued, pop and rock music festivals in France are a direct emanation of the renewal of local cultural policies. It is indeed significant that the most successful popular music festivals in France today do not take place in the traditional tourist regions. As opposed to the Côte d'Azur, which was chosen for the Cannes Film Festival precisely because it was already a glamorous destination (Mazdon, 2007, p. 16), the regions of the Centre (Printemps de Bourges), Brittany (Route du Rock, Vieilles Charrues) and to a lesser extent Charentes (Francofolies) were in economic decline in the 1970s. Precisely for this reason, local authorities found in music festivals an opportunity to compete with other holiday destinations, while cashing in on music consumption, the fastest-growing sector of cultural practice in the late twentieth century. This policy proved successful. By 2005, the revenues from live music performance in France had tripled since the early 1990s, reaching 400 million euros in 2005 (Dicale, 2006, p. 411). The fact that business acumen informed the creation of these events is also evident, for instance, in their taking place during holiday periods, be it the Easter break as in the case of Printemps de Bourges or, as is more common, the Summer months.

Strategic concerns were certainly central to the genesis of the Vieilles Charrues festival. Far from being driven by any specifically musical agenda, its organizers aimed to create an 'experience in economic solidarity' in the inland, isolated and economically depressed area of the Brittany region where they lived.[5] What started in 1991 as an end-of-year student party, with a few invited musicians, grew into a fragile but financially stable venture over the years, with the support of charity associations, unpaid volunteers and local subsidies. By the late 1990s, the festival had generated around one hundred new jobs, some of them permanent, linked to its upkeep.[6] More generally, the success of music festivals in France today is the result of a synergy between local, state and private initiatives, where music is essentially exploited for its potential to generate income. The Printemps de Bourges festival, set up in 1977, was initially meant to be a non-profit-making association, in partnership with the local Maison de la Culture. However, its legal status was quickly changed to that of a profit-making organization in order to cope with the steady increase in its takings, and in the process free itself from the constraints of its public partner. The festival founder, Daniel Colling, pragmatically recognized that his enterprise was indeed driven by the fluctuations of the market, and for this reason should be ready to take some commercial risks (Davet and Tenaille, 1996, p. 96).

Despite this, the state has remained motivated by the prospect of taxes on ticket entries, music copyrights and various indirect deductions, so much so that public subsidies amounted to 30 per cent of the budget of the Printemps festival in 1995, a sum shared between the Ministry of Culture, the region, the department and the local council. In 1995, the same festival brokered a partnership with the music major EMI for the promotion of young talent, taking its business savoir-faire to another level, and the state remained a willing partner in this new deal. In a similar spirit, the Francofolies festival was set up as a partnership between a private cultural association, bearing the festival's name, the state, through direct funding (20 per cent of the festival's budget in 1993), the Maison de la Culture of La Rochelle (state and locally financed), and local and international private sponsors. In 2002, the organizers proudly reported the 'highly positive economic impact' of the festival on the town of La Rochelle, with revenues estimated at

5 Le Festival des Vieilles Charrues, at www.vieillescharrues.asso.fr/media/telechargement/presse/presentation_impact_eco.doc, last accessed 24 March 2009. The original founder and current director of the festival, Christian Troadec, became mayor of Carhaix in 2001, winning the municipal elections with a loose left-wing agenda praising 'participant democracy', reminiscent of the Motivé-e-s electoral list run by the band Zebda in Toulouse the same year (Chapter 3).

6 Le Festival des Vieilles Charrues, at www.vieillescharrues.asso.fr/media/telechargement/presse/presentation_impact_eco.doc, last accessed 24 March 2009.

70 million francs and direct benefits to local trade (Bessaguet, 2002). The Route du Rock festival in Saint-Malo (North-Eastern Brittany), a more modest event created in 1990 and which attracted 17,000 participants in 1999, is a partnership between the cultural association Rock Tympans, with public subsidies reaching 20 per cent of the festival's budget in 1999 (split between the state and the municipality), and various private sponsors totalling 8 per cent of the budget (Valéro, 2002). These examples show that the proportion of public spending is sizeable in the finances of French music festivals, and that the state has helped spur local incentives in quite a significant way.[7]

Professionals are in general agreement that the music-playing situation greatly improved in France in the 1980s and 1990s, following this state-driven, region-based initiative. Serge Hureau, the director of the Centre National du Patrimoine de la Chanson [National Heritage Centre for *Chanson*], said in a 2000 interview: 'you can't complain when you've been travelling abroad a bit. When you come back to France you're very glad of the subsidies.'[8] The producers of the label Bondage were of the opinion that, since the late 1980s, 'lots of stuff has been happening in the regions' (Tellier, 1999, p. 36), allowing 'alternative' rock bands to perform on stages at local music festivals, including the Printemps de Bourges for Bérurier Noir, Mano Negra and Garçons Bouchers in 1987 and 1988. The members of Têtes Raides have also stated that touring outside Paris in the many provincial concerts and festivals of the 1980s and 1990s boosted their career.[9]

In addition to the decentralization factor, private companies have also sponsored festivals, attracted by the prospect of advertising at large venues, and on the attached documentation and websites. These included, for instance, Coca-Cola and Reebok as sponsors of the Francofolies festival (Lupieri, 1994). This combination of private sponsors with public subsidies has helped maintain relatively low entrance costs at French festivals. In 2001, a three-day pass for the Vieilles Charrues cost 320 francs (£32) and camping was free, while the three-day pass at Glastonbury in the UK in 2002 (no figures available for 2001), a comparable event in terms of music genre and attendance figures, was three times that at £97.[10] French festivals also tend to rely on the services of a large pool of unpaid volunteers.[11] Other factors play a part in maintaining relatively low fees

---

7   This is different from the UK, where local councils and new legislation (e.g. the Criminal Justice Act) have been instrumental in cancelling festivals in the 1990s (McKay, 2000, p. 3).

8   'On ne fait pas l'enfant capricieux quand on voyage, en revenant en France on est très content des subventions', interviewed for *Trafic d'influences*, France Inter, 28 February 2000. See Le Hall de la Chanson, www.lehall.com, last accessed 24 March 2009.

9   Grégoire Simon, interviewed by Albert Algoud for *La partie continue*, France Inter, 20 March 2001.

10   Perrin 2001b, and Glastonbury Festival, at www.glastonburyfestivals.co.uk/ uploadedFiles/Information/Student_Information_Pack/5%20Attendance%20Numbers.pdf, last accessed 24 March 2009.

11   Three thousand five hundred at Vieilles Charrues in 2000 (Allain, 2001).

and a high attendance rate, including the existence of a special benefits system in France for performing artists and arts technicians, facilitating their hire by small cultural organizations,[12] and the tendency of the French to listen to French music (as explained in Chapter 1), which orients the festival playlists towards 'cheaper', less well-known national artists than in the UK for instance. Their success shows that, far from being rare, spontaneous or marginal events, popular music festivals in France are a widespread, highly planned and regulated phenomenon (see also Hagen-Smith, 1995, p. 17).

Mikhail Bakhtin famously theorized the notion of 'carnival', in a literary context, as a 'licensed affair' that only entails a subversive edge to the extent that this is granted by the powers-that-be (Hitchcock, 1998, p. 104). In the 'real' social world, collective gatherings such as village fêtes and seasonal ceremonies have always been 'periods of sanctioned lawlessness' (Marcus, 1986, p. 1), controlled by the authorities, rather than moments of pure anarchy or power-reversal. In France, similarly, and especially given their heavy state input, popular music festivals fall squarely within the tradition of official festive celebrations that was established with the revolutionary and republican fêtes of the late eighteenth and late nineteenth centuries (Rearick, 1977). Consequently, contemporary festivals are well-organized and disciplined events, whose conformity to historical, social, economic and political conventions must be borne in mind when confronting this aspect of their reality with the impressions that participants have of them as principally evoking, and allowing to enact, the disruption of these very codes.

Furthermore, festivals are repetitive events, insofar as audiences often return to the same events year after year. At the 2001 Francofolies festival, 34 per cent of the participants had already attended the event at least three times (Bessaguet, 2002). At Vieilles Charrues in 2007, 42 per cent had previously attended the festival up to four times, and an impressive 27 per cent had been five times or more (GECE, 2007, p. 3). At Bourges in 1996, 36 per cent had been up to five times before, and 11 per cent had been more than ten times (Davet and Tenaille, 1996, p. 101). In these conditions, the connotations of 'alternativity' that popular music festivals still possess, and the pleasure of 'destabilization' that audiences claim they experience during these events, are enmeshed in expectedness and familiarity (Pitts, 2004, p. 152). Before exploring this contradiction further, however, it is worth returning to the tastes and ideology of this group of 'repeat offenders', for their experience of festivals as a moment of intense destabilization is, as we shall see, both at odds with the very concrete 'stability' of these events (in economic terms), and in keeping with their socio-cultural profile.

---

12   For an overview of the evolution of the legislative status of *intermittents* in France (performing artists and arts technicians), see the Coordination des Intermittents et Précaires d'Ile-de-France (CIP-IDF), www.cip-idf.org/IMG/doc/histoire_de_l_intermittence.doc, last accessed 24 March 2009.

Festival Audiences, Prestige and (Un)predictability

Popular music festivals in contemporary France are especially popular among a narrow sociological segment of the population, in conformity with the findings of Chapter 5 about rock music listeners in general. As tends to be the case elsewhere in North America (Hagen-Smith, 1995; Laing, 2004; Silverman, 2007) and in the UK (McKay, 2000; Pitts, 2004), popular music festivals principally attract a crowd of highly educated middle-class young adults, predominantly affiliated either to student or professional milieux such as the teaching profession (Benito, 2001, pp. 30–33). At the Route du Rock festival, 40 per cent of participants are university students (*Route du Rock*, p. 6, fig. 2); at Vieilles Charrues, 47 per cent hold at least a university degree-level qualification (GECE, 2007, p. 7); at Bourges, 50 per cent have at least two years of university education behind them (Davet and Tenaille, 1996, p. 101). In these, as indeed in most cases, the 18–25 and 26–35 age groups are the most heavily represented, with 82 per cent of Bourges festival-goers being between the ages of 18 and 34 (Davet and Tenaille, p. 101), 67 per cent of participants at Route du Rock being between 22 and 30 (*Route du Rock*, p. 6), and the average age of participants at Francofolies standing at 29 (Bessaguet, 2002).

This strong educational and generational homogeneity points, in France at any rate, towards a trend in the 'ageing of the young' (Dirn, 1998, pp. 36–7), whereby those who might have been considered 'adults' in the 1960s, when most people would either have secured a full-time job or started a family by their mid-twenties, are still sociologically 'young' today by virtue of being generally single, in further education and/or still in precarious employment well into their thirties (also Rambach and Rambach, 2001). As a result, a large proportion of the French population is today free to engage in cultural activities, and also has the intellectual training and inclination to do so. Their high level of cultural participation and large amount of free time makes them, in effect, the representatives of a cultural elite (see Chapter 5). If popular music festivals are 'popular' events in France, this does not make them democratic by the same token, at least not in the wide sociological sense, and we shall return later to the question of the exclusion that co-exists with feelings of social bonding.

This socio-cultural group is also characterized by its discourse of 'authenticity' and its elaboration of an 'alternative', vanguard or contestatory cultural identity, seen as opposing various dominant tendencies. Chapter 5 showed how interviewees belonging to this cultural elite tended to spurn 'mainstream' music and the overt profit-making strategies of the mainstream media. Instead, they favoured left-wing and politically committed artists, avoided the dominant media, relied on word-of-mouth recommendations, and generally expressed their preference for the vague notion of destabilization. For this specific cultural group, keen to locate a sense of 'alternativity' in their musical and cultural practices, festivals represent a further opportunity to do so. With their emphasis on 'live' performance, their history of left-wing connotations, their encouragement of communal living for a few days (in particular through camping), festivals function on a different level from 'mainstream' music practices, and fulfil these people's craving for the unexpected.

This perception that festivals break free of dominant social and cultural practices depends upon a binary opposition between live and mediatized music. Despite a wealth of evidence that domestic consumption of music can be very active indeed (Morley and Robins, 1995; Hennion, Maisonneuve and Gomart, 2000), and despite the fact that, since the advent of television, 'live' events have increasingly become mediatized in some way (Auslander, 1999), a discourse still exists, within elite cultural circles, which polarizes live performance against both televised retransmission and domestic entertainment. Indeed, this hierarchy is a contemporary Western topos, central to the edifice of 'alternative', supposedly more authentic or prestigious, music cultures (Laing, 2004, p. 3).[13]

This belief is perhaps even more systematic, and less questioned, in France, where the input of the state, the large proportion of 'intellectuals' attending festivals, and these festivals' historical development during the 1980s, have converged to reinforce this biased perspective. Indeed, popular music festivals were set up rather late in the day in France, after other types of festival had already accumulated social and cultural capital. The Cannes Film Festival, for instance, was launched in the post-war era by the state in an anxious and defensive bid to disseminate 'French cinematic prestige', and perceptions of quality have remained attached to this event ever since (Mazdon, 2007, p. 14). The links between festivals and 'high' culture are so ingrained in France that, according to one critic, the word 'festival' itself bears inherent 'connotations of prestige' and is 'a quality label' (Benito, 2001, p. i and p. 58). As a result, the polarization between high culture in live performance and low, seemingly passive culture in the home, has solidified. Secondly, music festivals became implanted in France in the 1980s, at a time when their credentials as places of 'authentic' protest were already firmly established, in particular via the paradigmatic example of Woodstock as a site of counter-culture (Schowalter, 2000; Bennett, 2004).[14] Furthermore, during the 1980s, France had appeared to be the 'victim' of the transformation of the music industry into a global and decidedly un-French system, especially with the rise of the charts system, the standardization of playlists on radio and television, and the consolidation of the major companies in this period (see Chapter 1). These factors combined to forge a strong climate of distrust, in some quarters, of 'mainstream' music and its relentless mediatization. The 1980s were therefore a catalyst in France for the notion that,

---

13   James (2007, p. 37) considered that 'festival people' were a class apart from the 'X-Factor' people' (a successful, prime-time TV music show), concluding that these were 'two incompatible cultures. It's better to be a festival person.'

14   A male interviewee in the Vieilles Charrues festival in 2000 explained his excitement at attending this event by comparing it to the illustrious American festival: 'it's crazy here, look, it's Woodstock in Brittany!' ['C'est l'orgie ici, regarde, c'est Woodstock en Bretagne!' – 'orgie' simply meaning craziness].

as live events, festivals could cater for the expression of less mediatized, 'alternative' values, and represent a form of 'authentic' engagement with music.[15]

The Printemps de Bourges festival, for instance, was launched with the express intention of 'confronting' the predominance of mainstream pop on the radio airwaves (Dicale, 2006, p. 288). In its first year, organizers invited French artists with radical left sympathies, including Colette Magny, Jacques Higelin and François Béranger, who helped establish the festival's 'protest' image. Equally, the team behind the music programming of the Route du Rock festival, who hail from the editorial board of the elitist rock magazine *Les Inrockuptibles* (see Chapter 5), select 'indie' artists who correspond to the event's self-styled 'niche, audacious and unexpected' identity.[16] Their aim, therefore, is to project a sense of rarity and high quality. This, however, appeals precisely to the educated and left-leaning middle classes, and guarantees the commercial success of these events. Nonetheless, many journalists and critics choose to ignore this socio-economic reality, insisting on the contrary upon the idea that quality and prestige can, and should, be separated from commercial imperatives.

In a 1996 publication on the Printemps de Bourges festival, released in the popular Gallimard Découvertes series, the authors accepted and praised the festival's intention to 'resolutely counter [the music programming] of the national and mainstream media', insisting that the festival could only be understood as a challenge to all 'profit-driven strategies' (Davet and Tenaille, 1996, p. 13).[17] They dismissed the fact that the Bourges festival had also been, from the start, a highly pragmatic venture, relegating the comments on this subject of its director, Daniel Colling, to tiny script in the appendix (pp. 96–9). Conversely, they emphasized, on page after page (e.g. p. 13, p. 26, p. 57) and with a selection of attractive colour pictures, the 'insolence' of the festival's line-up, the musical eclecticism of which was presented as evidence of its freedom from commercial preoccupations. In 2001, a review of the same Printemps festival, published in the well-known left-wing daily *Libération*, adopted a similarly slanted perspective. The journalist explained that the festival's gradual decline in popularity (only 46,000 tickets sold in 2001) was due to the 'mainstream drift' of its programming, caused by the creation of a partnership with the music major EMI (Bernier, 2001).[18] Colling, dismissively quoted by the journalist at the end of the article, explained more convincingly that this loss of income was due to particularly bad weather that week (which affects open-air concerts), and to an unexpected change in the academic calendar. This, in

---

15   The 'alternative' connotations of French festivals are thus partly reliant on the discourse of the Establishment, which is a different situation from the UK where popular music festivals are 'alternative' due to their associations with travellers and New Age followers (McKay, 2000).

16   '… pointue, audacieuse et surprenante' (*Route du Rock*, 1999, p. 2). The vocabulary is similar to that used by audiences in their definition of 'alternative' tastes (Chapter 5).

17   'Résolument le contre-pied des vitrines médiatiques nationales.'

18   'Egaré par les sirènes du show-biz.'

particular, had left a large proportion of the festival's habitual participants, teachers and students, unable to attend. His remark confirmed sociological analyses of festival-goers as generally belonging to 'superior intellectual backgrounds', while also stressing his own concern with profitability in his capacity as an organizer.

This example shows that there is a tendency, among French music critics, to ignore the fact that music festivals are strategically implanted within the commerce of music, and that the discourse of 'authenticity' overlaps, and indeed relies on, the broader structures of music production and consumption. For our purposes here, it will suffice to say that festivals are places of hidden contradictions, with local authorities, private sponsors and festival promoters considering them as opportunities for boosting their income, while a large proportion of the French media and, as we shall see, audiences, see them as places and moments in which a 'difference' from the mainstream can be experienced. Turning to the experience of audiences will now help bring these contradictions into sharper focus.

Routine and Disruption in Music Festivals

A prevalent academic interpretation of popular music festivals is that they are places of destabilization, whether of work-related, home-bound routines, or of the dominant conventions of consumer society. Hagen-Smith (1995, p. 17) expects festivals to challenge 'the order of [her] everyday life'. For Bennett (2004, p. xix), festivals are 'an opportunity to temporarily suspend the mundane predictability of normal everyday experience'. For Laing (2004, p. 7), festivals, unlike one-off concerts, demonstrate an 'impetus towards the reversal of everyday systems and structures'. An elaborate analysis of festivals' power of reversal is also provided by Michel Foucault (1986), who considers festivals to be examples of a 'heterotopia'. A heterotopia, literally an 'other space', is a real spatial location (in contrast to an imaginary utopia), which functions as a 'counter-site' to those other, more mundane, spaces that constitute our everyday environment. Heterotopic sites, such as museums, prisons or festivals, contrast, and at times contest, in a 'simultaneously mythic and real' fashion, the space of so-called normal social order. In particular, festivals offer dwellers 'a sort of absolute break' from their daily routine (1986, p. 26). While Foucault was probably not thinking of popular music festivals in this theorization of the heterotopia (his lecture was given in 1967), his model nonetheless applies faultlessly to the perceptions of contemporary audiences of these events.

Many interviewees saw music festivals as extra-ordinary places where, and moments when, their daily routines could be interrupted. At the Francofolies festival in La Rochelle, a female participant enthused that, during the festival, 'you don't do the same stuff as everybody else, and that's what's cool'.[19] Disregarding the fact that some 100,000 people were doing exactly what she was, she carved out

---

19   'En fait, on fait pas pareil que tout le monde, c'est ça qu'est cool.'

a sense of distinction for herself by implying that those who were not festival-goers fell into a series of homogeneous cultural practices. By contrast, she saw herself as standing out as an unusual person, participating in a rare and remarkable event. At Vieilles Charrues, a male interlocutor exclaimed that "the atmosphere is great here, it's not at all run of the mill". [20] Like the interviewee above, he erected a mental separation between the supposedly well-travelled roads where 'others' busied themselves, and the singularity of his own festival attendance. Many audiences also praised the liberal environment of festivals, where drugs (mainly hashish) were *de facto* authorized. One female informant summed up her impression of freedom thus: 'here it's really wild, you can just do whatever you want'.[21] Told with a joint between her lips, this comment implied that an array of constraints affected the speaker's everyday life, and that the festival was the only place where she could change, and perhaps subvert, the usual anti-drugs regulations. Along much the same lines, a male student interviewed in a bar, Jérôme, explained that music festivals gave him the opportunity to 'go mental, get stoned. Going mental means lots of things, like drinking or smoking [dope], but mainly it's having a break from everyday life'.[22] Jérôme derived great pleasure from the liberal drink and drug culture of festivals, quoting this as the main factor of interest before any mention of music. He also emphasized that a feeling of breaking from his daily routine was key to his experience of pleasure, suggesting that his everyday life was constrained in an unspecified, highly strenuous way.

These rather vague declarations are a direct echo of the more general discourse of 'alternative' music tastes observed in Chapter 5, being predicated upon a hierarchical binary system that credits festivals with the ability to bypass the supposedly banal and tedious forms of engagement with music in the home or through the media. In these formulations, participants construct their own 'alternative' identities in contrast both to a mass of undifferentiated, imagined 'others' (those who stay at home), and to themselves in their everyday lives, where they presumably suffer from a similar pattern of passivity and constraint. These perceptions must all be taken seriously, for festivals do provide a real rupture. During their time some habitual conventions *are* interrupted: drugs are liberally consumed, people sleep away from home (or do not sleep), television is not watched, audiences (but not artists) do not go to work, and so on.

Nonetheless, despite the participants' spontaneous assertions that festivals provide a break from routine, it is possible to regard this enjoyment in more relative and problematic terms. As noted earlier (and as acknowledged by Foucault and others), festivals are highly organized affairs, fitting into frameworks involving cultural organizations, local authorities and private sponsors. While this

---

20   'L'ambiance c'est bien, c'est pas du tout la même chose que les sentiers habituels.'

21   'Ici c'est sauvage, on peut faire ce qu'on veut.'

22   'Se lâcher, se retourner la tête. Se lâcher ça regroupe plein de trucs, boire ou fumer [du hash], mais c'est surtout faire un break par rapport à la vie quotidienne.'

organized element is largely invisible to, or consciously ignored by, participants, it is undeniable that regulation is a key factor in enabling feelings of 'extra-ordinariness' to take place. Moreover, and more crucially perhaps, the majority of participants in popular music festivals are already individuals with 'alternative' tastes and 'alternative' patterns of music consumption in their daily lives. As was clear from the material presented in Chapter 5, festival-goers tend to be university students, and generally highly educated, culturally minded individuals. Their routine is thus often already unconventional to an extent, involving, for instance, avoidance 'tricks' in record shops, and the expression of a sense of distinction from consumers of 'mainstream' pop music. Their everyday lives already challenge the dominant rules of consumer society and the more conservative positions of society, for example in relation to discourses on national identity (see Chapters 3 and 4). Furthermore, as university students and young professionals with a lot of free time, most participants have an everyday routine that is far from being difficult, commonplace or boring. Their everyday lives, then, already afford them an opportunity to escape feelings of oppression, and are ultimately characterized by a large dose of self-confidence and artistic satisfaction. In these conditions, festival-goers may ask of festivals to 'take them off from the real' (Dyer, 1985, p. 229), but festivals also extend and intensify their already non-conformist habits. Rather than exclusively challenging their everyday life, then, festivals are a prolongation of their own, pre-established 'alternative' routines.[23]

Upon reflection, the informant Jérôme moderated his earlier comments on the drug-taking liberality and sleepless nights of festivals, adding that 'yeah, except at the moment, every day's a bit like that for me'.[24] He explained that he was, in any case, a regular drug user, rarely got up early, partied most evenings, and certainly every weekend. His initial remark about a desire for a 'break' from routine may thus have been sincerely felt, but was in fact contradicted by his own real routine, the structure of which was already somewhat unusual, and certainly less conventional than if he had been working in a nine-to-five job. The response of two other interviewees revealed similar contradictions. Isabella, introduced in the previous chapter, evinced a disdainful attitude, explaining that festivals were

---

23   More research into 'mainstream' patterns of music reception would be needed at this stage, but this evidence at least suggests that audiences who belong to less intellectual backgrounds (such as those described by Dyer, 1985), do 'take off from the real' of their day-to-day routine more powerfully than 'alternative' audiences, when consuming 'mainstream' cultural products such as Hollywood films. It would seem that the educated and so-called vanguard audiences, on the contrary, prolong the already existing pleasures of their everyday lives into new realms. In this sense, an 'anti-mainstream' cultural identity could be summed up as a disdain for the pleasure of 'real difference' encountered by 'mainstream' audiences in their cultural practices, but it is also characterized by a more persistent element of facility and comfort than is the case for 'mainstream' identities, since their apparently out-of-the-ordinary musical experiences, such as going to festivals, actually extend, rather than simply disrupt, their already 'alternative' everyday lives.

24   'Ouais, sauf qu'en ce moment, c'est un peu tous les jours comme ça pour moi.'

'an escape for those who work'.[25] However, she disassociated herself from 'workers', people with the presumably trivial needs of making a living and having a rest, by implying that festivals were not, for her, an 'escape' from everyday life, since she found her everyday life satisfying. Rather, festivals gave her the opportunity to extend her identity as a discriminating and hard-working, not leisurely, consumer. As a result, there was a seamless transition between the festival and her everyday life.

At Vieilles Charrues, I also met Julie, a female trainee teacher who played in a rock band at weekends. Humorously, yet I suspect also quite seriously, she commented on the festival by wishing for a quick return to her ordinary life: 'it's lucky that there's everyday life to interrupt festivals; they're kind of a series of rather extreme situations, and all that'.[26] Referring to the constant sound level, the swarming crowds and rampant drug use, Julie was overwhelmed and longed for a break from this 'special place'. Inverting the usual binarism between daily life and the festival experience, she attributed positive values to indoor, restful and individual environments. These examples show that viewing popular music festivals as heterotopic sites, or as places of 'absolute' disruption and potential subversion, can only go so far. Participants may feel, spontaneously, that festivals constitute a break from their everyday lives and from the 'mainstream' world of non-festival-goers. However, in-depth audience research also complicates this initial impression, since the transition between everyday routine and festival-going, for audiences who already define themselves as 'alternative', tends to be comparatively smooth.

Camping, Nomadism and 'Gypsy' Authenticity

One of the best ways to disrupt one's daily routine is, arguably, to interrupt one's work and rest rhythms. Festivals achieve this by offering concerts throughout the day and most of the night, therefore keeping people awake and 'active' longer than usual. Festivals also take place over several days, encouraging participants to stay nearby in campsites. In rural locations, all festivals have dedicated camping areas and, even when participants live locally, the large majority choose to spend the night(s) in the campsites (GECE, 2007, p. 6). With its association with open-air holidays, camping is a break from domestic habits. It involves sleeping more or less outdoors, in a supposed 'communion' with the natural elements. It also involves a (relative) lack of comfort, being a crowded, noisy and often damp experience. In festivals, moreover, campsites are adjacent to the concert arena and it is therefore impossible to sleep until the last concert has finished because of the

---

25   'Un [sic] échappatoire pour ceux qui travaillent.'
26   'Heureusement qu'il y a la vie quotidienne pour faire une parenthèse aux festivals; c'est quand même des situations un peu extrêmes tout ça.'

sound level. Finally, festival camping is particularly unhygienic because of the absence of purpose-built washing and sanitation facilities.

Since we are dealing with festival-goers in search of a form of destabilization, however, the very rural location of camping, its lack of cleanliness and its inevitably collective character are precisely what generates pleasure (also Hagen-Smith, 1995; McKay, 2000, p. 13). First, festivals set in the countryside offer the chance to live the pastoral dream, especially for audiences who come, in bulk, from large urban centres (*Route du Rock*, 1999, p. 9, map 2; Davet and Tenaille, 1996, p. 101). The interviewee Isabella recalled a music festival in Montaigu (Vendée), where money had been traded in at the entrance for acorns. She used the adjectives 'champêtre' ['rustic'] and 'primitive' to describe the event, enthusiastically evoking the festival's attempt to provide an alternative to capitalistic exchange. Of course, this 'natural' atmosphere was only created artificially by the organizers, as participants with more acorns were still richer than the rest, and their money was presumably returned at the end. Nonetheless, this simple trick had enchanted her, and is an example of the profound need, for some people, to idealize the countryside and to simplify the forms of social and economic exchange of the past. Similarly, just as the presence of cows, grazing fields and a 'real' farmer are key in promoting the rural idyll of Glastonbury (McKay, 2000, p. 118), so the names of some French festivals play with expectations of pastoral authenticity, notably the Vieilles Charrues ('The Old Ploughs'). Nonetheless, it is telling that, among festival participants, farmers are the least represented socio-economic category (Benito, 2001, p. 33; *Route du Rock*, p. 5, table 3; GECE, p. 7). Spending two days outdoors, in what is essentially their workplace, would not be much of a break for them.

Proximity to mud and dirt, along with poor levels of hygiene, is another important element in the festival-goers' experience of a break from routine. For Westerners used to 'clean' urban and domestic settings, dirt can signal a disruption of the 'normal', 'disciplined' social order (Fiske, 1989, p. 99), even a 'threat' to majority culture (McKay, 2000, p. 6). Many interviewees, pointing out the groups of grubby, stoned and drunk campers, declared with glee that camping was indeed the biggest thrill, leading to unusual, illegal and potentially primal behaviours ('it's just like wild camping, here').[27] In addition, the physical movement involved in travelling to the festival can be exhilarating in itself. A young man interviewed in La Route du Rock festival recounted at length the journey that had brought him there, car-sharing with friends. He told of the gradual collective excitement that came over them as they compared themselves to itinerant artists and travellers ('we're a bit like troubadours, aren't we?').[28]

Responding to temporary displacement enthusiastically is nothing new. As early as the 1890s, when cabarets were located on the outskirts of Paris, city-centre bourgeois were already experiencing the 'thrill' of journeying to relatively far-off, semi-seditious places, which also felt like the countryside given the presence

---

27   'C'est un peu le camping sauvage, ici.'
28   'On est comme des troubadours, un peu, non?'

of fields and gardens in the 'zone' (Calvet, 1981, p. 69; Rifkin, 1991, p. 206). The persistence of this feeling for many urban dwellers today, then, is indicative of a deep human need to temporarily distance oneself from one's surroundings, physically and mentally, in both real and imaginary terms. During the momentary break of the festival, rural surroundings can provide excitement, and displacement can feel like danger.

In France, this general enthusiasm for transience, deregulation and the semblance of a lack of civilization is often mediated through the figure of the 'Gypsy'.[29] Among the festival-goers I interviewed, several compared their experience in festivals to the supposed lifestyle of *tsiganes*, *gitans* and *manouches* (all French terms for Roms), making comments such as 'we're playing at being Gypsies here, it's cool', or 'it looks like a Gypsy camp, here, doesn't it?'[30] Easy parallels can indeed be drawn between the use of tents in festivals, poor hygiene and geographical displacement, and the stereotypical representation of 'Gypsies' as non-sedentary people, lacking in 'civilization' or, more generally, not fitting into dominant society (Silverman, 2007, p. 336). However stereotypical, this recasting of 'Gypsies' as positive examples of social marginality embodies many of the 'alternative' and counter-modern aspirations of these French audiences particularly well, and is also echoed by many artists.

Chiefly among them are the *néo-réaliste* band Ogres de Barback (Chapter 2), who in 2002 commissioned the creation of a *chapiteau* (a large circus tent), where their concerts would henceforth be performed. This tent symbolized a rejection of the purpose-built structures of concert halls, and enabled the group to tour in relatively small towns with poor concert facilities. In the group's own words, the tent answered their 'visceral need for independence and total freedom' by echoing the freedom of *tziganes*, whose music and lifestyle they sought to emulate, in a discourse reminiscent of that of festival-goers.[31] The *chapiteau* tour of Ogres

---

29   See McKay (2000, pp. 15–20) for the 'Gypsy' trope in UK festival culture. I use the term 'Gypsy' with inverted commas throughout this chapter to denote the lack of fit between the homogeneous usage prevalent among interviewees, and the complex socio-ethnic, linguistic and political reality it covers (Silverman, 2007). Besides, the idea that economic hardship and artistic marginality go hand in hand belongs to the Romantic tradition, evident in the linguistic evolution of the term 'Bohemian', from being a term of geographical description relating to the westernmost area of the Czech Republic (Bohemia), where many 'Gypsies' hail from, to referring to struggling and vanguard artists on the fringes of mainstream success and recognition. See also Dicale (2006, p. 148) for the 'bohemianism' ['la vie de bohème'] of French singers in the post-war cabarets of central Paris, and Charles Aznavour's song 'La Bohème' (1966), which romanticizes, over a slow waltz played on the piano and violin, the links between social non-conventionality, artistic originality and economic poverty.

30   'On se la joue gitans, là, c'est cool'; 'Ça fait un peu romano, ici, hein?' (two male interviewees at Vieilles Charrues).

31   'Nécessité viscérale d'indépendance et de totale liberté'; 'les musiques tziganes, reflet d'un mode de vie dans lequel ils se retrouvent', 'Bio', Les Ogres de Barback,

de Barback was, furthermore, entitled *Latcho Drom*, in homage to Tony Gatlif's 1993 film which focused on a Romanian 'Gypsy' community of musicians, its title referring to the Romani phrase for 'bon voyage'. Ogres also invited Hurlements d'Léo, another French band, to perform with them in the tent. The latter explained that, as musicians, they were influenced by 'Gypsies' and that what mattered most to them was 'the primacy of travelling, ... wonderful human contact and sharing new experiences'.[32]

The similarity between these evocations and the statements by our interviewees demonstrates that, despite being simplistically associated with exclusion, freedom and protest, the figure of the 'Gypsy' is enthusiastically mobilized by 'alternative' French artists and audiences at the turn of the twenty-first century.[33] Clearly, a whole series of clichés persist in their use of this trope, including the representation of Roms as a uniform community, and the notion that travelling entails, *per se*, the opportunity for artistic creativity and social bonding. Their invocations also amounted to little more than a playful pose, and reflected an imagined lifestyle rather than any concrete preoccupations with the economic, ethnic, linguistic or political status of Roms. In this, French artists and audiences are, like other Westerners with an inclination towards 'authentic' or 'protest' music cultures, complicit in the marketing of 'Gypsy' identity as exotic (Gocić, 2001, p. 112; Silverman, 2007, p. 349). Nonetheless, at their own enthusiastic and naive level, they construct a cultural identity revolving around the possibility of conviviality and unconventionality, and the 'Gypsy' figure is for them an obvious emblem, as well as a problematic fashion accessory.

Collectivity, Utopianism and Exclusion

Just as this cultural borrowing is essentially imaginary (few audiences are interested in, or meet with, 'real' Roms), so the notion of conviviality that the 'Gypsy' trope conjures up is only partly, and ambivalently, materialized during the time of festivals. Generally speaking, the experience of collectivity on a large scale

---

www.lesogres.com/main.htm, last accessed 25 March 2009 .

32   'Contacts humains et le partage d'experience'; 'la primeur du voyage', at Hurlements de Léo, www.hurlements.com ('Bio'), last accessed 25 March 2009.

33   The place of an imagined 'Gypsy' identity in French popular music of the 1990s and 2000s could well be developed further, taking into account the influence of the films by Emir Kusturica in France (and their soundtracks), whose critical and commercial success, as well their presentation of a 'Gypsy' culture as a site of resistance, converged with cultural prestige via prizes at the Cannes Film Festival (Gocić, 2001, p. 129). France is also the home of the *manouche* jazz guitarist Django Reinhardt, whose music was reappraised by French 'indie' bands, including Paris Combo and Sansévérino, in the 1990s. Ogres de Barback only follow in a long line of leftist, 'alternative' artists who have favourably adopted the figure of the 'Gypsy' in that decade, and co-opted it as a symbol of 'authenticity' and 'protest', following the demise of the Eastern bloc (Silverman, 2007).

during concerts and festivals is often introduced by critics as conducive to intense pleasure. This is firstly because physical closeness between thousands of people is a rather unusual experience, often actively sought by participants. Secondly, this very proximity allows participants to experience, in a real-life situation, the utopian ideal of fraternity. Keith Negus (1992, p. 77), Simon Frith (1996, p. 123) and Benedict Anderson (1981, p. 145), among others, have formulated this idea as, respectively, the 'shared sense of being', the 'real experience of what the ideal could be' and the 'physical realization of the imagined community' that takes hold of concert audiences. In France, the notions of fraternity and utopianism are perhaps more poignant and ideologically loaded than elsewhere, due to the continuing relevance of humanism in the formation of official discourse on national identity. These philosophical concepts are certainly central to the cultural identity of the French 'alternative' music scene, the lyrics and declarations of many *néo-réaliste* and *rock métis* artists expressing explicitly critical views against individualism and exclusionary practices (see Chapters 2, 3 and 4). It is not surprising, therefore, to find that French festival audiences, on the whole, replicate this type of discourse, considering festivals as particularly significant moments when togetherness can be achieved, uniting individuals beyond their habitual (domestic, urban) isolation. "Everybody speaks together, it's really convivial'; 'we came here for the atmosphere, everybody speaks with everybody, it's cool and everybody just mucks in'; 'a festival is just an excuse with some music to be with others'.[34] These participants' reactions implied that the mere proximity to thousands of people, and the potential for social interaction with strangers, was desired and realized. Attempting to account for the sheer incommensurability of festival crowds, their vague terminology (everybody, everyone) echoed the abstract formulation of republican universalism.

I asked interviewees to expand on these initial, vague declarations, and to reflect on the composition of a typical festival crowd. To this, participants would immediately emphasize inclusivity, and the realization of social, generational and taste mixing, stressing that the crowds were 'very varied', 'with lots of different styles'.[35] For one male interviewee, festival audiences were made up of 'all sorts, guys into ska, punks, old rockers, young people more into reggae, everything'.[36] Nonetheless, just as the latter list of 'differences' only covered subtle sub-divisions within the specific rock music scene, the sociological composition of the festivals was, as we have seen, narrow, with festival-goers tending to come from similar backgrounds in terms of class, education, age and ethnic group, but

34 'Tout le monde se parle, c'est hyper convivial'; 'On est venu pour l'ambiance, tout le monde qui parle avec tout le monde, c'est cool, c'est la bonne franquette'; 'le festival, c'est une excuse avec de la musique pour être à plusieurs'.

35 'Y'a de tout, c'est très varié'; 'c'est ça qu'est bien dans les festivals, tu rencontres de tous les styles'.

36 'Y'a de tous les types, des mecs branchés ska, des punks, des vieux rockers et des jeunes plus ska-reggae, de tout.'

with an equal gender split. In longer interviews, respondents tended to reveal that their interaction with others during the time of the festival was in fact limited to a clique of already-gathered friends. For Isabella, 'what's great is the reunion of a certain category of people, there's an osmosis between people of the same generation'.[37] Her perception of, and pleasure in, social transcendence was actually limited to a narrow age-based community. For an interviewee in Vieilles Charrues, 'the main thing is being with your friends'.[38] Also in Vieilles Charrues, a female interviewee stated that she only met with people she knew: 'the year before, there were more people, it was excellent [because] you could bump into someone you knew from elsewhere'.[39] For these participants, the sense of universal bonding and shared collectivity was thus restricted to their pre-existing social networks. These interviews make transparent the fact that these festival-goers constructed a mental image of a 'universal' community, while experiencing in reality a rather limited form of human interaction. Further, they demonstrate that festivals are an extension of the participants' everyday lives, rather than a disruption of them.

This overlap between the imagined festival and its real experience is perhaps most evident in terms of ethnicity. Visible (post-colonial) ethnic minorities are conspicuous by their absence in French pop and rock music concerts and festivals. The overall absence of black people and *beurs* is not an intentional exclusion on the part of organizers, artists or audiences, but rather the result of the imbrication of ethnicity within social practices, which corresponds to the general lack of visibility of post-colonial minorities in the French cultural landscape – and particularly within elite circles (Hargreaves and McKinney, 1997). There is unfortunately no official data available on the ethnic composition of cultural audiences in France, since ethnicity is officially classed as irrelevant in defining identity and practices. This being said, some observations exist which back up this impression. In a 2007 interview, the French-Algerian singer Rachid Taha (see Chapter 3) remarked that during his participation in KO Social, the charity concert set up by the *néo-réaliste* band Têtes Raides, the crowd was 'only made up of nice white middle-class kids' (Pascaud, 2007, p. 14).[40] The discrepancy between the event's agenda, promoting solidarity with the destitute and marginalized of society, including ethnic minorities, and the actual make-up of its audience, is indicative of the somewhat counterproductive strategies that 'alternative' artists

---

37   'Ce qu'est bien, c'est les retrouvailles entre une certaine catégorie de personnes, y'a une osmose entre les gens de même génération.'

38   'La musique on s'en tape un peu, finalement. Le tout c'est d'être entre copains.'

39   'L'année dernière, y'avait plus de monde; c'était excellent, tu rencontrais des gens que tu connaissais d'ailleurs'. Pitts (2004, p. 149) corroborates this evidence, noting the gap between her respondents' self-perceptions as a disparate, inclusive group, and their strong age and social homogeneity, suggesting that they interact within a 'tightly-knit community'.

40   'Dans la salle, il n'y avait ni beurs ni blacks, rien que des gentils petit-bourgeois blancs.'

develop when attempting to raise the profile of socio-political issues, as they refuse to 'go mainstream' (Lebrun, 2005a). In any case, it took the *beur* Taha to notice the absence of black people and *beurs*, as Têtes Raides, an all-white band, have never commented on the ethnic composition of their audiences. Similarly, the concerts of anti-globalization activist and pro-migration exponent Manu Chao (see Chapter 4) are primarily attended by 'clean-cut, white university students' (Cassavetti, 2007, p. 31).[41] This reflects the wider absence of socially disadvantaged and ethnic minority youths from events and debates that supposedly concern them, as left-wing activism tends to be the prerogative of well-integrated, 'invisible' white people (also Waters, 2006).

During my fieldwork, the only *beurs* I interviewed were one woman, Rachida, whose educational profile closely matched that of the majority of interviewees (see Chapter 2), and two male security guards on duty at the Saint-Nolff and Francofolies festivals. The latter's reflections on the ethnic composition of festivals shed interesting light on the place of that untold, supposedly irrelevant 'difference'. In Saint-Nolff, the guard commented that the style of rejoicing in festivals was typically middle-class and therefore white, and suitable for people who sought to 'let their hair down'. Festivals were for 'people from a nice background if you see what I mean'. He added: 'you see, I'm from a Maghrebi background, I'd never go camping like that for three days, I just wouldn't fancy it... in fact they're just posh kids slumming it.'[42] By contrast, when participating in an 'extra-ordinary' event, he claimed that he would rather go clubbing.[43] His perspective on festivals, doubly external as an ethnic-minority worker (not an audience member), differs considerably from that of most festival-goers, who are overwhelmingly white. This young man felt, and rightly so, that people from different ethnic backgrounds tended to engage in different cultural practices, a fact that other interviewees, all white, passed over completely in their praise of a 'universal' bonding. He also remarked upon and dismissed the artifice at play in attending festivals, considering that camping was a pose ('slumming it', 'let their hair down'), and not an authentic experience of autonomy, contestation, collectivity or nomadism. In La Rochelle, another *beur* bouncer made similar points, also contrasting the performance of contestation in festivals with that in nightclubs: 'here, even those who cheat [jumping over fences] are rich kids, why do they play at being rebels? I know they can afford their entry. It's not like in a club where people fight. They don't do fights,

---

41   'Un public essentiellement d'étudiants blancs, plutôt propres sur eux.'

42   'Des gens de bonne famille entre guillemets'; 'tu vois, moi je viens d'un milieu maghrébin, j'irais jamais camper comme ça pendant trois jours, ça me dirait rien... en fait c'est un peu des snobs qui se lâchent'.

43   A study on the usage and connotations of French *boîtes* (nightclubs) has yet to be written, but would constitute a fascinating foray into mainstream popular culture, where equally competing discourses and heterogeneous audiences presumably co-exist.

here, they're just nice people.'[44] Disregarding the issue of ethnicity in this case, he concentrated on financial power and argued that 'authentic' rebellion concerned those without economic means, who could not afford the cultural practice of festival-going (or had little taste for it). Moreover, he equated marginality and rebellion with violence and fraud. Attending a festival was therefore not a sign of contestation in his view, since 'real' protest actively contravened and threatened the social order.

These remarks revolved around a different understanding of 'rebellion' and 'marginality' than most interviewees' comments so far. Both security guards could see that festival-goers, overall, attempted to construct an 'authentic' cultural identity for themselves by engaging in a degree of behavioural originality, and a form of social marginality by camping and even, for some, jumping over fences (!). However, they also disparaged this practice as a playful, inconsequent game, in contrast to their understanding of what constituted 'real', 'authentic' rebellion. For them, real rebellion was a sharp reversal of the established societal norms, including being financially poor rather than 'slumming it', and acting violently rather than being respectful towards others. In both cases, they also suggested that 'rebellion' was not a cultural activity worth pursuing, but a mindless, angry response to society's economic injustice.

It is a reassuring fact that most rock and pop festival-goers abide by the dominant social rules. Festival participants are 'nice, on the whole' (James, 2007, p. 34), even 'very, very nice' (Hagen-Smith, 1995, p. 18). They put consideration of others at the heart of their social interactions, even if limiting this to their acquaintances, and have, following the Bakhtinian analysis of carnival participants, 'no intention of obliterating the Other' (Yol Jung, 1998, p. 107). Indeed, real violence always ends the precarious balance of festivity, and luckily, in France so far, no popular music festival has had to report a fatal incident – unlike the infamous US festival of Altamont (1969), where one man was mobbed to death and three others died accidentally, or the 1994 Glastonbury festival where five people were shot, and one man died from an overdose (McKay, 2000, p. 93 and p. 109).

Nonetheless, that the issue of violence should be significant in these bouncers' account of 'rebellion', and completely absent from the discourse and practices of festival-goers who see themselves as cultural rebels, is indicative of the wider socio-cultural discrepancies that shape French society. For these *beurs*, standing on the periphery of 'alternative' music identities, festivals were firstly a place of work, and secondly the sites of an artificial, luxurious cultural pursuit for the well-integrated ethnic majority. They were also a bewildering irrelevance for those who thought of themselves as socially excluded.

A similar approach was expressed by a white male interviewed in Saint-Nolff, a mechanic in his early twenties who had never been to a festival before. Laurent

---

44 'Ici, même les fraudeurs c'est des riches, pourquoi ils s'amusent à jouer les rebelles? Je sais bien qu'ils ont de quoi payer. C'est pas comme en boîte où t'as d'la baston. Y'a pas de bagarre ici, c'est des gens de bonne famille.'

had spent most of his time in the campsite, smoking joints and listening to the concerts from a distance. He was quite content with this experience, comparing it to 'having the radio in the background', not seeing the point of watching the live performances.[45] His view was quite unrepresentative of the wider festival-going population, and possibly anathema to many festival-goers for whom live music should be regarded more highly than radio broadcast. Laurent also stated that 'a rebel is someone looking for trouble, but here there's none of that',[46] directly echoing the remarks by the two bouncers about the general lack of violence in festivals. Without commenting on ethnic exclusion, then, he still understood 'contestation' as a serious and aggressive breach of social conventions, and not at all as a cultural, ideologically loaded musical identity.

Despite the evident need to carry out further research into the reception of festivals in particular, and so-called alternative music more generally, by more 'mainstream' audiences with less political and personal investment in 'protest', these initial findings are interesting for the contrast they highlight between self-declared 'alternative' audiences and others. Firstly, on a basic level, the existence of competing discourses among interviewed audiences underlines the relative heterogeneity of festival crowds, and relativizes the pleasure of destabilization that many audiences experience. Secondly, in closer relation to this book's discussion of the constitutive features of an 'alternative' music identity, this fieldwork reveals that self-declared non-mainstream audiences are drawn for the most part from a social, educational and cultural elite, and usually belong to the dominant ethnic group. This stresses once more the central paradox of 'alternative' identities, which involves belonging to 'dominant' social, cultural and economic structures (being white, highly educated, usually well-off, and so on), while seeking at the same time to challenge other 'dominant' patterns in society, be they the mass-mediatization of *variété* (Chapters 1 and 5), neo-liberalism (Chapter 4), the exclusionary practices and 'abstract' interpretation of republicanism (Chapter 3), or the persistence of economic disparities and the perceived increase in individualism and consumerism (Chapter 2).

Audience research also allows us to stress that 'alternative' identities do exist, by virtue of what some people do (such as attending live music festivals, camping, spending time collectively) and what they say (such as disparaging 'mainstream' music and audiences, praising notions of destabilization and autonomy). This method also allows us to emphasize the idea that the pleasure of destabilization encountered in festivals by a certain class (in every sense of the word) of audiences is very real to them. At the same time, audience research also highlights the fact that 'alternative' identities can be, and indeed usually are, imaginary constructs, for participants' expression of protest is in fact highly regulated, situated in a historical tradition and shaped by political and economic factors, as well as, to a certain extent, normative, despite being premised upon ideas of distinction. Moreover,

---

45 'C'est comme la radio en bruit de fond.'
46 'Le rebelle, c'est celui qui cherche des embrouilles, mais ici c'est pas du tout ça.'

'alternative' music identities are, at their core, non-aggressive and non-rebellious, if 'true' rebellion means physically hurting others. They are truly insurrectionary, however, if, as Yol Jung argues (1998, p. 107), 'the true rebel is the one who senses and cultivates his or her allegiance to dialogue and human solidarity'. Following closely on the renewal of a left-wing project of solidarity (see Chapters 2 and 4 in particular), France's 'alternative' community of music listeners indeed contests some dominant dogma and unpleasant realities. That it should take members of the 'elite' to do so, and to do so only tentatively, is not a sign of inauthenticity, but a social fact that testifies to the appeal and welcome resilience of discourses of 'protest' in contemporary society.

Conclusion

This book has sought to demonstrate that there is such a thing as a 'protest' music culture in late twentieth- and early twenty-first-century France, that this culture is largely shaped by material determinants and historical contingency, and affects people in both real and imaginary ways (see Frith, 1996, p. 275). This music culture exhibits a number of identifiable features, including the tendency for participants to reject key commercial media outlets, to question profit-seeking commercialization, to challenge traditional republicanism, to deplore anti-immigration policies and global inequalities. Yet it is also heterogeneous, able to express itself in musically diverse forms (the waltzing accordion of *chanson néo-réaliste*, the reggae and Arab-influenced mix of *rock métis*), and it groups together, in more or less loose collectivities, individuals with varying music tastes, who constantly redefine their understanding of 'alternative' identities in the face of changes in the production, mediatization and success of artists. The main constant in this fluid music culture, then, is the perception on the part of artists, producers, critics and audiences, that a powerful, ubiquitous and nefarious force of 'mainstream' music exists. Their investment in terms of time and energy, words and actions, ideals and symbols, in their attempt to escape from, and/or challenge, this negative force, is what defines their contestation.

France's 'protest' music culture thus opposes a number of dominant trends in French society. This is done both actively, for instance when artists achieve fame thanks to word of mouth rather than prime-time television, and symbolically, as when song lyrics and declarations criticize social inequalities and generally question the mainstream media's emphasis on youth, beauty and success. Yet, an analysis of this music culture which takes into account, as this book has, the evolution of the music industry and of state policy, and incorporates the findings of audience reception research, also reveals that there is nothing inherently, independently 'authentic' about this mode of engagement with popular music, however sincerely felt this opposition may be. For instance, we saw that expressing alternative ideas and protest in French popular music is dependent on the same structures of production that also gave rise to mainstream music, with private businesses, state subsidy, and the factors of competition, fashion and entrepreneurship all playing a large part in the construction of resistance. We saw, too, how the rather different notions of nostalgia and *métissage* could achieve the same goals of contesting the mainstream, while both entailing various limitations, ranging from the possibility of ethnic exclusion, to an emphasis on pure festivity and the consideration of marginality as a simple fashion accessory.

Furthermore, the apparent need that 'alternative' artists and audiences have for an identifiable enemy can lead them to adopt a tone of moral superiority that is not always attractive. In premising their identity upon an 'anti-mainstream' distinction, the participants in this music culture closely resemble the UK dance music fans of the 1990s who, more than anything, 'jockey[ed] for social power' (Thornton, 1995, p. 163). In so doing, neither the UK clubbers nor the French rockers succeed in developing a progressive, radical or subversive identity. Rather, as Chapters 5 and 6 in particular underlined, dogma, conformity and exclusions also contribute to shaping 'alternative' feelings and 'alternative' social meanings. This said, elements of snobbery and exclusion do not necessarily invalidate cultural identities, even if they feature prominently within them, and are probably to be found in all cultural groupings, including 'mainstream' ones.

By concentrating on self-defined 'alternative' music professionals and audiences, this study has confirmed the existence of a constellation of individuals who consider that the expression of anti-mainstream resistance is important, and who construct their cultural and social identities to a large extent around this binary. The production of the most successful French popular music by foreign major companies, its broadcast on radio stations with a limited playlist, and its tendency to reproduce a conservative view of society (see Chapters 1 and 5), certainly justify the claims of non-mainstream music listeners that they feel dominated by the mainstream media, and gives them grounds for lumping together commercial success with reactionary politics. Nonetheless, the place and definition of the mainstream, although a central element in this investigation, has only been touched on in very general terms. Future research would do well, therefore, to examine the constitution of the 'mainstream' according to 'non-alternative' music consumers, and gauge more precisely how those who regularly listen to chart music, as well as those who are indifferent or oblivious to processes of distinction between mainstream and non-mainstream identities, construct the mental and social category of *variété* music. In particular, does left-wing protest music exist for them in the same way that mainstream music exists for 'protest' music listeners? Do 'mainstream' and 'non-mainstream' music exist as separate categories for listeners of mostly chart music, and are they pitted against each other as implacably as they are by 'alternative' participants when they pass judgement on music?

Since its creation in 1992, the self-proclaimed *variété* magazine *Platine*, mentioned in Chapter 5, has never reviewed the albums of Têtes Raides, Zebda or Manu Chao, artists who are admittedly not the biggest sellers in the French market, but who also happen to take openly leftist positions (see Chapters 2, 3 and 4). This absence would suggest that audiences with a self-declared interest in 'mainstream' music (or at any rate, the publishers with an interest in selling a magazine dedicated to chart music), consciously reject those musicians who might be considered as 'protest' artists. Given that these artists are effectively excluded from a magazine of this sort, and that they are less mediatized overall than their *variété* counterparts, one can imagine how the category of 'alternative' music might be relatively invisible from a mainstream standpoint. If listeners of *variété* music engage with popular music only through mass-media consumption or avowedly 'mainstream' outlets, such as the magazine *Platine*, then the alternative/mainstream binary vanishes for them, the 'non-mainstream' pole being non-existent. However, this binary continues to exist for 'alternative' music connoisseurs, who cannot escape having a certain awareness, voluntary or otherwise, of mainstream music, due to the pervasiveness of mass-mediatization.

This basic contrast, however, is only hypothesized from the content of a single magazine, and does not constitute a scientific demonstration. Other questions might therefore be fruitfully asked in the future, including the following: who are the listeners of 'mainstream' music, and do they think they engage with music in an artificial, conservative or submissive way? Are there people able to see past the fact that Carla Bruni is married to a right-wing President, and still enjoy her music today (and when, where, with whom, etc.)? Does anyone deliberately listen to Johnny Hallyday and to Têtes Raides on the same day, although perhaps not in the company of the same people? Who, furthermore, are the (French) music artists who manage to avoid being placed on the mainstream/non-mainstream axis, rendering processes of social distinction irrelevant, even if only temporarily? Answering these kinds of questions would bring a more nuanced understanding of the mainstream, and help establish when and under what conditions the mainstream/alternative binary is useful and significant to people (and not just to 'alternative' audiences), and when it is not, or is no longer so. A more accurate knowledge of the real meanings attached to music categories in France would also answer questions about the ways in which individual tastes develop and relate to existing social structures and ideologies.

The parallels between non-mainstream identities in France and the UK also emphasize how placing value on the notion of 'protest' in popular music is not specific to France. Nonetheless, this study has demonstrated that the rhetoric of authenticity is particularly fierce, enduring and prestigious in France, where it is state-funded and institutionalized to a large extent, as well as frequently commercially successful (in relative terms), given the receptive audience it finds in the left-wing and educated segment of the purchasing public. This audience, which we called the vanguard both with reference to Bourdieu's theoretical model and by virtue of its belonging to a cultural elite, tends to be highly educated yet also relatively precariously situated in economic terms. This balance constitutes something of a French speciality, due to the relatively cheap cost of remaining in further education in France, and the relatively high rate of unemployment in recent decades, including among highly qualified people (Rambach and Rambach, 2001; Maurin, 2005, p. 104). As a result, there is an argument for recognizing the relatively strong national character of 'protest' cultural identities in contemporary France, this identity being understood – as the various chapters in this book have outlined – as the distillation of left-wing intellectualism, defensive self-protection and serious political commitment.

In this context, it also worth making a quick observation on the links between the notions of youth, protest and seriousness. In 1960s France, young people roughly between the ages of 15 and 25, who had access to the new technology of portable radios and turntables, were the audiences of *yéyé* music, but also of *chanson à textes*. For one female respondent of 25, interviewed by Bourdieu in the 1960s, Jacques Brel had been her 'most important teenage crush', while she despised the *yéyé* singer Sheila (Bourdieu, 1979, pp. 412–13).[1] This underlines how young people may be attracted by seriousness, and see 'protest' as a reaction not against adulthood, but against the formidable presence of youth itself on the mainstream media. In this case, the contrast between Brel and Sheila could not be more telling. Sheila was born in 1946 and posed as a young schoolgirl in her 1963 hit 'L'école est finie', aged only seventeen, while Brel (born in 1929), was seventeen years her senior and his songs tackled such complex subjects as anti-clericalism and death (Tinker, 2005).

Casting aside the relative banality of young girls developing crushes on older men, the fact that an 'old' and 'serious' artist such as Brel could and did appeal to young audiences points to the importance of maturity and seriousness in the expression of 'authenticity' and 'protest' for some young people. Philippe Teillet (2003, p. 177) makes a similar point when he explains that France's rock music culture developed in a profoundly intellectual manner, due to the role of the rather literary and erudite monthly music press as a mediator.[2] If both *chanson* and Anglo-American rock already thrived on intellectualism and maturity in France in the 1960s, it is easy to see the legacy of this opposition in contemporary French rock music, whose twin influences are punk-rock and *chanson* (see Chapters 1 and 2).

In the 1960s, the likes of Jacques Brel and Georges Brassens were 'enlisted as a national gold standard' (Looseley, 2003, p. 203) against which to gauge the authenticity or artificiality of other popular music genres. This study showed, then, that the broad genre of French rock music perpetuated this discourse of prestige and its embedded polarization, from the 1980s onwards, in its various incarnations as *rock alternatif*, *chanson néo-réaliste* and *rock métis*. French rock music also continues to juxtapose 'protest' sentiments with seriousness and an (ageing) youth culture. The respondents interviewed for this research, most of whom were in their early twenties at the turn of the twenty-first century, disparaged youth culture when it simply involved following dominant consumption patterns, and encouraged a more intellectually and politically significant way to make and listen to music.

In contrast to the 'aestheticization of politics' (Thornton, 1995, p. 167) observed in British rave culture of the same period, then, French popular music of the 1990s and 2000s showed its renewed commitment to political activism, as all the artists discussed here have used their songs and their fame (however small) to argue for more social justice and the respect of ethnic minorities, and to highlight the dangers of unquestioned mass-mediatization. The enduring character of this 'worthy' protest discourse in contemporary France may be the sign of a certain degree of

---

1   'Le grand amour de mes quinze ans.' Sheila had a worldwide hit in 1977 with 'Spacer', a Chic-produced disco track released under the name of Sheila B. Devotion.

2   This was the case for the transmission of Anglo-American rock music, though not for the home-grown derivative genre of *yéyé*.

wishful thinking on the part of artists and audiences, but also shows that thought and politics continue to play an active role in French popular culture. The moral character of this endeavour can be somewhat double-edged, appearing joyless and naive for some, whereas for others it is a fundamental part of the artist's role in society. Certainly, a national specificity here is the vast number of artists who have managed to achieve reasonable sales through their engagement with such issues, dealing seriously (if sometimes superficially) with notions of 'resistance' and 'utopia' in songs, despite working in what remains, essentially, the entertainment industry. The pointing out of social and moral insuffiencies in society, and the questioning of the economic and cultural status quo is a mode of protest which grants French artists occasional success as well as a veneer of respectability, in a way that is possibly more immediate, widespread and unproblematic than elsewhere.

So, is France's protest music culture healthy in these consumerist and morally vacuous times, or is it just an old-fashioned relic in the post-modern age? The findings displayed here would suggest that the answer lies somewhere in between. While the performance of Sébastien Tellier, the French entry for the 2008 Eurovision Song Contest, showed that it is perfectly possible for French music artists not to take themselves too seriously, the fervour and earnestness with which his selection was commented upon in the national press implies that it remains somewhat difficult for a popular music artist in France to be playful and still be critically acclaimed (see Cassavetti, 2008). Music culture is arguably the most 'classifying' culture in terms of its creation of social distinctions (Bourdieu, 1979, p. 17), and the intense debate surrounding the country's Eurovision entry shows that popular music certainly remains a weighty matter in France today. This book, at least, has tried to show that it is possible to be fun and serious at once.

Bibliography

Allain, Pierre-Henri (2001), 'Carhaix: le sillon du patron des Vieilles Charrues', *Libération*, 21 February, 14.

Anderson, Benedict (1991), *Imagined Communities. Reflections on the Origin and Spread of Nationalism* (London and New York: Verso).

Andrews, Chris (2000), 'The Social Ageing of *Les Inrockuptibles*', *French Cultural Studies*, 11, 235–48.

L'Année du disque 1999 (1999) (Music Business Publishing/SNEP).

Anon. (2007), 'Manu Chao', *The Independent. The Information*, 7 September, 6.

Arteta, Stéphane (2003), 'NRJ ou le triomphe de la FM', *Le Nouvel Observateur*, 16 January, 16–18.

Aubel, François (1999), 'Zebda: le chant des partisans', *L'Evénement du jeudi*, 15 April, 62–5.

Auslander, Philip (1999), *Liveness. Performance in a Mediatized Culture* (Abingdon and New York: Routledge).

Austin, Guy (2003), *Stars in Modern French Film* (London: Arnold).

Austin, Thomas (2002), *Hollywood, Hype and Audiences. Selling and Watching Film in the 1990s* (Manchester and New York: Manchester University Press).

Balibar, Etienne, Monique Chemillier-Gendreau, Jacqueline Costa-Lacoux and Emmanuel Terray (eds) (1999), *Sans-papiers: l'archaïsme fatal* (Paris: La Découverte).

Barbot, Philippe (2002), 'Zebda: "Pas des rebelles à trois sous"', *Télérama*, 2744, 16 August, 30–2.

Barbot, Philippe (2003), 'Un courant d'air frais', *Télérama*, 2770, 12 February, 46–51.

Barbot, Philippe (2004), 'Le chant des opposants', *Télérama*, 2832, 24 April, 14–22.

Barbot, Philippe and Christian Sorg (2001), 'L'été sera Chao', *Télérama*, 2681, 30 May, 72–4.

Barker, Martin (2006), 'On Being Ambitious for Audience Research', in Isabelle Charpentier (ed.), *Comment sont reçues les œuvres* (Grâne: Creaphis), 27–42.

Barnel, Jeff (2005), *Dalida, la femme de cœur* (Paris: Editions du Rocher).

Belén Luaces, María (2003), 'Manu Chao al margen', *Al Margen, Revista Digital de Cultura e Historia*, www.almargen.com.ar/sitio/seccion/entrevistas/mchao, last accessed 22 March 2009.

Belhaddad, Souâd (2003), *Manu Chao et la Mano Negra* (Paris: Librio Musique).

Bell, Laurence (1997), 'Democratic Socialism', in Christopher Flood and Laurence Bell (eds), *Political Ideologies in Contemporary France* (London and Washington: Pinter), 16–51.

Benetollo, Anne (1999), *Rock et politique* (Paris: L'Harmattan).

Benito, Luc (2001), *Les festivals en France* (Paris: L'Harmattan).

Bennett, Andy (ed.) (2004), *Remembering Woodstock* (Aldershot: Ashgate).

Bernier, Alexis (2001), 'A Bourges, le Printemps reverdit', *Libération*, 23 April, 38.

Berrian, Brenda F. (2000), *Awakening Spaces. French Caribbean Popular Songs, Music, and Culture* (Chicago and London: University of Chicago Press).

Bessaguet, Maryse (2002), PR of the Francofolies festival (La Rochelle), personal email communication, 15 April.

Béthune, Christian (2003), *Le rap. Une esthétique hors la loi* (Paris: Editions Autrement, coll. Mutations).

Bhattacharyya, Gargi, with John Gabriel and Steven Small (2002), *Race and Power: Global Racism in the Twenty-First Century* (London and New York: Routledge).

Birgy, Philippe (2001), *Mouvement techno et transit culturel* (Paris: L'Harmattan).

Bonnaud, Frédéric (2001), 'The *Amélie* Effect', *Les Inrockuptibles*, 11 December, article translated online at: www.filmlinc.com/fcm/11–12–2001/amelie.htm, last accessed 21 March 2009.

Bonnieux, Bertrand, Pascal Cordereix and Elizabeth Giuliani (2004), *Souvenirs, souvenirs... Cent ans de chanson française* (Paris: Gallimard/BNF, La Découverte, no. 454).

Boucher, Manuel (1998), *Le rap. Expression des Lascars* (Paris: L'Harmattan).

Bouledogue Rouge (2003), 'Manu Chao', *Ce Qu'il Faut Détruire (CQFD)*, 4, 15 September, www.cequilfautdetruire.org, last accessed 24 March 2009.

Bourdieu, Pierre (1979), *La distinction. Critique du jugement social* (Paris: Les Editions de Minuit).

Bouton, Rémi (1999), 'A l'écoute des tendances', *L'Année du disque 1999* (Paris: Music Business Publishing/SNEP), 64.

Breatnach, Mary and Eric Sterenfeld (2000), 'From Messiaen to MC Solaar: music in France in the Second Half of the 20th Century', in William Kidd and Siân Reynolds (eds), *Contemporary French Cultural Studies* (London: Arnold), 244–56.

Brocard, Véronique (2008), 'Ondes positives', *Télérama*, 3029, 30 January, 9.

Bruneau, Ivan (2006), 'La Confédération paysanne', in Xavier Crettiez and Isabelle Sommier (eds), *La France rebelle* (Paris: Michalon), 234–48.

Brunstein, Laurent (1997), 'S'approprier le rock', in Anne-Marie Green (ed.), *Des jeunes et des musiques. Rock, rap, techno...* (Paris and Montreal: L'Harmattan), 113–67.

Byrne, Ciar (2007), 'Major Record Labels "Stifling Creativity" Say Independents', *The Independent*, 5 October, 9.

Calvet, Louis-Jean (1981), *Chanson et société* (Paris: Payot).

Calvet, Louis-Jean and Jean-Claude Klein (1978), *Faut-il brûler Sardou?* (Paris: Editions Savelli).

Cameron, Deborah (2001), *Working with Spoken Discourse* (London: Sage).

Cassavetti, Hugo (2007a), 'Les Rita Mitsouko', *Télérama*, 2986, 4 April, 14–18.

Cassavetti, Hugo (2007b), 'Et pourquoi pas l'Amérique?', *Télérama*, 3007, 29 August, 30–3.

Cassavetti, Hugo (2008), '53ème concours Eurovision de la chanson', *Télérama*, 3045, 21 May, 85.

Cavicchi, Daniel (1998), *Tramps like Us. Music and Meaning among Springsteen Fans* (New York and Oxford: Oxford University Press).

Cecchetto, Céline (2007), 'Popularité et mémoire dans la chanson française contemporaine. Analyse croisée de trois albums de Têtes Raides, Les Ogres de Barback et Weepers Circus', IASPM branche francophone d'Europe, first conference, Leuven, February, unpublished paper, www.iaspmfrancophone. online.fr select 'colloque 2007', scroll down to 'Cecchetto'. PDF available.

Certeau, Michel de (1990), *L'invention du quotidien (1)* (Paris: Folio/Gallimard).

Chamberland, Roger (2002), 'The Cultural Paradox of Rap Made in Quebec', in Alain-Philippe Durand (ed.), *Black, Blanc, Beur. Rap Music and Hip-Hop Culture in the Francophone World* (Lanham: Scarecrow Press), 124–36.

Chérel, Guillaume (1992), 'Le parrain des bouchers', *L'Humanité*, 12 May, online at http://www.humanite.fr/journal/1992–05–12/1992–05–12–653473, last accessed 18 March 2009.

Coffey, Amanda and Paul Atkinson (1996), *Making Sense of Qualitative Data* (Thousand Oaks: Sage).

Cole, Alistair (1998), *French Politics and Society* (Hemel Hempstead: Prentice Hall).

Collin, Claude (1982), *Ondes de choc. De l'usage de la radio en temps de lutte* (Paris and Grenoble: L'Harmattan).

Connell, John and Chris Gibson (2003), *Sound Tracks. Popular Music, Identity and Place* (London and New York: Routledge).

Conway, Kelley (2004), *Chanteuse in the City. The Realist Singer in French Film* (Berkeley, Los Angeles and London: University of California Press).

Cornick, Martyn (1998), 'The Silence of the Left Intellectuals in Mitterrand's France', in Mairi Maclean (ed.), *The Mitterrand Years* (Basingstoke: Macmillan), 300–13.

Crisp, Colin (1997), *The Classic French Cinema, 1930–1960* (Bloomington and London: Indiana University Press and I. B. Tauris Publishers).

Cyran, Olivier (2000), 'Zebda: "Y'a pas d'arrangements avec la télé"', *Charlie Hebdo*, 397, 26 January, 10–11.

D'Angelo, Mario (1997), *Socio-économie de la musique en France* (Paris: La Documentation française).

Dahan, Béatrice (2004), 'Livret de famille (suite)', *Empan*, 56 (4), 170–71.

Dalbavie, Juliette (2003), 'Exposer des objets sonores: le cas des chansons de Brassens', *Volume!*, 2 (2), 145–61.

Dauncey, Hugh and Steve Cannon (eds) (2003), *Popular Music in France from Chanson to Techno* (Aldershot: Ashgate).

Davet, Stéphane and Frank Tenaille (1996), *Le Printemps de Bourges. Chroniques des musiques d'aujourd'hui* (Paris: Découvertes Gallimard).

Delaroche, Philippe (1994), 'Musées, parcs, festivals: l'envers du décor', *Enjeux, Les Echos*, 94, July-August, 48–9.

Deschamps, Stéphane (2001), 'Un indien dans la ville', *Les Inrockuptibles*, 290, 15 May, 36–43.

Deschamps, Stéphane (2002a), 'L'auberge espagnole', *Les Inrockuptibles*, 11 September, 46–9.

Deschamps, Stéphane (2002b), 'Quelqu'un m'a dit', *Les Inrockuptibles*, 31 October, www.lesinrocks.com, key in 'Carla Bruni', then select 'Carla Bruni-Quelqu'un m'a dit'.

Désir, Harlem (1985), *Touche pas à mon pote* (Paris: Bernard Grasset).

Dicale, Bertrand (2006), *La chanson française pour les nuls* (Paris: First Editions).

Dirlik, Arif (1994), 'The Post-Colonial Aura: Third World Criticism in the Age of Global Capitalism', *Critical Inquiry*, 20, 328–56.

Dirn, Louis (1998), *La société française en tendances, 1975–1995: deux décennies de changement* (Paris: Presses Universitaires de France).

Donnat, Olivier (1998), *Les pratiques culturelles des Français, Enquête 1997* (Paris: La Documentation française).

Drake, Philip (2003) '"Mortgaged to Music": New Retro Movies in 1990s Hollywood Cinema', in Paul Grainge (ed.), *Memory and Popular Film* (Manchester and New York: Manchester University Press), 183–201.

Dubois, Laurent (2000), '*La République métissée*: Citizenship, Colonialism, and the Borders of French History', *Cultural Studies*, 14 (1), 15–34.

Duffy, Michelle (2000), 'Lines of Drift: Festival Participation and Performing a Sense of Place', *Popular Music*, 19 (1), 51–64.

Durand, Alain-Philippe (ed.) (2002), *Black, Blanc, Beur. Rap Music and Hip-Hop Culture in the Francophone World* (Lanham: Scarecrow Press).

Dyer, Richard (1985), 'Entertainment and Utopia', in Bill Nichols (ed.), *Movies and Methods: An Anthology*, vol. 2 (Berkeley: University of California Press), 220–32.

Dyer, Richard (1990 [1979]), 'In Defense of Disco', in Simon Frith and Andrew Goodwin (eds), *On Record. Rock, Pop, and the Written Word* (London and New York: Routledge), 410–18.

Ervine, Jonathan (2008), 'Citizenship and Belonging in Suburban France: The Music of Zebda', *ACME. An International E-journal for Critical Geographies*, 7 (2), May, 199–213.

Farchy, Joëlle (1999), *La fin de l'exception culturelle?* (Paris: CNRS Editions).

Ferenczi, Aurélien (2008), 'Carla punie', *Télérama*, 3035, 12 March, 14.

Finkielkraut, Alain (1987), *La défaite de la pensée* (Paris: Folio).

Fiske, John (1989), *Understanding Popular Culture* (Boston: Unwin Hyman).

Flick, Uwe (1998), *An Introduction to Qualitative Research* (Thousand Oaks: Sage).

Fontana, Céline (2007), *La chanson française. Histoire, interprètes, auteurs, compositeurs* (Paris: Hachette).

Forrest, Emma E. (2002), 'Busker in Babylon', *The Guardian Weekend*, 13 April, 37–8.

Foucault, Michel (1986 [1967]), 'Of Other Spaces', *Diacritics*, 16 (1), Spring, 22–7.

Frith, Simon (1981), *Sound Effects. Youth, Leisure, and the Politics of Rock'n'Roll* (New York: Pantheon Books).

Frith, Simon (1992), 'The Industrialization of Popular Music', in James Lull (ed.), *Popular Music and Communication* (Newbury Park and London: Sage), 49–74.

Frith, Simon (1996), 'Music and Identity', in Stuart Hall and Paul Du Gay (eds), *Questions of Cultural Identity* (London: Sage), 108–27.

Froissart, Alain and Antoine de Gaudemar (2004 [1974]), 'Nougaro: "Je suis un négro-grec"', *Libération Hors-Série*, 'Chanson française, 1973–2006: paroles, musiques et polémiques', 6–9.

Fumaroli, Marc (1992), *L'état culturel. Essai sur une religion moderne* (Paris: Editions de Fallois).

Fysh, Peter (1998), 'The Failure of Anti-Racist Movements in France, 1981–1995', in Mairi McLean (ed.), *The Mitterrand Years. Legacy and Evaluation* (Basingstoke: Macmillan), 198–214.

Garapon, Paul (1999), 'Métamorphoses de la chanson française, 1945–99', *Esprit*, July, 89–118.

Gasnault, François (1986), *Guinguettes et Lorettes. Bals publics à Paris au 19ème siècle* (Paris: Aubier).

Gastaut, Yvan (2006), 'Chansons et chanteurs maghrébins en France (1920–1986)', *Migrations Société*, 18 (103), 105–15.

GECE (2007), *Etude des publics du festival des Vieilles Charrues 2007*, Groupe d'Etudes Culturo-économiques, Rennes, www.vieillescharrues.asso.fr/media/telechargement/RapportInternet07.pdf, last accessed 24 March 2009.

Gildea, Robert (1994), *The Past in French History* (New Haven and London: Yale University Press).

Gilroy, Paul (1993), *The Black Atlantic. Modernity and Double Consciousness* (London: Verso).

Gocić, Goran (2001), *The Cinema of Emir Kusturica. Notes from the Underground* (London and New York: Wallflower Press).

Gonot, Jean-Philippe (2003), *Têtes Raides* (Paris: Seghers).

Les goûts musicaux des Français (survey Sofrès for SACEM), January 1999.

Green, Anne-Marie (ed.) (1997), *Des jeunes et des musiques. Rock, Rap, Techno...* (Paris and Montreal: L'Harmattan).

Gustave, Anne-Marie (2003), 'Les liens du son', *Télérama*, 2770, 12 February, 152–3.

H.M. (1991a), 'Allez les Vertes!', *Rock & Folk*, 285, May, 36–7.

H.M. (1991b), 'Mano deluxe', *Rock & Folk*, 290, October, 42–3.

H.M. (1992a), 'La Mano Negra. Amerika Perdida', *Rock & Folk*, 293, January, 78.

H.M. (1992b), 'Les Négresses Vertes. Famille nombreuse', *Rock & Folk*, 293, January, 79.

H.M. (1992c), 'Alternactif (Bondage)', *Rock & Folk*, 299, July, 52–5.

H.M. (1992d), '7 à Toulouse (Zebda)', *Rock & Folk*, 302, October, 32–3.

H.M. (1992e), 'Négresses with Attitude', *Rock & Folk*, 303, November, 56–9.

Hache, Victor (2002), 'Patrick Bruel entre-deux javas', *L'Humanité*, 12 July, www.humanite.presse.fr/journal/2002–07–12/2002–07–12–37052, last accessed 21 March 2009.

Hache, Victor (2006), 'Grégoire Simon: "Artistiquement et socialement, il y a des choses à dire"', *L'Humanité*, 15 September, www.humanite.fr/popup_imprimer.html?id_article=836729, last accessed 21 March 2009.

Hagen-Smith, Lisa (1995), 'On Your Mark… The Audience Place and the Winnipeg Folk Festival', *Canadian Folk Music Bulletin*, 29 (3), 16–19.

Hakem, Tewfik (1999), 'Métèque et mat', *Les Inrockuptibles*, 206, 7 July, 40–41.

Hardt, Michael and Antonio Negri (2000), *Empire* (Cambridge and London: Harvard University Press).

Hare, Geoff (2003), 'Popular Music on French Radio and Television', in Hugh Dauncey and Steve Cannon (eds), *Popular Music in France from Chanson to Techno* (Aldershot: Ashgate), 57–76.

Hargreaves, Alec (1997), 'Multiculturalism', in Christopher Flood and Laurence Bell (eds), *Political Ideologies in Contemporary France* (London and Washington: Pinter), 180–99.

Hargreaves, Alec (2007), *Multi-Ethnic France. Immigration, Politics, Culture and Society* (London and New York: Routledge).

Hargreaves, Alec and Mark McKinney (1997), 'Introduction', in Hargreaves and McKinney (eds), *Post-Colonial Cultures in France* (London and New York: Routledge), 3–27.

Harrison, Kim (2003), 'Putain d'camion: Commercialism and the *Chanson* Genre in the Work of Renaud', *Volume!*, 2 (2), 69–82.

Hawkins, Peter (2000), *Chanson. The French Singer-Songwriter from Aristide Bruant to the Present Day* (Aldershot: Ashgate).

Hazera, Hélène (1999), 'Raides, caustiques et acoustiques', *Libération*, 26 January, 38.

Hennion, Antoine (1990 [1983]), 'The Production of Success', in Simon Frith and Andrew Goodwin (eds), *On Record. Rock, Pop, and the Written Word* (London and New York: Routledge), 185–206.

Hennion, Antoine, Sophie Maisonneuve and Emilie Gomart (2000), *Figures de l'amateur. Formes, objets, pratiques de l'amour de la musique aujourd'hui* (Paris: La Documentation Française).

Hesmondhalgh, David (1997), 'Post-Punk's Attempt to Democratise the Music Industry: The Success and Failure of Rough Trade', *Popular Music*, 16 (3), October, 255–74.

Hesmondhalgh, David (1999), 'Indie: The Institutional Politics and Aesthetics of a Popular Music Genre', *Cultural Studies*, 13 (1), 34–61.

Hesmondhalgh, David (2002), 'Popular Music Audiences and Everyday life', in David Hesmondhalgh and Keith Negus (eds), *Popular Music Studies* (London: Arnold), 117–30.

Hidalgo, Fred (1991), *Putain de chanson* (Nantes: Editions du Petit Véhicule).

Hitchcock, Peter (1998), 'The Grotesque of the Body Electric', in Michael Mayerfeld Bell and Michael Gardiner (eds), *Bakhtin and the Human Sciences* (London, Thousand Oaks and New Delhi: Sage), 78–94.

Hopkins, Nic (2004), 'EMI and Warner Merger "Back on Agenda"', *The Times*, 21 June, http://business.timesonline.co.uk/tol/business/article447993.ece, last accessed 25 March 2009.

Howarth, David and Georgios Varouxakis (2003), *Contemporary France. An Introduction to French Politics and Society* (London: Arnold).

Huq, Rupa (2006), *Beyond Subculture. Pop, Youth and Identity in a Postcolonial World* (London and New York: Routledge).

Hutnyk, John (2000), *Critique of Exotica. Music, Politics and the Culture Industry* (London and Sterling: Pluto Press).

James, Alex (2007), 'Mud, Sweat and Beers', *The Independent Magazine*, 12 May, 34–7.

Jameson, Fredric (1984), 'Postmodernism, or the Cultural Logic of Late Capitalism', *New Left Review*, 146, July–August, 53–92.

Jammet, A. (1999), 'Argent, or ou diamant? Les salaires du disque', *L'Année du disque 1999* (Music Business Publishing/SNEP), 28–35.

Jarno, Stéphane (1999), 'Les gringos parigots', *Télérama*, 2567, 24 March, 66.

Jarno, Stéphane (2003), 'Carla Bruni, une pure épure', *Télérama*, 2770, 12 February, 50.

Jordana, Huguette (2004), 'Livret de famille', *Empan*, 56 (4), 169–70.

Jouvenet, Morgan (2006), *Rap, techno, électro... Le musicien entre travail artistique et critique sociale* (Paris: Editions de la Maison des sciences de l'homme).

July, Joël (2007), *Esthétique de la chanson française contemporaine* (Paris: L'Harmattan).

Kaganski, Serge (2001), 'Amélie pas jolie', *Les Inrockuptibles*, 31 May.

Kelly, Michael (ed.) (2001), *French Culture and Society. The Essentials* (London: Arnold).

Kernel, Brigitte (1987), *Chanter Made in France* (Paris: Michel de Maule).

King, Stephen A. (2006), 'Protest Music as "Ego-Enhancement": Reggae Music, the Rastafarian Movement and the Re-Examination of Race and Identity in

Jamaica', in Ian Peddie (ed.), *The Resisting Muse: Popular Music and Social Protest* (Aldershot: Ashgate), 105–18.

Klein, Jean-Claude (1995), 'Chanson et société: une "passion française"?' in Ursula Mathis (ed.), *La chanson française contemporaine* (Innsbruck: Verlag des Instituts für Sprachwissenschaft), 63–76.

Klein, Naomi (2001), *No Logo* (London: Flamingo).

Kun, Josh (2004), 'Esperando La Ultima Ola / Waiting for the Last Wave. Manu Chao and the Music of Globalization', in Deborah Pacini Hernandez, Héctor Fernández L'Hoeste and Eric Zolov (eds), *Rockin' Las Américas. The Global Politics of Rock in Latin/o America* (Pittsburgh: University of Pittsburgh Press), 332–46.

Lacoeuilhe, Eric (1987), 'Le Top 50: Fumisterie?' in Brigitte Kernel (ed.), *Made in France* (Paris: Michel de Maule), 95–102.

Laing, Dave (1986), 'The Music Industry and the "Cultural Imperialism" Thesis', *Media, Culture and Society*, 8, 331–41.

Laing, Dave (2004), 'The Three Woodstocks and the Live Music Scene', in Andy Bennett (ed.), *Remembering Woodstock* (Aldershot: Ashgate), 1–17.

Le Guern, Philippe (2003), 'The Study of Popular Music between Sociology and Aesthetics: A Survey of Current Research in France', in Hugh Dauncey and Steve Cannon (eds), *Popular Music in France from Chanson to Techno* (Aldershot: Ashgate), 7–26.

Le Vaillant, Luc (2007), '"Pipolitique": Nicolas Sarkozy et Carla Bruni à l'affiche', *Libération*, 17 December, www.liberation.fr/actualite/societe/298392.FR.php, last accessed 23 March 2009.

Leahy, Sarah (2005), 'Mireille Mathieu', in Bill Marshall (ed.), *France and the Americas. Culture, Politics and History*, vol. 2, 782–3.

Lebrun, Barbara (2002), 'A Case Study of Zebda: Republicanism, *Métissage* and Authenticity in Contemporary France', *Volume!*, 1 (2), 59–69.

Lebrun, Barbara (2005a), 'Charity and Political Protest in French Popular Music', *Modern and Contemporary France*, 13 (4), November, 435–47.

Lebrun, Barbara (2005b), 'Mind over Matter. The Under-Performance of the Body and Gender in French Rock Music of the 1990s', *French Cultural Studies*, 16 (2), 205–21.

Lebrun, Barbara (2006a), 'Banging on the Wall of Fortress France: Music for *Sans-Papiers* in the Republic', *Third Text*, 20 (6), November, 709–19.

Lebrun, Barbara (2006b), 'Majors et labels indépendants. France, Grande-Bretagne, 1960–2000', *Vingtième Siècle*, 92, October–December, 33–45.

Lebrun, Barbara (2007), 'Le bruit et l'odeur... du succès? Contestation et contradictions dans le rock métis de Zebda', *Modern and Contemporary France*, 15 (3), August, 325–37.

Lebrun, Barbara (forthcoming 2009), 'René, Ginette, Louise et les autres: nostalgie et authenticité dans la chanson néo-réaliste', *French Politics, Culture and Society*.

Leclère, Thierry (1999), 'Zebda, les chanteurs de la contestation festive', *Télérama* 2566, 17 March, 31–2.

Lefeuvre, Gildas (1998), *Le guide du producteur de disques* (Paris: Dixit).

Lefeuvre, Gildas (1999), 'Indépendance cha-cha-cha!', *L'Année du disque 1999* (Music Business Publishing/SNEP), 45–52.

Lehoux, Valérie (2004), 'Le baby boom', *Télérama*, 2862, 17 November, 54–61.

Lehoux, Valérie (2008a), 'Attention, fragile!', *Télérama Sortir*, 3049, 18 June, 4–5.

Lehoux, Valérie (2008b), 'Padam', *Télérama*, 3049, 18 June, 65.

Lehoux, Valérie and Hugo Cassavetti (2008), 'L'épreuve du lancer de disque', *Télérama*, 3050, 25 June, 11.

Liauzu, Claude and Josette Liauzu (2002), *Quand on chantait les colonies. Colonisation et culture populaire de 1830 à nos jours* (Paris: Editions Syllepse).

Lin, Zoé (2001), *Zebda 100% Motivés* (Paris: Agnès Vienot Editions).

Liperi, Felice (1988), 'Sound Waves from the Edges of the Empire: The Ethno-Wave', *Cultural Studies*, 2 (2), May, 247–50.

Lledo, Eugène (1991), 'Rock et séduction', in Patrick Mignon and Antoine Hennion (eds), *Rock: de l'histoire au mythe* (Paris: Anthropos), 121–46.

Looseley, David (1995), *The Politics of Fun. Cultural Policy and Debate in Contemporary France* (Oxford: Berg).

Looseley, David (2003), *Popular Music in Contemporary France: Authenticity, Politics, Debate* (Oxford and New York: Berg).

Looseley, David (2005), 'Fabricating Johnny: French Popular Music and National Culture', *French Cultural Studies*, 16 (2), 191–204.

Lorton, Patrice with Laurent Ciron and Emmanuel Charriéras (2002), 'Manu Chao: Incognito', TV documentary for *Envoyé Spécial*, France 2, May.

Loupias, Bernard (2001), 'Le retour du clandestino', *Le Nouvel Observateur*, 31 May, 124–6.

Lowenthal, David (1985), *The Past Is a Foreign Country* (Cambridge and New York: Cambridge University Press).

Lupieri, Stéphane (1994), 'Francofolies, le triomphe de la chanson', *Enjeux, Le mensuel de l'économie*, 94, July–August, 54.

MacDonald, Raymond, Dorothy Miell and Graeme Wilson (2005), 'Talking about Music: A Vehicle for Identity Development', in Dorothy Miell, Raymond MacDonald and David J. Hargreaves (eds), *Musical Communication* (Oxford: Oxford University Press), 321–38.

Manche, Philippe (2004), *Manu Chao: Destinación Esperanza* (Paris: Le Serpent à Plumes).

Marc Martínez, Isabelle (2008), *Le rap français. Esthétique et poétique des textes (1990–1995)* (Bern: Peter Lang).

Marcil, Erwan (1997), *Bérurier Noir. Conte cruel de la jeunesse* (Maisonneuve: Camion Blanc).

Marcus, Leah S. (1986), *The Politics of Mirth. Jonson, Herrick, Milton, Marvell, and the Defense of Old Holiday Pastimes* (Chicago and London: University of Chicago Press).

Marx-Scouras, Danielle (2004), 'Rock the Hexagon', *Contemporary French and Francophone Studies*, 8 (1), January, 51–61.

Marx-Scouras, Danielle (2005), *La France de Zebda, 1981–2004. Faire de la musique un acte politique* (Paris: Editions Autrement).

Mason, Jennifer (1996), *Qualitative Researching* (London: Sage).

Mathis-Moser, Ursula (2003), 'L'image de "l'Arabe" dans la chanson française contemporaine', *Volume!*, 2 (2), 129–43.

Maurin, Louis (2005), 'Inégalités sociales. Grandes tendances', in Serge Cordellier and Elizabeth Lau (eds), *L'Etat de la France, Edition 2005–2006* (Paris: La Découverte), 99–105.

Maxwell, Ian (2002), 'The Curse of Fandom: Insiders, Outsiders and Ethnography', in David Hesmondhalgh and Keith Negus (eds), *Popular Music Studies* (London: Arnold), 103–16.

Mazdon, Lucy (2000), *Encore Hollywood. Remaking French Cinema* (London: British Film Institute).

Mazdon, Lucy (2007), 'Transnational "French" Cinema: The Cannes Film Festival', *Modern and Contemporary France*, 15 (1), February, 9–20.

McClary, Susan (2000), *Conventional Wisdom. The Content of Musical Form* (Berkeley: University of California Press).

McKay, George (2000), *Glastonbury. A Very English Fair* (London: Victor Gollancz).

McMurray, David A. (1997), 'La France arabe', in Alec Hargreaves and Mark McKinney (eds), *Post-Colonial Cultures in France* (London and New York: Routledge), 26–39.

Meouak, Mohamed and Jordi Aguadé (1996), 'La Rhorhomanie et les Beurs: l'exemple de deux langues en contact', *Estudios de dialectología norteafricana y andalusí* (EDNA), 1, 157–66.

Mermet, Gérard (1985), *Francoscopie. Les Français: qui sont-ils? Où vont-ils?* (Paris: Larousse).

Mermet, Gérard (1998), *Francoscopie 1999. Qui sont les Français? Faits, Analyses, Tendances, Comparaisons* (Paris: Larousse).

Mermet, Gérard (2000), *Francoscopie 2001. Comment vivent les Français* (Paris: Larousse).

Meunier, Alexandre (1998), 'Du rififi chez les indépendants : un état des lieux du mouvement indépendant français', Mémoire de Licence, IUP Ingénierie documentaire, Département Archives et Médiathèque, Université de Toulouse II-Le Mirail, France. Available online : http://membres.lycos.fr/discographies/le_rock_independant.htm

Micaeli, Corinne (1990), 'Suivez le boeuf! Boucherie en Amérique', *Rock & Folk*, 280, December, 74–8.

Mongeau, Olivier (2002), '*Les Inrocks* ont gagné en maturité', *Stratégies*, 1230, 29 March, 18.

Monnin, Isabelle (2000), 'Zebda: la colère en chantant', *Le Nouvel Observateur*, 23 March, 10.

Moores, Shaun (1993), *Interpreting Audiences. The Ethnography of Media Consumption* (London: Sage).

Moreira, Paul (1987), *Rock métis en France* (Paris: Souffles).

Morley, David (2006), 'Unanswered Questions in Audience Research', in Isabelle Charpentier (ed.), *Comment sont reçues les œuvres* (Grâne: Creaphis), 263–81.

Morley, David and Kevin Robins (1989), 'Spaces of Identity: Communications Technologies and the Reconfiguration of Europe', *Screen*, 30 (4), 10–34.

Morley, David and Kevin Robins (1995), *Spaces of Identity. Global Media, Electronic Landscapes and Cultural Boundaries* (London: Routledge).

Mortaigne, Véronique (1998), 'Toulouse, capitale de la résistance musicale des quartiers', *Le Monde*, 8 November, 27.

Mucchielli, Laurent (2006), 'Les émeutes urbaines', in Xavier Crettiez and Isabelle Sommier (eds), *La France rebelle* (Paris: Michalon).

Murphy, Timothy and Daniel Smith (2001), 'What I Hear Is Thinking Too: Deleuze and Guattari Go Pop', *Echo: A Music-Centered Journal*, 3 (1), Spring, www.humnet.ucla.edu/echo/volume3-issue1/smithmurphy/deleuze_and_guattari.pdf, last accessed 22 March 2009.

Negus, Keith (1992), *Producing Pop: Culture and Conflict in the Popular Music Industry* (London and New York: Edward Arnold).

Negus, Keith (1999), *Music Genres and Corporate Cultures* (London and New York: Routledge).

Norot, Anne-Claire (1999), 'L'un dans l'autre', *Les Inrockuptibles*, 206, 7 July, 42–5.

Paddison, Max (1996), *Adorno, Modernism and Mass Culture. Essays on Critical Theory and Music* (London: Kahn and Averill).

Pantchenko, Daniel (2004), 'Têtes Raides. Bouffe tes morts', *Chorus*, 49, Autumn, 95–118.

Paquotte, Anne-Marie (1999), 'Paris Combo', *Télérama*, 2580, 23 June, 74.

Paquotte, Anne-Marie (2001), 'Têtes Raides', *Télérama*, 2667, 21 February, 56–9.

Paquotte, Anne-Marie (2002), 'Rue de la Muette', *Télérama*, 2713, 9 Janvier, 53.

Pascaud, Fabienne (2007), 'Rachid Taha: "La France est un pays de plus en plus féminin"', *Télérama*, 2977, 31 January, 14–18.

Pasqualini, Jean-Pierre (2007), 'Chanson et politique. Les lendemains qui déchantent', *Platine*, 142, July–August, 3.

Péchu, Cécile (2006), 'Le rock alternatif', in Xavier Crettiez and Isabelle Sommier (eds), *La France rebelle* (Paris: Editions Michalon), 609–16.

Pecqueux, Anthony (2002), 'Common Partitions: Musical Commonplaces', in Alain-Philippe Durand (ed.), *Black, Blanc, Beur. Rap Music and Hip-Hop*

Culture in the Francophone World (Langham and Oxford: Scarecrow Press), 33–44.

Peddie, Ian (ed.) (2006), *The Resisting Muse: Popular Music and Social Protest* (Aldershot: Ashgate).

Pellerin, Hélène (2003), 'Crisis? What Crisis? The Politics of Migration Regulation in the Era of Globalization', in Eleonore Kofman and Gillian Youngs (eds), *Globalization: Theory and Practice* (London and New York: Continuum), 177–84.

Perrin, Ludovic (2001a), 'Têtes-à-Têtes raides', *Libération*, 13 March, 38.

Perrin, Ludovic (2001b), 'Carhaix d'as', *Libération*, 23 July, 29.

Perrin, Ludovic (2005), *Vincent, Carla, M et les autres. Une nouvelle chanson française* (Paris: Editions Hors Collection).

Pinçon, Michel and Monique Pinçon-Charlot (2000), *Sociologie de la bourgeoisie* (Paris: La Découverte).

Pinsard, Laurence (2001), 'Le monde selon Manu Chao', available on www. bestofmanuchao.com/manu-chao/interviews.php (select 'presse écrite', then 'Article de Laurence Pinsard Septembre 2001', and click 'la suite'), last accessed 25 March 2009.

Pinto, Diana (1988), 'The Atlantic Influence and the Mellowing of French Identity', in Jolyon Howorth and George Ross (eds), *Contemporary France: A Review of Interdisciplinary Studies*, vol. 2 (London: Pinter), 116–33.

Pires, Matt (2003), 'The Popular Music Press', in Hugh Dauncey and Steve Cannon (eds), *Popular Music in France from Chanson to Techno* (Aldershot: Ashgate), 77–98.

Pitts, Stephanie E. (2004), '"Everybody Wants to Be Pavarotti": The Experience of Music for Performers and Audience at a Gilbert and Sullivan Festival', *Journal of the Royal Music Association*, 129 (1), 143–60.

Plummer, Ken (1995), *Telling Sexual Stories. Power, Change and Social Worlds* (London: Routledge).

Powrie, Phil (ed.) (1999), *French Cinema in the 1990s: Continuity and Difference* (Oxford: Oxford University Press).

Prévos, André J. M. (1991), 'Le "mouvement alternatif", un renouveau de la chanson populaire française? Le cas de Bérurier Noir et des Garçons Bouchers', *Contemporary French Civilization*, 15 (1), Winter/Spring, 35–51.

Provencher, Denis (2003), 'Press' in Hugh Dauncey (ed.), *French Popular Culture* (London: Arnold), 34–47.

Rambach, Anne and Marine Rambach (2001), *Les Intellos Précaires* (Paris: Fayard).

Reader, Keith A. (1987), *Intellectuals and the Left in France since 1968* (Basingstoke: Macmillan).

Rearick, Charles (1977), 'Festivals in Modern France: The Experience of the Third Republic', *Journal of Contemporary History*, 12, 435–60.

Reijasse, Jérôme (2002), *Zebda, Guide Musicbook* (Paris: Prélude et Fugue).

Reins, Sacha (2003), 'Y a-t-il une nouvelle chanson française?', *Le Point*, 18 July, 70–3.

Renault, Gilles (1999), 'Mouiller la chemise', *Libération*, 6 September, 31–2.

Revel, Renaud (2008), 'Carlamania ou Sarkopub?', *L'Express*, 2974, 3 July, 26.

Reynolds, Simon (2005), *Rip It Up and Start Again, Post-Punk 1978–1984* (London: Faber and Faber).

Rifkin, Adrian (1991), 'French Popular Song: Changing Myths of the People', in Brian Rigby and Nicholas Hewitt (eds), *France and the Mass Media* (London: Macmillan), 200–19.

Rigoulet, Laurent (1998), 'Louise Attaque par surprise', *Libération*, 6 April, 32–3.

Robecchi, Alessandro (2002), *Manu Chao* (Paris: Plon).

Robine, Marc (1994), *Anthologie de la chanson française. Des trouvères aux grands auteurs du XIXème siècle* (Paris: Albin Michel).

Rosello, Mireille (1998a), 'Representing Illegal Immigrants in France: From *clandestins* to *L'Affaire des sans-papiers de Saint-Bernard*', *Journal of European Studies*, March–June, 28 (1–2), 137–52.

Rosello, Mireille (1998b), *Declining the Stereotype. Ethnicity and Representation in French Cultures* (Hanover and London: Dartmouth College/University Press of New England).

Ross, David A. (2007), 'Madame Souza's *Casa Portuguesa* in France: The Portuguese Element in Sylvain Chomet's Multicultural, Animated Film, *Les Triplettes de Belleville* (2003)', in Francisco Cota Fagundes and Irene Maria F. Blayer (eds), *Tradições Portuguesas / Portuguese Traditions: in Honor of Claude Hulet* (San Jose: Portuguese Heritage Publications of California, 2007), 463–77.

Roussel, Daniel (1995), 'L'état, le rock et la chanson', *Regards sur l'actualité* (Paris : La Documentation française), 218, 41–55.

Route du Rock report (1999), Unpublished survey, forwarded by Alban Coutoux, PA for La Route du Rock festival.

Saka, Pierre and Yann Plougastel (eds) (1999), *La chanson française et francophone* (Paris: Larousse/HER).

Santolaria, Nicolas (2002), 'Zebda. Les agités du vocal', *Epok*, 28, July–August, 9–14.

Schowalter, Daniel F. (2000), 'Remembering the Dangers of Rock and Roll: Toward a Historical Narrative of the Rock Festival', *Critical Studies in Media Communication*, 17 (1), March, 86–102.

Schuster, Liza (2004), 'The Exclusion of Asylum Seekers in Europe', Working Paper for *Compas* Research Centre, University of Oxford, March, www.compas.ox.ac.uk/publications/papers/WP0401.pdf, last accessed 22 March 2009.

Scott, Derek (2001), *The Singing Bourgeois. Songs of the Victorian Drawing-Room and Parlour* (Aldershot: Ashgate).

Scott, Derek (2008), *Sounds of the Metropolis. The 19th-Century Popular Music Revolution in London, New York, Paris and Vienna* (Oxford: Oxford University Press).

Seca, Jean-Marie (2001), *Les Musiciens Underground* (Paris: Presses Universitaires de France).

Seery, Mairéad (2001), 'Essence ordinaire de Zebda: carburant pour une République en panne', *The Irish Journal of French Studies*, 1, 15–24.

Seery, Mairéad (2007), 'Echoes, Images and Myths of the Entre-Deux-Guerres in French Popular Music of the 21st Century', PhD thesis, National University of Ireland, Galway, 108–33.

Shuker, Roy (1998), *Key Concepts in Popular Music* (London, Routledge).

Silverman, Carol (2007), 'Trafficking in the Exotic with "Gypsy" Music: Balkan Roma, Cosmopolitanism, and "World Music" Festivals', in Donna A. Buchanan (ed.), *Balkan Popular Culture and the Ottoman Ecumene* (Lanham: Scarecrow Press), 335–61.

Silverman, Max (1995), 'Rights and Difference: Questions of Citizenship in France', in Alec G. Hargreaves and Jeremy Leaman (eds), *Racism, Ethnicity and Politics in Contemporary France* (Aldershot: Edward Elgar), 253–64.

Sorgue, Pierre (1998), 'Liberté, égalité, fraternité!', *Télérama*, 2548, 14 November, 15.

Spencer, Neil (2007), 'Manu Chao', *The Observer*, 16 September, 20.

Tarr, Carrie (2005), *Reframing Difference.* Beurs *and* banlieue *Film-making in France* (Manchester: Manchester University Press).

Teillet, Philippe (1993), 'Sur une transgression: la naissance de la politique du rock', *L'Aquarium* (Rennes: CRAP), 73–85.

Teillet, Philippe (2003), 'Rock and Culture in France: Ways, Processes and Ambitions', in Hugh Dauncey and Steve Cannon (eds), *Popular Music in France from Chanson to Techno. Culture, Identity and Society* (Aldershot: Ashgate), 171–90.

Teillet, Philippe (2008), 'Le public "insaisissable" : la crise des festivals', *Les Cahiers de l'ORCCA*, 28, May, 28–30.

Tellier, Emmanuel (1999), 'Les joies du Bondage', *Les Inrockuptibles*, 206, July, 34–7.

Terrasse, Jean-Marc (1995), 'Le populisme dans la chanson française. De Damia à Renaud, aux Garçons Bouchers et aux Négresses Vertes', in Ursula Mathis (ed.), *La chanson française contemporaine: politique, société, médias* (Innsbruck: Verlag des Instituts für Sprachwissenschaft), 205–22.

Thornton, Sarah (1995), *Club Cultures. Music, Media and Subcultural Capital* (Cambridge: Polity Press).

Tinker, Chris (2005), *Georges Brassens and Jacques Brel. Personal and Social Narratives in Post-war Chanson* (Liverpool: Liverpool University Press).

Tinker, Chris (2007), 'Shaping Youth in *Salut les copains*', *Modern and Contemporary France*, 15 (3), August, 293–308.

Tournès, Ludovic (2005), 'L'électrification des sensibilités musicales: le disque, l'enregistrement électrique et la mutation du paysage sonore en France (1925–1939)', *French Cultural Studies*, 16 (2), 135–49.

Valéro, Vanessa (2002), 'Le festival de rock, entre passion et désenchantement', *Volume!*, 1 (1), 113–23.

Vandel, Philippe and Paul Rambali (1988), 'La java contre Le Pen', *Actuel*, 108, June, 105–15.

Verlant, Gilles (ed.) (2000), *L'encyclopédie du rock français* (Paris: Editions Hors Collection).

Vignol, Baptiste (2007), *Cette chanson qui emmerde le Front National* (Paris: Editions de Tournon).

Vincendeau, Ginette (1987), 'The *Mise-en-Scène* of Suffering. French *Chanteuses Réalistes*', *New Formations*, 3, 107–28.

Vincendeau, Ginette (2001), 'Café Society', *Sight and Sound*, 11 (8), August, 22–5.

Von Badaboum, Hermann (1999), 'Hasta siempre la techno', *Charlie Hebdo*, 350, March, 10.

Walser, Robert (1993), *Running with the Devil. Power, Gender, and Madness in Heavy Metal Music* (Hanover and London: University Press of New England).

Walsh, John (2008), 'A Really In Tents Experience, Man', *The Independent Magazine*, 26 April, 20–5.

Warne, Chris (1997), 'The Impact of World Music in France', in Alec Hargreaves and Mark McKinney (eds), *Post-Colonial Cultures in France* (London and New York: Routledge), 133–49.

Waters, Sarah (2006), 'A l'Attac. Globalisation and Ideological Renewal on the French Left', *Modern and Contemporary France*, 14 (2), May, 141–56.

Wolton, Dominique (2003), *L'autre mondialisation* (Paris: Flammarion).

Yee, Jennifer (2003), '*Métissage* in France: A Postmodern Fantasy and Its Forgotten Precedents', *Modern and Contemporary France*, 11 (4), November, 411–26.

Yol Jung, Hwa (1998), 'Bakhtin's Dialogical Body Politics', in Michael Mayerfeld Bell and Michael Gardiner (eds), *Bakhtin and the Human Sciences* (London, Thousand Oaks and New Delhi: Sage), 95–111.

Yonnet, Paul (1985), *Jeux, Modes et Masses* (Paris: Gallimard).

Selective Discography

Bérurier Noir (1987), *Abracadaboum* (Le Folklore de la Zone Mondiale, re-edn 2006).

Birkin, Jane (2007), *Best Of* (Mercury).

Blanchard, Gérard (1982), *Rock Amadour* (Barclay, re-edn 1989).

Brassens, Georges (2006), *Les 100 plus belles chansons* (5 vols) (Mercury).

Bruel, Patrick (2002), *Entre-deux* (RCA).

Bruni, Carla (2002), *Quelqu'un m'a dit* (Naïve).

Bruni, Carla (2008), *Comme si de rien n'était* (Naïve).

Buena Vista Social Club (1997), *Buena Vista Social Club* (World Circuit).

Casse-pipe (1998), *La Part des Anges* (Kerig).

Chao, Manu (1998), *Clandestino* (Virgin/EMI).

Chao, Manu (2001), *Proxima Estacíon: Esperanza* (Virgin/EMI).

Chao, Manu (2007), *La Radiolina* (Because Music/Wagram).

De Palmas, Gérard (1995), *La dernière année* (Chrysalis).

Dion, Céline (1998), *S'il suffisait d'aimer* (Columbia/Tristar).

Les Escrocs (1997), *C'est dimanche* (Virgin/EMI).

Farmer, Mylène (2002), *Les mots* (Polydor).

Garçons Bouchers (1992), *Vacarmélite* (Island, re-edn 2002).

Général Alcazar (1998), *La position du tirailleur* (Verdier, MSI).

Gnawa Diffusion (1997), *Algeria* (GDO Records).

Goldman, Jean-Jacques (1997), *Singulier 81–89* (2 vols) (Columbia/Tristar).

Hallyday, Johnny (2008), *Triple Best Of* (3 vols) (Mercury).

Hurlements d'Léo (2000), *La belle affaire* (Madame Léo/PIAS).

Jack O'Lanternes (1998), *Mines de rien* (Kerig/MSAï).

Lo'Jo (1998), *Mojo Radio* (Emma Production/Night & Day).

Louise Attaque (1998), *Louise Attaque* (Atmosphériques/Warner).

Macias, Enrico (2006), *20 chansons d'or* (EMI).

Mano Negra (1988), *Patchanka* (Boucherie Production).

Mano Negra (1989), *Puta's Fever* (Virgin).

Massilia Sound System (1995), *Commando Fada* (Adam, re-edn 2002).

Négresses Vertes (1989), *Mlah* (Delabel, re-edn 1992).

Négresses Vertes (1991), *Famille nombreuse* (Delabel).

Nougaro, Claude (2007), *Les 50 plus belles chansons* (3 vols) (Universal).

Ogres de Barback (1997), *Rue du Temps* (Les Ogres de Barback/PIAS).

P18 (1999), *Urban Cuban* (VIF Production).

Paris Combo (1997), *Paris Combo* (Polydor).

Piaf, Edith (2006), *20 chansons d'or* (EMI).

Pigalle (1990), *Regards affligés sur la morne et pitoyable existence de Benjamin Tramblay, personnage falot mais ô combien attachant* (Island, re-edn 2002).
Sardou, Michel (2004), *Anthologie* (3 vols) (AZ).
Sergent Garcia (1999), *Un poquito quema'o* (Labels).
Têtes Raides (1988), *Not Dead but bien raides* (Tôt ou Tard, re-edn 2004).
Têtes Raides (1998), *Chamboultou* (Tôt ou Tard).
Têtes Raides (2000), *Gratte-poil* (Tôt ou Tard).
La Tordue (1995), *Les choses de rien* (Mody Dick/Média 7).
La Tordue (2000), *Le vent t'invite* (Epic/Sony Music France).
Various Artists (1992), *Ma grand-mère est une rockeuse* (Boucherie).
Various Artists (1999), *Aux suivants* (Barclay/Universal).
Various Artists (1999), *Chansons du bord de zinc* (vol.1) (Inca).
Various Artists (2001), *Chansons du bord de zinc* (vol. 2) (Inca/EMI).
Various Artists (2001), *Les oiseaux de passage* (Mercury).
Various Artists (2002), *Cuisine non-stop* (Luaka Bop).
Various Artists (2003), *Avec Léo* (Barclay/Universal).
Various Artists (2006), *Zic de zinc* (vol. 1) (Wagram).
Various Artists (2007), *Zic de zinc* (vol. 2) (Wagram).
Les Wampas (2003), *Never Trust a Guy Who, after Having Been a Punk, Is Now Playing Electro* (Atmosphériques/Warner).
Zebda (1995), *Le bruit et l'odeur* (Barclay/Universal).
Zebda (1998), *Essence ordinaire* (Barclay/Universal).
Zebda (2002), *Utopie d'occase* (Barclay/Universal).
Zen Zila (1999), *Le mélange sans appel* (Eva Luna/Naïve).

Index